D0213738

Constructing Capitalism

Constructing Capitalism

The Reemergence of
Civil Society and Liberal Economy
in the Post-Communist World

EDITED BY

Kazimierz Z. Poznanski

Westview Press

BOULDER • SAN FRANCISCO • OXFORD

All rights reserved. No part of this publication may be reproduced or transmitted in any form or by any means, electronic or mechanical, including photocopy, recording, or any information storage and retrieval system, without permission in writing from the publisher.

Copyright © 1992 by Westview Press, Inc.

Published in 1992 in the United States of America by Westview Press, Inc., 5500 Central Avenue, Boulder, Colorado 80301-2847, and in the United Kingdom by Westview Press, 36 Lonsdale Road, Summertown, Oxford OX2 7EW

Library of Congress Cataloging-in-Publication Data
Constructing capitalism : the reemergence of civil society and liberal
   economy in the post-communist world / edited by Kazimierz Z. Poznanski.
      p.   cm.
   ISBN 0-8133-1481-X — ISBN 0-8133-1482-8 (pbk.)
   1. Europe, Eastern—Economic conditions—1989–   . 2. Civil society—
Europe, Eastern.   3. Soviet Union—Economic conditions—1985–   .
4. Civil society—Soviet Union.   I. Poznański, Kazimierz.
HC244.C67   1994
338.947—dc20   91-35237
                                                                        CIP

Printed and bound in the United States of America

 The paper used in this publication meets the requirements
of the American National Standard for Permanence of Paper
for Printed Library Materials Z39.48-1984.

10   9   8   7   6   5   4   3   2   1

HC
244
.C67
1992

Contents

PART THREE
Dilemmas of Democratization

Acknowledgments

This volume is the product of an International Political Economy Colloquium series held at the Henry M. Jackson School of International Studies. The colloquium was chaired by Kazimierz Z. Poznanski from the school and Janice Thomson, Political Science. The effort has benefitted greatly from the encouragement and advice of Joel Migdal, director of the International Studies Program at the school. The volume would not have been finished without invaluable assistance from Karen Walton throughout the whole process of preparation of the manuscript for publication.

Kazimierz Z. Poznanski

Introduction

Kazimierz Z. Poznanski

The collapse of communism in Eastern Europe and its near total collapse in the former Soviet Union (subsequently renamed the Commonwealth of Independent States) has forced scholars in the field to revisit some basic issues and raise many new ones. The rapid pace of recent change makes it difficult to grasp the economic or political reality of the region, but the search for answers must not be further prolonged. The countries of Eastern Europe and the former Soviet Union are now engaged in building a replacement for the communist experiment. There is thus an obviously important need for scholarship addressing both the nature of the communist demise and the meaning of these recent developments.

The collapse itself seems less surprising, or less difficult to explain, than the way in which it happened. Many social theories have been advanced to demonstrate that the system based on centralized rule and isolation from the rest of the world could not survive, but less has been done in terms of identifying the exact mechanics of inevitable collapse. Those arguing that the structure would break down because of economic decline have to be surprised, then, by the fact that no economic calamity preceded the recent collapse of the political order, and that indeed some countries actually did rather well economically (for example, Czechoslovakia with its low foreign debt, negligible inflation and quite respectable growth rates). Contrary to popular arguments on the inevitable breakup of the system, the region, particularly the Soviet Union, did not suffer from some "humiliation" in the world power game, one that would make leaders lose their confidence in their projects (even the withdrawal from Afghanistan was not a complete military defeat, since a friendly government has been left in place).

What may also come as a surprise to many is that the system—which has typically been described as nonreformable—broke down without bloodshed, if some few isolated cases are discounted. Moreover, the power transfer away from the party/state has not taken the indigenous populations from traditional apathy, so that they have behaved mostly as bystanders during the shift of leadership away from the communists. Because the developments were so "casual," it is also unclear which social group provided the greatest momentum for this "quiet death" of the system. While the system had been typically predicted as heading for a nasty, spectacular finale, the party/state nevertheless put up little resistance when it confronted a fatal threat to its power base.

Almost three years ago Eastern Europe, and more recently the independent parts—states—of what used to be called the Soviet Union, witnessed the collapse of the communist system, but this has not ended the troublesome development of the region. This collapse seemed to conclude an unfortunate episode in the region's move to modernity, a sort of detour, a deviation from otherwise well-directed efforts by these societies to create an industrial system, market structures, and a civil society, the main building blocks of modern nations. If anything, the experience of the post-Communist period suggests that success is not going to be instant, and that predispositions for radicalism are not yet gone.

In the brief time span that has elapsed since the rejection of the Communist system—either through active opposition forces (e.g., in the cases of Poland or Hungary), or by the elite themselves (e.g., in Russia or some other parts of the former Soviet Union)—the economies of the region have fallen into a deep recession, or in some cases even into depression. In 1990 Eastern European industry output declined by almost 15 percent, and it continued to decline even further throughout 1991. In Poland the crisis had already begun in 1989, around the time of political power transfer through "roundtable" negotiations. The national output continued to drop through 1991, with the cumulative loss in industrial output in Poland close to 40 percent and a decline in the national product of around 20 percent.

Not only has output declined but all the economies in the region have also entered into a period of great instability, including high inflation. In mid-1989 Poland experienced price escalation bordering on hyperinflation. After drastic monetary/fiscal measures were applied in 1990, inflation rates subsided but still remained on a high level (e.g., around 70 percent in 1991). In the former Soviet Union the state budgets have become heavily imbalanced, with all the excess expenditure being monetized, thus fueling enormous inflation—possibly already reaching the level of hyperinflation in late 1991. While the radical transition has eliminated remaining shortages in some countries, most notably Poland and Hungary, the situation has deteriorated in others, like Russia and Ukraine. There, prices have escalated in 1992 but goods have become even less available then in the recent past ("shortage economies" have turned into "chaos economies").

This book intends to provide an analytical framework to better understand why the "real" socialist systems disintegrated in the way they did, and also what patterns of change have already begun to emerge in the recent period of transition to more market-oriented, pluralistic structures. Almost all contributions here may be categorized as works in empirical theory, namely building broad generalizations regarding the region on the basis of quantitative research. The focus is on some more universal trends in the evolution of these countries and a comparison of individual patterns of change in particular countries, but also on the possible relations between the patterns detected in the region and elsewhere. The main themes and theoretical propositions of this volume are summarized again in the epilogue.

The book opens with a discussion of the primary forces that have caused the collapse of the communist system; the discussion centers upon the near-unanimous consensus that the extinction is more readily attributed to ideological erosion rather than economic deterioration, despite the difficulty of separating the two. The ideology of communism—which presented the party as a vanguard entrusted with executing certain inevitable "laws of history" in order to attain ultimate socialist harmony, i.e., communism—was so critical for the stability of that system that only through the "loss of faith" by the supporters, inside and outside of the party, was its decay possible. However, with the progressing erosion of the communist ideology, economic performance became the primary source of legitimacy for the party—the stagnation in production could then also be cited as a reason for the system's collapse.

Leszek Kolakowski's analysis offers the strongest argument for the decisive role of the ideological factor in the decay of communism, without denying that the economic record of that system—where economics in the true sense of the word was ruled out—was miserable. Economic sufferings do not easily, or frequently, turn into social protest but rejection of a value system, or "world view," does. In the case of Eastern Europe and the Soviet Union, this rejection had been slow, stepwise, until it eventually culminated in widespread frustration and surrenders by the party.

In the neo-institutional approach applied by Kazimierz Z. Poznanski to examine the same question of collapse, ideology is recognized as a factor, but only as one of three that contributed to the decay. These three forces at work have been, first, dilution of property rights, which led to continually greater waste of resources; second, disintegration of the party/state apparatus, which was fragmented by interest groups; and third, diminished appeal of the official ideology, which made it more and more difficult for the party/state to enforce public property rights.

Valerie Bunce takes yet another perspective on the breakup of what she calls two-tiered Stalinism by identifying not factors of decay but rather contradictions built into the communist system that brought it down. Her argument is that the same features that made the party/state system strong were sources of its weakness. She stresses in particular the fact that the more power was shifted to the apparatus, the greater was the pressure put on it by society at large, and the more unified the masses became, so that the party/state eventually lost the ability to control people.

Still, when Bunce analyses the final moments of the communist system, she recognizes the primacy of ideology over economics. The two-tiered structure—with the Soviet leaders controlling national parties and the parties controlling their populations—broke down before the potential for economic growth was exhausted because of Soviet leaders' anticipation of an even greater—possibly fatal—threat to their national ambitions. Jozef C. Brada also finds strong evidence that ideological concerns rather than cold economic calculations dominated recent developments, at least in the case of the decay of the regional trade regime—the CMEA—originally imposed by the Soviet Union on Eastern Europe.

The next group of issues analyzed in this volume relate to the current efforts by Eastern Europe and the former Soviet Union, the Commonwealth of Independent States, to reestablish competitive markets, particularly for capital. This often seems to be a rather straightforward and short-term task whose completion depends mostly on the will by post-communist leaders to embark upon it. Without doubt, there seem to be many ready-to-go patterns of capitalist markets available and they appear to have been successfully tested as well. Still, all the contributors to this volume who are concerned with market reconstruction present this process as the most complicated and time-consuming.

In his account of market-type reforms during the region's communist past, Janos Kornai points out that many institutional changes not only had their own basis, contrary to party/state preferences, but that these processes moved very much at their own pace. Thus, while the communist leaders were reluctant to acknowledge private activities, they nevertheless expanded spontaneously, while attempts to curb the central bureaucracy continuously failed. A lesson could be drawn from that account that there is little the post-communist elites can accomplish by rushing with radical programs of reform.

The transition to capitalist liberal markets is likely to be difficult, and there is no reason to assume that it will be linear or uniform throughout the region. The collapse of the communist economy is not yet total, and its immediate substitute will not necessarily be a liberal market. As Poznanski argues, between these two economic orders—structuring individual choices in the allocation of productive resources—there are many potential variants, and it is these models or their hybrids that are most likely to emerge first, with particular countries not necessarily pursuing the same sequence.

Among the possible ways of reintroducing markets is the so-called third road, combining public, or other nonprivate, ownership with market coordination. Kornai argues that such a combination represents a "weak form" that goes against economic logic, and Poznanski turns attention to the political impracticability of such forms. Jozef M. van Brabant presents a different view, as he finds the question of who has the right to dispose of a given property less important than that of control over assets. This, as he submits, leaves room for a diversified rather than uniform ownership structure.

The final group of issues discussed in this volume focuses on the political dimension of transition away from the Soviet-type system, including the question of whether market structures produce democratic pluralism automatically. In the tradition of liberal economics, markets are seen as having a strong "moralizing force" that turns individuals into responsible citizens who participate in the political process and respect diversity. The contributors to this volume tend, however, to perceive politics as having very much its own dynamics, as stressed, for instance, by Mira Marody.

Democratic institutions cannot function without an established democratic tradition, which has never been very strong in most of Eastern Europe and has been even less so in the former Soviet Union and its predecessor—tsarist Russia. The experience of the anti-communist opposition in the past did not improve the situation dramatically, since, as George Kolankiewicz argues, these political struggles were aimed mostly at regaining group rights (e.g., trade union representation, national sovereignty) rather than individual rights. The latter, however, are essential, since democratic politics is sustained only by the recognition that individual freedom of expression and enterprise are primary to all other rights.

The emerging political structures are free of many specific features of the communist system but have not yet assumed a form of its antithesis. In the final stages of communist rule in the region, the nationalist ideology completely resurfaced as segments in the party/state bureaucracy discovered its great practical clout (as was clearly the case in the political fight between elites in the republican and the federal establishment under Mikhail Gorbachev). In fact, Communism did not do away with nationalism but rather was a form of "suppressed nationalism," as it recognized the superiority of countries that had converted to the communist idiom, and it also gave them the right to enforce its revolutionary program on the latecomers. Nationalism, according to Jadwiga Staniszkis, has also become critical in the post-communist phase of political evolution in the region—a good illustration is the cycle of elections in post-1989 Poland.

PART ONE

Regional Political Economy

1

Mind and Body: Ideology and Economy in the Collapse of Communism

Leszek Kolakowski

The question of whether the economic or the ideological failures of Communism are mainly responsible for its present collapse can be easily shrugged off as an example of the proverbial and futile hen and egg problem; it is indeed obvious that those two sides of the disintegration process reinforce each other. I would like to argue, however, that the question is not meaningless and that trying to cope with it might be helpful in understanding the current events in the Communist world.

An Instant Failure

"Without" Economy. How do we, in fact, identify what the economic "failure" of Communism is? In a basic sense, it was a failure from the very beginning. Its goals included the abolition of the economy, that is, the replacement of economic relationships between people by the orders of Party and state functionaries, as well as the total prohibition of any economic activity apart from that initiated and commanded by the state.

This resulted inevitably in drying up the sources of the spirit of technical innovation, in real prices being fundamentally incalculable so that prices had to be arbitrarily set up by planning bodies, in the killing of incentives that would stimulate economic growth and in the necessity to replace them by sheer physical coercion. The restoration, under other names, of slavery and serfdom was the fateful effect of the idea, impracticable but tried time and again with a desperate obstinacy, of all-encompassing planning.

9

The first and paradigmatic failure of the communist economy was, of course, the so-called war communism; it was not, in fact, a by-product of civil war (as it was to be claimed later on); it was supposed to be established as a permanent form of socialist economy. It was replaced, thanks to Lenin's moment of sobriety by NEP one minute before the ultimate calamity that would have almost certainly brought about the collapse of the Soviet state and the victorious re-emergence of counter-revolution.

The pattern was to be repeated many times during the history of communist states, including all the Central European countries, China, Vietnam and Cambodia. Whenever the imminent catastrophe had become obvious, concessions were made by Communist rulers, and their meaning was invariably the same: a margin for the market, for free trade and private property, that is to say, for "capitalist" order, was opened, usually in the hope that the concessions would be abrogated again and the full command economy restored after some "mistakes" had been corrected.

In reality, a command economy has never been and never could be, because of physical impossibility, fully implemented. Over all the decades of its existence, it could survive only thanks to the so-called black economy, whereby the real economy brought corrections into the structure based on an impossible project. The economic history of Communism may be seen as alternating periods of dogmatic attempts to assert the full-fledged totalitarian system of production and exchange and some reluctantly made concessions to the market.

Communist countries did develop, of course; their productive effects were not simply stagnant or declining except in agriculture, which was left in ruins wherever wholesale collectivization was carried out. However, since the technological and organizational innovations had to be imposed from without, by the Party and state organs, and since more often than not they ran counter to the interests of both the workers and the managerial class, the development, apart from military industry, was first, slow, wasteful and chaotic; second, mainly extensive; and third, involving social costs of enormous dimensions, incomparable with the cost of any other known industrialization process.

System's Resilience. And what is indeed the mechanism whereby economic failures bring about the collapse of a political regime? It appears that no such mechanism that works automatically is in existence. A regime may, or so we think, crumble under the impact of a war it has lost as a result of its technological inferiority. Even if this happens, in most cases it is arguable that it is moral rather than technical collapse that is decisive, and this is obviously not how the present disintegration of communism can be explained.

Do economically inefficient regimes collapse simply because the poverty of the population provokes revolts? Hardly. Poverty can be defined either relatively, by contrast with more developed countries, or absolutely, that is, in terms of basic physiological need. But even if the regime fails to satisfy the most elementary requirements, it doesn't thereby provoke the destructive reactions of the people. In fact, communist regimes have survived their highly inefficient and wasteful economy, and only now do we witness their dismantlement, which, though seemingly rapid, will probably be painful, dangerous and long-lasting.

It is difficult to imagine more disastrous economic measures than the collectivization of agriculture in the Soviet Union (and then in China), with millions dying of hunger. There might have been some local outbursts of violent despair, but no resistance that would at any time threaten the power system. In terms of life standards, all communist countries have always been poor by comparison with western democracies, but they have differed significantly from one another. East Germany and Czechoslovakia have been relatively well off, while Rumanian citizens lived in the utmost misery; and anti-communist upheavals occurred in all three countries almost simultaneously. It seems clear that it was changes in mentality and not the level of absolute or even relative material satisfaction to which the collapse of the regime may be attributed.

Nor can police repressions explain the resilience of the system. One can hardly imagine a regime that was better protected by the police network, more efficiently controlled by fear, universal spying, and all sorts of oppressive measures than Ceausescu's fiefdom; and it fell apart almost overnight. The best-organized, the most bestial and ruthless police turn out to be helpless if social pressure is strong enough, and this simple truth has been borne out by innumerable examples in modern history. Depending on the circumstances, despair may make people apathetic and inert or courageous and unmindful of danger and death. But both apathy and courage are mental events.

The point here is not the trivial and incontestable observation that in order to overthrow a regime, people have to be mentally ready to do so. It is rather that no particular economic factor, repeated failures, or the misery of the population either a sufficient or the necessary condition for political upheaval of the kind we were witnesses to recently. It is invariably the case, of course, that once a popular movement begins, all sorts of economic grievances come up to the surface of social life, and they often seem preponderant in the way people voice their dissatisfaction and anger; all the unfulfilled promises and dashed expectations of a better life fuel the revolutionary energy. But the real source of this energy is to be looked for in changes of mentality.

The Role of Ideology

When we say "mentality," we mean a much larger realm than "ideology." The latter has to be, by definition, a distinct doctrinal body that is known as such to people who either accept or oppose it, whereas mentality does not need to be thus articulated, and people do not even need to be well aware of changes that occur in their minds. In communist regimes, however, the fate of ideology—the way in which it operates and the depth of its penetration into human minds—is of decisive weight in shaping the historical process. Perhaps the strongest case against Marx's immortal phrase that "social being determines consciousness" is provided by the history of the states that have assimilated this very phrase as part of their ideology.

It is a commonplace that totalitarian regimes imperatively need an ideological foundation in the form of an obligatory doctrine with all-embracing pretensions—and it has been a commonplace for years that the communist ideology either died away or was facing imminent extinction. These two statements now reduced to banalities are certainly not wrong, and the recent course of events seems to confirm them, but they do not add up to the whole truth.

It is no doubt true that a totalitarian communist regime could not survive without taking its legitimacy from the ideological principles that established its place in history and its unlimited rights both to keep its subjects in eternal serfdom and to expand as much as feasible. This ideology, Marxism-Leninism, codified by Stalin and baptized by him, was absolutely indispensable regardless of whether or not anybody believed in it. This does not imply, however, that being or not being believed was irrelevant to this ideology's efficiency and thus to the social and political history of communist states. Ideology was not an abstract entity having an independent life of its own and fulfilling its legitimizing function mechanically. It was an aspect of culture, and its erosion is of great importance in the process of the gradual dissolution of communism.

It is simply untrue to say that communist rule, from the very beginning, had nothing at its disposal except pistols, prisons, and concentration camps or that ideology was nothing but a necessary though inert decoration. For a long time, this was genuinely believed by large segments of the intelligentsia, especially Party members and Party appa-ratchiks. Those people might have been victims of what Marxists used to call "false consciousness," but what they believed really determined their behavior and reactions.

As with most closed ideological systems, communism was for a long time immune to criticism, and no empirical evidence to the contrary made a difference, since the ideology could easily absorb any facts that seemed to falsify it and dismiss them as irrelevant. The "essence" of the system was immutably sound and conformed to ideological principles, no matter how many obvious facts one could cite that displayed the grotesque incongruity of reality with ideological slogans. To be sure, the promises included in the doctrine failed to be kept (they have never been kept), the historical prognoses of Marxist philosophy proved to be false (they were never confirmed) and the anticipated kingdom of freedom turned out to be one of extreme despotism and all-pervading mendacity.

And yet all these facts cannot explain by themselves the collapse of the regime and of its ideological foundations; since they could be easily explained away and reduced to irrelevance by ideological means, there is no reason why such pseudo-explanations could not have worked indefinitely, not unlike in Millennarist sects, which can always adjust themselves, no matter how painfully, to the persistent failures of prophecies announcing the imminent day of *parousia* and survive. Still, this adjustment system in the case of communist doctrine proved to be vulnerable, and the whole edifice eventually had to collapse, not at one stroke but step-by-step over a long period.

It needs stressing that even though the communist idea has been fre-quently compared to religious faith, the comparison is apt only in part. The way in which it operated in minds might indeed have been similar to that of religion: It demanded blind obedience to the actual verdicts of the ideological authority and it was immune to falsification, but all the time it boasted of being a rationally grounded, scientific theory. This made it a parody of religion rather than a religion proper, and its self-contradictory characteristic "scientific blind faith," was one of the reasons it was exposed to rational criticism.

Invisible Decomposition

So what happened? The entire post-Stalinist era was marked by the slow but inexorable erosion of Communism as a living faith and ended in its total ruin, at least in Europe. The death of Stalin was not insignificant, as it robbed Communism of the single, immutable and unquestionable source of truth; this single authority had worked for a quarter of a century quite efficiently, but the Party apparatus was not ready, for obvious reasons, to invest another single ruler with this sort of personal despotic might, as such a concentration of power reduced all members of the privileged class to the status of slaves whose lives and privileges depended at every moment on the whims of the tyrant. The throne stood empty and thereby the infallible criterion of truth evaporated. Confusion in ideology was inevitable.

Revisionist Critique. One of the factors that strongly contributed to the ideological decomposition of Communism was the so-called revisionist movement, which had been expanding since the mid-fifties first and in the strongest form in Poland and then in other communist countries with varying intensity. This movement was an intellectual phenomenon not to be explained by economic deficiencies of the system. It was self-contradictory in that it tried to graft onto the body of Communism respect for truth, moral rules independent of political expediency, acceptance of democratic values and economic rationality, without destroying the core of the communist idea. However, since this core did in fact include, as was unmistakably admitted in the founding documents of Leninism, everything opposite to these values, that is the ideal of total power to which the entire realm of culture, science and economy was to be strictly subordinated, the hope for a Communism that would assimilate respect for truth, democracy, human rights and economic efficiency was roughly the same as the alchemist's ambition to invent dry water.

Revisionism could be therefore only a short-lived phenomenon, but it played an important role in the destruction of the ideology. Because the Party and the party apparatus were still sensitive to ideological changes and shocks, the voice of revisionism, which appealed to the same ideological stereotypes and traditions, was audible within the party, unlike the attacks and strictures from without. This kind of internal ideological criticism was fading away in the 1960s, along with its efficacy in dismantling the body of the communist idea and the awareness of its own inconsistency. The officially binding doctrine still remained as a fossilized collection of meaningless slogans. The rulers were increasingly aware of the incurable cancer devouring the legitimizing bases of their power and desperately looked for other devices to justify the system.

Ideology of Apathy. A restriction, however, is necessary at this point. The Communist ideology consisted of two parts. One of them may be summed up in a brief saying: "Communism is the radiant future of mankind." After decades of material and cultural misery, of serfdom, fear and lies, of so many disappointments and so much suffering, the idea of Communism as a hope for a glorious future was irreversibly exhausted and lost all traces of vitality; it subsisted in the form of a few vague phrases that served to embellish the oppression and privileges and, indeed, to provide people with guidelines about what was or was not permissible and ordered. Otherwise, nobody expected that anybody would give credence to these phrases, or even note their content.

The other half of the ideology may be summed up in the saying, "Communism (that is, Sovietism) is historically inevitable." In contrast to the first half, this one was really important in its very content and the ruling party made a serious effort to convince people of its truth. From the schools onward, the propaganda was concentrated on this task: Make people believe that the Soviet regime including its slightly different offshoots or mutations in Europe and Asia was invincible because the natural succession of historical phases destined it to spread and to conquer the world.

This particular half of the ideology had two functions: It legitimized the imperialist expansion of the Soviet Union and it taught the population that any resistance to the Soviet regime was doomed to failure as it ran counter to "historical laws" laid out (scientifically, needless to say) in the classics of Marxism-Leninism. Briefly, this was an ideology of apathy and despair, designed to rob people of the will to resist their serfdom. The idea seemed to be cleverly devised, but there was a flaw in it; it made the system vulnerable. Any defeat of the Soviet Union and, in particular, any territorial loss amounted to an ideological defeat; it showed people that Sovietism was not invincible after all, and that the supposed "historical laws" were no more than a clumsy forgery.

Loss of Faith. And so the present process of the collapse of Communism, which is far from being completed and might yet suffer dramatic regressions and reversals, has not been caused by the loss of faith in Communism as a promise of a better world (this faith having died away long ago) but, at least in part, by the loss of the depressing belief that Sovietism is bound to be victorious. Everybody sees that it is not and that it can be crushed. One understands as well why this process of crumbling takes the form of the domino effect, that the disease is very contagious.

In the 1970s, there were among well-placed Russian (and Polish) observers different views on the actual relevance of ideology to Communism. People like Sakharov argued that ideology does not matter since nobody takes it seriously and no political decisions are made on an ideological basis. This seems to apply to the first, and not to the second, part of the doctrine. Solzhenitsyn, on the contrary, saw in ideological prejudices the chief source of all the catastrophes that befell Russia, and he believed that if the rulers got rid of them, without even giving up their power, they could save the country. This seems to overlook the fact that power and ideology are coupled into one thing in this system and that, in fact, the aspiration to total power was ultimately the very meaning of the ideological framework of the regime.

Zinovyev argued that Soviet people do not believe, to be sure, in the doctrine they are supposed to profess; they do not even perceive its content, but they accept it nevertheless almost as a natural phenomenon. They got used to it and the system did efficiently produce the "Soviet man" or the "new man of Socialism," an inert, ignorant mannequin unable to revolt or to think critically. Zinovyev thought that the task of the system was so properly and irreversibly performed that there were no reasons to expect any significant movement of protest or rebellion in the Soviet Union. This prophecy by Zinovyev, fortunately, proved to be wrong.

To say this, of course, is not to deny the enormous cultural and mental harm brought about by decades of indoctrination. In Poland, Czechoslovakia and Hungary, the results of indoctrination have proved to be much more superficial and relatively easy to reverse, but in the former Soviet Union itself this process will certainly last much longer.

Ideological Crisis

Wave of Nationalism. The awareness of ideological crisis caused attempts to seek other instruments for the legitimization of power. In Poland, this took the form of an officially permissible nationalism and the idea of the state; it was more and more the state rather than the Party or the doctrine that was supposed to be the supreme value and the focus of loyalty of the citizens. In Communist regimes in conformity with the doctrine, the state has always been an organ of the party. One may even say that the Marxist prophecy of the withering away of the state was realized in a grotesque and perverse manner; indeed, when we say "the state," we add automatically the idea of sovereignty. But the Communist state, including the Soviet Union, has never been sovereign; it has always been the property of the party.

Already by the 1970s, the Polish party was trying to build what might seem a monstrosity: a communist state without ideology. The series of cataclysmic events that followed—including, in particular, the emergence of "Solidarity"—proved that the attempt failed, but it was impossible and too late to go back to the ideological state.

Moreover, we observed analogous efforts in the Soviet Union under

Gorbachev: the restoration of the state as a seemingly autonomous entity, an attempt to reinforce and to stabilize the state machinery at the expense of the party apparatus. This aims, of course, at making it easier for Gorbachev himself to concentrate the supreme power in his own hands and largely diminish his dependence on political apparatchiks, but the goals are not only personal. The point is also to fortify professionalism in the administration of the country and even to achieve, at least in part, the rule of law. This latter goal is clearly incompatible with the communist regime, where the law has always been a malleable tool of the party and has had no force of its own; the rule of law simply contradicts the illimitable and arbitrary power of the Party, supposedly the great achievement of Socialism.

But the worship of the state is a double-edged weapon. While it might help leaders get rid of the absurdly inefficient ideology, it is naturally associated, by force of tradition, with the idea of the national state; this encourages national feelings. Nationalism can do without an explicitly elaborated ideology, although it might use it. Nationalism is, rather, a visceral, almost instinctive, reaction aimed at the reinforcement of tribal cohesion with the help of xenophobia and the hatred of other tribes; a few simplistic slogans are usually quite sufficient for it to flourish.

The waves of nationalism that now convulse and jolt the former Soviet Union—and, less strongly, Central Europe, in conformity with the predictions that many people have been making for a long time— were both predictable and explicable. They are even justifiable to the extent that they have to be seen as a natural reaction to the decades-long brutal oppression of the national culture and tradition of all the communist nations, including (and this needs stressing) Russia.

It goes without saying that those waves carry an enormous danger to the world and are obviously the most destructive threat to the Soviet empire. Of course, we hoped for the fall of the Soviet empire, and we feared exactly what is happening right now. If indeed the demise of the empire is going to come about through chaotic massacres and the war of all against all, we should agree with those who expect that in the coming years the world will not be a safer place, alas. A political regression in the former Soviet Union is quite possible: it might halt for awhile the explosion of nationalism by military and police repressive measures but since regression cannot resolve any economic, national, or cultural problems, it cannot be long-lasting and will probably usher in even more violent explosions sometime later. The West has no efficient means to control this process and is restricted to impotent sermons.

While the ideological confrontation between totalitarianism and the desire for freedom is practically finished in Europe, social forces that have their vested interests in the totalitarian system are far from being dead and will probably try to express themselves in nationalist form, that is, in the former Soviet Union in the form of Great-Russian chauvinism; this can only enhance national tensions and bring them to the critical point. One can see already a kind of alliance between chauvinist forces and neo-Stalinism, joined to one another by their hatred of western culture.

It would be improper to say that nationalism has replaced or is going to replace Communism as another ideology. Nationalist feelings have always been there; the oppressive regime has prevented them from expressing themselves. They were not created as a result of the decline of the communist idea. When we say "ideology," we normally mean a global worldview that pretends to be capable of answering all philosophical, historical and political questions with a caricatural substitute for religion in its medieval theocratic form.

Religious Revival. The West and East were not offering, properly speaking, competing ideologies; democracy is not a global ideology in this sense, it is a method, the best invented so far, to channel and resolve social conflicts. It includes, of course, a number of values, but by itself it does not create a community that human beings need. What can compete with the expiring communist ideology is not the democratic idea but perhaps religious faith, insofar as it provides people with answers to the issues concerning the meaning of life and of the universe, and the destiny of man. Nationalisms fight against each other, to be sure, but they do not compete with each other because by definition they do not address the same audience.

The religious revival that can be seen in countries that free themselves from Communist fetters is not without dangers, though. Considering the totalitarian potential of Islam and the fact that Eastern Christianity has not been noted for its spirit of tolerance, to put it mildly, the regimes that are going to emerge in the post-Communist countries will not necessarily warm the hearts of those who treasure the values of pluralism and freedom, especially where religious and nationalist fanaticisms fuse into one thing. Nevertheless, one may be cautiously optimistic about Central Europe.

But there is another and more comforting side to these processes. They seem to confirm the view that people want freedom not because freedom promises more material goods but because they want freedom, freedom *tout court*, without qualifications. In the countries that have been kept for decades in strict isolation, having hardly an access to other sources of information other than those provided by the ruling party, being fed with endless lies under the guard of the omnipresent secret police, the longing for freedom has not been forgotten; whenever the slightest opportunity appears, people prove that their minds have not been properly Sovietized, after all, and that the desire for freedom cannot be eradicated. Does this not suggest that the powerful need to be free is perhaps more than a contingent product of peculiar historical circumstances, that it is, so to say, anthropologically rooted, that it belongs to the permanent spiritual constitution of humanity?

Dismantlement of the Soviet Empire

Postscript. The above arguments seem to be borne out, I daresay, or at least not falsified, by recent events, in particular by the pathetic failure of the putsch in August 1991. Everybody was naturally flabbergasted by the almost incredible ineptitude of the putschists. How could it have happened, all analysts asked, that they, including experienced commanders of the Army and KGB, failed to arrest the obvious candidates for leaders of the opposition, let telephones and faxes work, did not immediately expel foreign journalists and TV crews, set up no operational centers in non-Russian republics, did not tell soldiers exactly what they were supposed to do, etc. Although many details of the attempted coup are still shrouded in darkness, the blunders of the would-be new rulers were patent even to people who by no means can claim to be experts in such matters.[1]

The answer, we may guess, is simple. While the putschists were of course anxious not to acquaint too many people with their plan or at any rate with the timing (rumors and warnings about the imminent coup had been circulating in Russia for months) and risk early detection, they probably believed that the number of initiated did not matter much because they acted on the premises of the old regime: "We run well-disciplined police and army troops, as well as the party machinery; they obey orders, whatever those orders might be, and the whole operation will be completed in no time." The putschists probably drew up their plans in the secrecy of their offices, without bothering much about the state of mind of the country or even of the power apparatus. One might think they would have known better.

Nothing worked. Even the gigantic machinery of repression proved to be unreliable. Like everything in the Soviet Union, the inherited and seemingly well-proven instruments of power just refused to operate in the old manner. And the reason was changes in the mentality of the Russian (or Soviet) people. They, at least very many of them, stopped being and feeling like puppets, passively carrying out the wishes of the

master. In spite of the gloomy assessments of those who had lost faith in
the possible awakening of the corpse of Russia, the majority wanted to
be human creatures endowed with free will.

It was not economic considerations that prompted them to defend
their freedom; what made freedom possible was the fact that the lifeless
body of the oppressive ideology had been reduced to the same state as
Lenin's mummy in Red Square, and buried. Indeed, people had been
dead-weary with the misery of Gorbachev's last years and bitterly
disappointed by the unfulfilled promises of perestroika; one could
expect that in desperation they would give credence to the new, however hollow, promises of the putschists who even displayed some
ridiculous signs of their prowess (for one day one could buy caviar in
Moscow). But this did not happen. Too many people realized that their
human status had not been irreversibly crushed by decades of serfdom
but could still be restored.

One cannot even say that they got rid of fear. Fear is a normal, instinctive, animal reaction and one can hardly imagine that an unarmed
man facing a tank is simply free of fear. What makes fear a paralyzing
force is the feeling that our effort and bravery are in vain, that nothing
can be done in the face of the invincible dragon. This was what the
ideology had tried to convince people, and with a considerable measure
of success. Ruthless repressions instilled fear, of course, but what made
it disabling was the ideology: "We, the oppressors," was the message,
"will always win; whatever you do against us is in vain because history
marches inexorably on our side."

Fear and Hope. During the genocidal German occupation, especially in
Poland, the horrors of oppression were much greater than even in the
Stalinist years in Poland or in the post-Stalinist years in Russia. Of
course, people feared torture, death, and concentration camps, and yet
many of them were ready to risk their lives fighting. This was possible
because nobody believed that the Third Reich might win the war and
everybody was convinced that its domination, however monstrous, was
temporary and that the beast would be done in eventually. Fear was not
paralyzing because it was not propped up by feelings of hopelessness,
whereas in the Soviet regime, the ideology of hopelessness made the
fear effectively overpowering.

One significant defeat of Sovietism could make this ideology empty
and without destroying the fear deprive it of its power. This is why the
example of Solidarnosc was of such extraordinary importance. It
showed the world, and especially the denizens of the Soviet bloc, that
there is no 'history' to protect the regime and that the regime can be
effectively brought to the brink of extinction by the sheer will to fight. In

spite of temporary defeat under the military dictatorship, this will could not be killed any longer. It reemerged and asserted itself later on and won. Inevitably, the precedent was of highest significance and proved to be deadly infectious.

This is not to say that the Russian coup was doomed to failure from the very outset and could not succeed no matter what the plotters might have devised. It could have succeeded, but even if it had, the victory would probably have been short-lived since the gang had no idea how to deal with any of the economic, social, national, or cultural problems of the country and their only aim was keeping power. Their failure on the third day of the attempted assassination of freedom proved that, even had they succeeded, they would have been defeated shortly thereafter.

The demise of communist ideology could be seen even in their own astonishingly clumsy pronouncements. They did not dare appeal to the glory of the regime or to the radiant future of communism. Neither did they dare to explicitly take up the slogans of Great Russian nationalism. They pretended to be the saviours not of communism, not of the Russian nation, but of the state as such, though the state had by then already begun the process of decomposition and nothing could save it in its existing shape.

Partial Victory. To be sure, the victory is not definitive; no victory is. There is no guarantee that in peculiar conditions no other coup might occur that would restore the dictatorial regime, not necessarily communist, in its ideological form. The remnants of totalitarian education are alive and not likely to be wiped out overnight. They survive in mentalities, rather than in conscious ideological patterns. After so many years of life in a fundamentally lawless regime, the contempt for law is deeply ingrained; establishment of the rule of law is an immensely difficult task, as it involves not only institutional but psychological changes. Various barriers are still there to hamper the transition to a market economy: the belief that the state is responsible for everything and nobody is responsible for the state or, for that matter, for himself; the nearly total evaporation of the "work ethic"; a reluctance to make long-term investments rather than quick gains that can be used for immediate consumption of luxuries; the difficulty of accepting the simple fact that the state can be ideologically uncommitted.

This last point needs stressing. The ideologically neutral state is under attack from two sides: nationalist and clericalist. The sinister dream of an ethnically pure society has gained popularity to various degrees; to be fair, all over the post-Communist world the idea of a Christian state reappears. One may hear the argument that once we get rid of an atheist state, its place should be taken by a Christian state, as there is no other choice; as if the state that does not include in its constitution the belief in God is duty bound to make atheism an obligatory ideology (in fact, in European communist states, apart from Albania, atheism was not officially established as a constitutional principle; on the contrary, religious freedom, as well as the separation of the Church from the state, was usually guaranteed on paper though hardly ever observed, especially in the Soviet Union and Czechoslovakia).

But the growth of nationalist passions is by far more dangerous. It seemed unbelievable that we would live to see fascist heroes resurrected to glory by some segments of the political spectrum: Tiso in Slovakia, Ante Pavelic in Croatia, Antonescu in Romania, Bandera in Ukraine (Poland and Bohemia, thank God, have no such figures to worship). The former East Germany has become a center of xenophobic violence, and the ghoul of anti-semitism, as it turns out, refuses to expire. It is impossible yet to measure the strength of such trends, and they are not universally dominating. But they carry an explosive force; the Soviet Union has only begun to disassemble itself, and several dozen small nations live on the territory of the Russian republic. We may only hope that the general weariness and misery will prevent those chauvinist energies, hostile to civilization, from exploding.

Human culture includes religion; it includes tribal or national communities that people inhabit; and it includes the awareness of living in historical time. From the fact that people need all these components of communal life, it does not necessarily follow that to survive they need a single all-embracing ideology that gives definitive answers to all religious, philosophical, historical, and political questions and a practical prescription about how to live. It has been proven that they can live without it. In favorable circumstances, as it turned out, they willingly adopt such ideologies, alas. Therefore, it is recommended that we all be ready to counter the destructive force of ideologies with universal pretensions, whatever their content might be. They never die away entirely.

Conclusion

To the question of why the events that started with the emergence of "Solidarity" in Poland in 1980 accelerated suddenly and reached a culminating point at the precise time they did, there is no answer. If we could explain the timing, we could predict it, which we certainly did not do. One may say, of course, that the changes occurring in the Soviet Union resulted from its economic failures, but there was no simple causal relation between the latter and the former; a certain state of mind was needed to initiate this movement, including the doubts of the leaders about the legitimacy, durability, and social justification of the system over which they presided.

In revolutionary changes, peaceful or violent, nothing is certain until the last moment, and a slight accident or one individual decision may entirely upset the course of events. An example: We learned that the Stalinist despot of East Germany, Mr. Honecker, decided to apply the full force of repression to stifle the peaceful revolt. This did not happen, fortunately; but who may state that it could not have happened, that this was just unfeasible? It was feasible.

And assuming that the streets of Leipzig, Dresden, and Berlin had been covered with blood and corpses, in what international situation would we now live? Various scenarios are imaginable, one of them being simply that the Soviet Union, however reluctantly, would have used its troops to keep East Germany from falling part and to restore the good order, old Soviet style. The entire international setting would have been upset, a cold war would have returned, the disarmament negotiations would have come to a halt, and what about Poland and Hungary? Who knows? The catastrophe was averted by a hair's breadth.

Therefore, we must not rely on irresistible forces of progress.

Notes

1. The imposition of military dictatorship ("martial law") in Poland in December 1981 appeared by comparison to be technically brilliant, almost impeccable. Couldn't the putschists have learned from this successful prototype? (To be fair, the comparison is apt only in part, as the Polish military did not need to remove the president, who was himself the chief organizer of the operation.)

2

Two-Tiered Stalinism: A Case of Self-Destruction

Valerie Bunce

Political systems are not in the habit of committing suicide.
—Milovan Djilas, 1988

It is by now evident that the Soviet bloc we once knew is no more. Instead of witnessing state socialism, which was defined by state ownership of the means of production, Leninist party rule and central planning, we now find competitive politics and regimes committed to privatization and marketization. Changes at the international level have been equally dramatic. Instead of allying themselves with the former Soviet Union, being hostile to the West and isolating themselves from the global economy, are now regimes committed to establishing an economic and political-military alliance with the West.

The economic and political monopoly long enjoyed by the Communist parties in Eastern Europe, therefore, has been dismantled. Politics and economics—at the domestic and at the regional level—have been deregulated. As a result, we can conclude that the house that Stalin built collapsed in Eastern Europe in 1989 and in the Soviet Union not long after. With that died the postwar division of Europe and the terminology that accompanied that division. The transformed Soviet Union and Eastern Europe can now be said to reside in a place called eastern Europe.

As to what to call these new states, the most accurate, albeit awkward, term is liberalizing regimes. They are no longer Stalinist systems since they have deregulated their politics and economics; but they are not yet capitalist liberal democracies. To be capitalist liberal democracies, the liberalization process would have to go much further and be institutionalized (see, for instance, Przeworski, 1986).

These dramatic changes in the "new" eastern Europe boggle the mind and the paradigm, thus presenting us with a number of difficult questions. For instance, if Soviet general secretaries are in the business of preserving their system, their bloc and their power, as we have long assumed, then why did Mikhail Gorbachev risk all three by deregulating politics and economics at home and in eastern Europe?

Further, how are we to explain the reactions of these societies and these parties to Gorbachev's policies? If these parties were so strong and these societies so weak, as many in the East as well as in the West presumed, then why did every regime topple, why were these clearly revolutionary changes so peaceful (except in Romania) and why were the changes always in the direction of communist parties giving up their powers to their assertive and well-organized societies?

Another pressing question is, why did economic and political liberalization—a virtual inversion of Stalinist economic and political arrangements—arise from the ashes of Stalinism? Finally, does all this mean that these so recently Stalinist systems are in the process of turning their histories upside down by evolving into capitalist liberal democracies?

The purpose of this chapter is to provide some answers to these questions. I will do so by analyzing the long-term dynamics of Stalinism—as a domestic and as a regional political economy. As we will discover, Stalinism destroyed itself and, at the same time, created the building blocks for a new and liberalized economic and political order.

The Two-Tiered Structure of Stalinism

Domestic Structure. Let us turn, first, to the structure of Stalinism as a domestic political economy (see, for instance, Bunce, 1989c; Nove, 1980a; Harding, 1984). This political economy rests on five pillars: state ownership of the means of production; central planning; isolation from the global economy; rule by a single Leninist party that operates in a climate of political certainty (by virtue of its controls over exit and voice, to borrow from Albert Hirschmann); and commitment to rapid socioeconomic development.

These five traits can be said to create a political economy that is distinct from both capitalist liberal democracies and authoritarian systems, either pre-capitalist or state capitalist. First, Stalinism—or what we can also term state socialism—erases the familiar boundaries separating politics from economics. As a consequence, authority relations are merged with exchange relations. The economy is fully politicized and, less often noted, the polity is fully "economized" (see, especially, Bunce, 1985; Harding, 1984). In this sense, Stalinism resembles pre-capitalist state formations.

Next, Stalinism combines this "old-fashioned" characteristic with a number of others that are distinctly modern. In particular, Stalinism erases the boundaries between the state and civil society. Indeed, Stalinism could be said to have been committed to the eradication of civil society. As a result, social relations are fully politicized. Public swallows up private. Moreover, this veritable fusion of politics, economics and society is joined with an extraordinary degree of centralization. By eliminating all those who might compete for political power or economic resources at home through creation of a single party enjoying complete control over the creation and distribution of power and privilege, Stalinist systems allow the party to function as a political, social and economic monopoly (see, especially, Csanadi, 1989; Jowitt, 1971).

Finally, Stalinism is "ultra-modern" in its commitment to rapid development. This goal, when combined with the traits already listed, means that Stalinist systems are propelled by a need to expand. Here, I do not refer to the argument that "communism" seeks world domination. After all, both Stalinist and liberal democratic systems want an international system composed of states just like them. Rather, I refer to pressures for domestic expansion (see Csanadi, 1989). These were dictatorships that could never rest on their laurels. There was never enough growth, so there was never enough power—and vice-versa. Small wonder, then, that Stalinism was notable for its "excesses" (Cohen, 1985).

External Aspects. Let us now turn our attention to the international side of Stalinism; that is, the structure of the Soviet bloc (see, for instance, Bunce, 1985). The Soviet bloc has been termed a regional hierarchical system featuring isolation from the international system; extraordinary redundancy with respect to the domestic political economic structure of the bloc states;[1] considerable interstate coordination of domestic and foreign policy; and a single and powerful hegemon, the Soviet Union, which dominated the smaller and weaker states within the regional system.

The final trait requires some amplification. Hegemon in this case refers to the powers enjoyed by the Soviet Union as a consequence of Soviet control over bilateral relations within the bloc and bloc relations in turn with the international system, and Eastern European dependence on the Soviet Union for power, security, markets and primary products. As regional hegemon, therefore, the Soviet Union enjoyed sufficient economic, ideological and military resources to function within the region as *the* mediator among states and between these states and the international system as *the* guarantor of political stability, ideological purity, national security and economic growth.

There are a number of striking similarities, then, between the structure of Stalinism as a domestic political economy, on the one hand, and the structure of the Soviet bloc as a regional hierarchical system, on the other. For instance, just as these parties could be said to have enjoyed a domestic monopoly because their systems fused economics, politics and society and guaranteed at the same time party control over the production and distribution of power and privilege, so the Soviet Union could be said to have enjoyed a regional monopoly by virtue of its fused assets and the absence of competition within or outside the region.

Moreover, just as "consumers" could be said to have been captive at home, having to "buy" whatever power and privilege the party chose to distribute, so Eastern European states functioned within the bloc as "captive consumers" of whatever the Soviets manufactured or distributed. Finally, just as the joining of monopoly with the commitment to rapid growth leads to continuous pressures to expand power and growth in the domestic sphere, so a regional monopoly and a commitment to rapid growth at home and in the region led the Soviets to continually press for expanding power and plenty in Eastern Europe.

Stalinism, therefore, is best understood as a two-tiered system combining a Stalinist domestic political economy with a Stalinist regional political economy. Such a two-tiered structure produces parallel domestic and regional dynamics. Just as these parties are in a position to ride roughshod over their societies, so the Soviet Union in turn is endowed with sufficient resources to ride roughshod over Eastern Europe. Next, this two-tiered structure creates an integrated hierarchy that works to the benefit of Soviet hegemony, since by controlling parties in Eastern Europe, the Soviets could control their societies as well. Finally, such a structure is by definition opposed to liberalization, since it would break up the very monopoly upon which the system is based.

Of course, such a structure would seem to be unusually capable of self-reproduction. The system is sealed off from any "contaminant" given the monopolistic position enjoyed by these parties and, in turn, by the Soviet Union (Hirszowicz, 1988; Horvat, 1984). But something clearly did push these systems to stop reproducing and, what is more, to liberalize their politics and economics. And "that something" was in fact Stalinism itself. Let us now reexamine Stalinism with our attention focussed on its self-destructive qualities and their contributions in turn to the transition from Stalinism to liberalization.

Domestic Redistribution of Power

Elite Conflict. The domestic structure of Stalinism had the peculiar effect over time of gradually reducing the power of the party and expanding, just as gradually, the power of society. This occurred in part because of the intense nature of intra-elite politics, due, in turn, to the fact that political—party—monopoly created here a monopsony. Just as the party was the sole allocator of power and privilege, and that gave the party tremendous powers, so the party necessarily functioned as the market for any and all claims to power and privilege. Because political and economic fortunes are fused in Stalinist systems, the stakes attached to winning or losing are very high indeed, consequently the elite stratum feels very insecure. With but one arena for the mediation of conflict (economic and political), high stakes, and insecure politicians, Stalinism produced an extraordinarily conflictual elite environment.

In all political systems, of course, a divided elite has important consequences for public policy and regime-society relations, since elites make policy and a divided elite encourages defections from the elite stratum and expanded room for maneuver by the society in general and the opposition in particular. However, Stalinist systems are unusually "elite-sensitive" because the party generates an elaborate system of dependent relationships. Thus, if the elites are stable, economics and politics, power and personnel, are stable.

This can lead to incrementalism, or, from a less charitable perspective, to stagnation. But if elites in a Stalinist system conflict, as they often do, tremors are sent throughout the system and the result is extreme change. Whether these changes suggest innovation or chaos (again, depending on one's perspective), the consequences are the same. Intra-elite conflict wrecks havoc on all (see, especially, Link, 1989), and it makes the system unusually open to change—from within and outside the elite stratum.

Because they want to protect themselves and their system, though, Stalinist elites devise means to reduce the costs of conflict. The Soviet case is instructive. After Stalin (and Beria) died, the Soviet leadership decided to eliminate death as a punishment for ending up on the wrong side of a political battle. After all, they knew, so to speak, that "there but for the grace of God go I." Providing security of life, of course, increased intra-elite conflict by keeping winning very attractive while lowering the costs of losing. Moreover, conflict came to be expressed in other unsettling ways—for instance, the rapid personnel turnover, hare-brained schemes and radical shifts in public policy of the Khrushchev era. This led the Soviet political leadership to depose Khrushchev in 1964 and install Brezhnev.

Brezhnev further reduced the costs of intra-elite conflict by, for instance, agreeing to stability in cadres, stability in policies and use of the surplus as a mechanism for absorbing conflict. What this meant in practice, of course, was that intra-elite conflict was still encouraged but that the resolution of this conflict became more and more a matter of money. And money, unlike power, is scarce and has a visible metric. Intra-elite conflict, therefore, was not ended; it was simply rechanneled.

Control Capacity. If Stalinism encourages intra-elite conflict and makes such conflicts expensive, both literally and figuratively, it also encourages a decline in the capacity of the political leadership to control the system. This is, first, because Stalinist bureaucracies are built to maximize the power of the top leadership, not to maximize efficiency. As Elemer Hankiss (1988) has argued, Stalinist bureaucracies are set up to protect and expand the power of the top leadership. Patronage as a method of allocating bureaucratic positions, provisional mandates extended by those at the top of the hierarchy to all those below them and the sheer size of the nomenklatura all serve this function, as does the absence of either a rational bureaucracy or rule of law.

The end result is that bureaucrats are quite insecure, since they are dependent on capricious officials above them in the hierarchy and since they are, at the same time, mired in conflicts with each other as a consequence of having neither job security nor standard operating procedures. Such bureaucratic arrangements also leave the public in a vulnerable position. They are held hostage to capricious officials who are in turn held hostage. In this way, the costs of uncertainty of the top leadership are passed down, first to bureaucrats and then to the clienteles the bureaucrats purportedly serve. Stalinist elites, therefore, derive much of their power from manipulating uncertainty (and see Whyte, 1989).

This arrangement did concentrate power at the top in the short run, but in the longer run it began to have the opposite effect. One problem was that battling bureaucrats are not very good at implementing policy. Another problem was that such a system encourages bureaucrats to seek some insurance as a guard against uncertainty. This meant, for instance, a marked propensity to squelch "bad news," to carve out islands of autonomy wherever possible, to resist any and all changes in policy, to engage in corruption and to pass all these costs on to their clienteles (see Bruszt and Redi, 1989). Their clienteles, in turn, engaged in similar behavior in order to ward off uncertainty. In this way, the "insecurity blanket" of the Stalinist state led in fact to less efficiency and less penetration over time. The power of the political leadership was more and more compromised, and manipulating uncertainty, therefore, proved to be an asset of declining value.

This leaves us with a final elite asset, turned liability in Stalinist systems: socioeconomic development. Development created two major problems that directly undercut the power of elites: complexity and reduced capacity for economic growth. Complexity expanded the bureaucracy, enhanced the capacity of bureaucrats to carve out areas of autonomy, multiplied economic goals and diversified economic interests. The economy, as a result, was less "plannable" (see Nove, 1980b). Economic policy was a product more and more of decision-makers who had trouble setting priorities and trouble implementing policies and who had to reach outside their immediate environs in order to mobilize support, gather needed information and coopt those who were most likely to block implementation of policy.

At the same time, development led to a maturation of these economies, and the inevitable slowdown in growth fanned intra-elite conflict. This was in part because there was less surplus to distribute, and elites divided over the question of how to get the economy moving again. Moreover, the party had lost some of its capacity to control economic policy and had at the same time come to rely more and more on economics as the arbiter of politics. And development had expanded the number of claimants to the surplus.

Thus, what appeared to be elite assets in a Stalinist system became in fact liabilities insofar as the power of the elites was concerned. What Stalinist elites thought they created was a system that maximized their powers by combining certainty in political and economic outcomes— that is, creating a monopoly that could plan politics as well as economics—with uncertainty in political and economic processes by keeping everyone in the dark, on the edge and, therefore, without power, reliable and permanent allies or rights. This is, of course, precisely opposite to what we see in capitalist liberal democracies; that is, uncertain results but certain procedures (see Bunce, 1990).

However, in joining uncertain procedures with certain results, Stalinism created, instead, a system that generated intra-elite conflict, systemic instability and a decline in the control the party in general and the elites in particular could exercise over the system. The system, in short, encouraged compensatory effects. It generated over time pressures to make economic and political outcomes more uncertain. At the same time, it generated over time pressures to make political and economic processes more certain. The system, in short, was liberalizing in spite of—that is, in reaction to—itself (see, for instance, Przeworski, 1986 and Bunce, 1990).

Society, of course, took advantage of the situation. Declining state autonomy and rising societal autonomy are, after all, two faces of the same coin. But the ability of society to capitalize on elite weakness was greatly enhanced by the impact of Stalinism on societal resources. Society benefitted, in particular, from the homogenization of these resources. Here I refer not just to the constraints on differentiation of wages and standards-of-living which, are typical of Stalinist systems, once the initial phase of industrialization is achieved. I also refer to the ways in which Stalinism places members of society in an unusually (but not completely) similar structural position.

What makes members of these societies uniform is that everyone within society is an employee of the state and deprived simultaneously of economic or political resources. Moreover, they all are dependent on the state for access to all scarce goods, including jobs, apartments and political rights. Also, people are affected by changes in state policy in similar ways at the same time and therefore quite willing and able to hold the party responsible for all that happens, good and bad.[2] In doing so, Stalinist systems also tend to create relatively similar societal values and interests. In spite of its intentions to the contrary, Stalinism homogenizes society. It gives the weak one crucial weapon (to borrow from Scott, 1985): a great deal in common.

This is only enhanced by the fact that Stalinist systems are very successful in promoting literacy and urbanization: two contributors to collective action. Stalinist development also leads to rising expectations for a number of reasons. The party has promised rewards for the sacrifices of rapid industrialization and the regime has sold socialism on primarily economic grounds and defined these economic benefits as rights, not privileges. At the same time, younger generations expected improvements in their material conditions equal to those enjoyed by their parents and grandparents.

All this translates into anger, and, what is more important, a widespread sense of injustice—a feeling of being denied what is one's due (see Moore, 1977; Scott, 1985). It also translates into less compliance, both in economic and political terms. This is because fusion of the economy and the polity in Stalinist systems renders the party responsible for whatever happens in economics as well as in politics. Stalinism marries economic to political dissatisfaction—within the society as a whole as well as within the elite.

Socioeconomic development, therefore, leads society to begin to outgrow the confines of its Stalinist "britches" (see, especially, Lewin, 1988).

The declining autonomy of the party-state, outlined above, is matched by a growth in societal autonomy (see, for instance, Bunce, 1989c; Lapidus, 1989; Kelliher, 1989). Stalinism redistributes power over time from the party to society—in spite of itself. Pressures for liberalization—that is, a deregulation of politics and economics—grow.

Regional Redistribution

Regional Monopoly. A similar process takes place at the regional level. Since I have developed this argument at length elsewhere (Bunce, 1985), I will be brief. The strength of the Soviets within the bloc, like the strength of these parties at home, leads over time to weakness. This occurs precisely because the Soviets are in the same position within the region as communist parties are at home. In particular, the Soviet regional monopoly creates a monopsony. Eastern European demands, therefore, converge on the Soviet Union as a consequence of Soviet control over all the resources these states need to meet their goals of national security, economic growth and domestic political stability.

Moreover, the regional "game," like the domestic "game," is one of high stakes, insecure politicians and but one arena for the mediation of conflict. This produces, quite predictably, a lot of disagreements between the Soviets and the Eastern Europeans, and, given the structure of the bloc, easy translation of these disagreements into dramatic shifts in power, policy and personnel—which in turn stokes conflicts among these parties and undercuts Eastern European compliance with Soviet demands.

Just as these parties seem to wreck havoc on their systems at home as a consequence of the system's "elite" sensitivity, so the Soviet Union wreaks havoc on the bloc as a consequence of the region's "Soviet" sensitivity. And in both cases, these ripple effects are as much by accident as by design. Indeed, just as these parties seem to influence their societies precisely when they do not want such influence (for example, when elites are locked in disputes), so the Soviet Union has often influenced Eastern Europe precisely when the Soviets would have preferred less influence—for example, when the Kremlin is divided over questions of power and policy.

The Soviets also paid a price for creating a bloc that had the sole purpose of maximizing Soviet control over the region. The decision to place power over performance had predictable effects. Just as the bureaucracies within Stalinist systems sought to reduce the costs of dependence and uncertainty, so Eastern European parties responded to Soviet power and caprice by creating islands of autonomy (e.g., hiding negative information, resisting Soviet efforts to make the bloc more rational). That which enhanced the power of the hegemon in the short term, therefore, ended up undermining that power in the longer term.

Finally, rapid maturation undercut the power of the Soviet Union within the bloc precisely because it generated complexity and reduced the capacity of the bloc economies to grow as fast as they once did. Coordinating the economic policies of all these countries was a problem in itself, but coordination of increasingly complex economies was even more of a headache. At the same time, lower growth meant an increase in conflicts between Soviet and Eastern European elites for all the reasons noted above with respect to the domestic arena—for example, the tensions generated by tying the stability of the domestic systems and the regional system to growth in a period when there was less growth and yet more and more claimants to the surplus.

The capacity of Eastern Europe to benefit when bargaining with the Soviets grew, of course, as Soviet control over the region declined. But the structure of the bloc also allocated to the Eastern Europeans some independent resources that allowed them to exploit the Soviet Union. First, like the role of society at home, the role of Eastern Europe within the bloc was enhanced by the homogenizing effects of Stalinism. For example, the bloc structure allowed the Eastern European regimes to present a united front with respect to their needs, their interests and their demands. If nothing else, geographical proximity and redundant domestic structures, assets and liabilities made it very easy for the Eastern Europeans to convince the Soviets that problems in one Eastern European country could very easily become problems in all the Eastern European countries unless the Soviets extended help to everyone in crisis or, purportedly, "on the verge" of crisis.

The structure of the bloc also married politics and economics. Because politics was less and less effective as a promoter of political stability (its currency had been devalued), economics became *the* basis for regional as well as domestic stability. As a result, just as publics at home gained autonomy and raised their economic expectations, all at growing costs, political and economic, to the state, so Eastern European regimes gained autonomy and raised their economic expectations, all at growing costs to the Soviet Union. "Weakness," in short, became a source of strength.

Thus far, I have treated regional and domestic dynamics as parallel. However, they also intersected, meaning in practice that parties were weaker and societies stronger in Eastern Europe than in the Soviet Union. Redistribution of power went further in Eastern Europe for a number of reasons, including the facts that in Eastern Europe socialism was younger and imposed by the Soviets, Stalinization was briefer, and socialism carried no "extra" benefits such as an increase in international influence. Moreover, dependence on the Soviets for power, money and security left these parties in the unenviable position of being continually torn between Soviet demands and those of their restive citizens.

Power Redistribution. For the reasons already noted, the Soviets hardly benefitted from the weakness at home of their allies. Instead, fearing instability and its easy spread in a regional hierarchical system, the Soviets were forced to take on considerable regional burdens. The two-tiered structure of Stalinism, therefore, had left the Soviets with multiple burdens. There were burdens at home, the consequence of a more pressing society, the burdens of weak parties in Eastern Europe and, finally, the burdens imposed by fickle Eastern European societies making demands on their parties—which were, of course, passed on to the Soviets.[3]

Creating a domestic political economy that "guaranteed" the autonomy of the party and the dependence of the society and creating a regional bloc that "guaranteed" the power of the Soviet Union and the weakness of Eastern Europe, therefore, had quite the opposite effects over time. Penetrative and despotic states—that is, autonomous states (see Mann, 1986)—became decidedly less so. This is indicated by, for instance, the decline over time in the number of political prisoners and the severity of punishment for political deviance. The "zone of political indifference," in short, grew over time (Hankiss, 1988).

Moreover, there was the growing inability of these states to make, let alone implement, their policies. This was most evident with respect to the many economic reforms in the bloc, beginning with the Liberman reforms in the Soviet Union in 1953. Finally, there was the growing sensitivity of the party to mass concerns, as registered in the political consumption cycle, with temporary priming of public consumption (see Bunce, 1981). This was also registered in the social compact, particularly in Eastern Europe, where political leaders made peace with their publics by trading economic security—minimal work norms, job security, subsidized consumer goods—for political compliance or, more accurately, public acquiescence (see Pravda, 1981; White, 1986; Szelenyi, 1989).

The penetration and despotism of the Soviet Union within the bloc also declined over time. This is apparent, for example, in the contraction in the size of the bloc over time as a consequence of various state defections, the inability of the Soviets to get what they wanted from the bloc with respect to trade, the defense burden and regional economic specialization, and, finally, the clear decline in the capacity and/or willingness of the Soviet Union to use its full coercive powers to punish deviant behavior in the bloc—for instance, the violence that accompanied the invasion of Hungary in 1956 versus the minimal violence in Poland as a consequence of declaring martial law in December, 1981.

As a result, it can be argued that the social compact at home was matched by a version of the social compact within the region. The center—that is, the party at home and the Soviet Union abroad—traded a more lax political and economic environment and considerable economic security for a commitment on the part of the periphery—that is, the society in the domestic sphere and Eastern Europe in the regional sphere—that they would comply with the now scaled-down demands of the hegemon. That acquiescence, not enthusiastic support, became the new standard that tells much of the story.

In this way, the redistribution of power carried several costs beyond the obvious ones of weakening the party at home and the Soviet Union abroad. One was forcing the economy to perform the function of political integration. In particular, these economies were forced to perform not just their usual tasks but also a variety of political tasks such as ensuring elite and bloc cohesion and ensuring mass and Eastern European compliance. The end result was that politics was seen by more and more to be bankrupt (and that included ideology), and these economies, carrying additional political burdens, began to show some signs of bankruptcy as well (Golubovic, 1988).

Another cost of domestic and regional redistribution of power was the creation of a base for economic and political liberalization—at the domestic and the bloc levels. This base was laid in part by the ways in which the tug of war between the party and the society, the Soviet Union and Eastern Europe, and the changes in policies that resulted from that war, linked economic to political liberalization. This base was also laid by the growing autonomy of these societies and these economies in the domestic realm and Eastern Europe in the regional realm. Autonomy, of course, disperses resources. And dispersion of resources through deregulation is the essence of economic and political liberalization.

Economic and Governability Crises

Multiple Crises. Stalinism also produced an economic crisis in the Soviet Union and Eastern Europe. Czechoslovakia, reflecting in part its comparatively high level of socioeconomic development, was the first country in the bloc to register the economic costs of the Stalinist model of development. This crisis, which took place in 1962, foreshadowed the joint party-society reform movement of 1967–1968, which was abruptly terminated by Soviet intervention. The Czechoslovak crisis also foreshadowed the very close linkages indeed between economic and political liberalization and their role as necessary partners in any process that would seek to reform the system.

By the late 1970s, it became increasingly apparent that in addition to the problems in Czechoslovakia, serious economic difficulties began to present themselves in virtually all of the other states in the bloc and, indeed, in Yugoslavia as well (see, for instance, Vanous, 1982). The sources of the economic crisis were multiple and included rapid industrialization giving way to slower rates of growth as new sources of labor and capital were eventually depleted and as development generated powerful "distributive coalitions" (see Olson, 1987). But much of the decline was due to Stalinist practices that exaggerated these constraints on growth while adding a few more peculiar to these centrally planned and state-owned economies.

Stalinist economies are good at mobilization of resources, especially in early stages of development when economic goals are "plannable," economic interests are few, labor and capital are in abundant supply (see, for instance, Lindblom, 1977 and Nove, 1980). However, once these conditions pass from the scene, such economies show all the problems of having strong thumbs but weak fingers—their inefficiencies begin to show. Such economies distort information, perpetuate shortage, encourage "soft" budgets and provide few incentives (as demonstrated by Kornai, 1989), all undermining economic growth.

The Stalinist system also breeds unusually powerful "distributive coalitions"—albeit of a type specific to these economies. In addition to obvious vested interests, such as planners and the party, there are also all those who benefit from what might be termed domestic protectionism (Bogomolov, 1985; Brus, 1983, 1980). The latter include enterprises that depend on state subsidies, workers who depend on job security and consumers who depend on low prices. Stalinist economies, therefore, practice an extreme version of moral hazard wherein economic risk is transferred from individuals and enterprises to the state (see Loriaux, 1991). As a consequence, societal pressures on the surplus are considerable, and this produces severe economic problems.

These difficulties were only enhanced by what was happening in the CMEA. In creating a bloc based on barter trade, redundant economic strengths and weaknesses and isolation from the global economy, the Soviet Union ensured that the bloc structure would merely reinforce, rather than counteract, the problems of Stalinist economies. Moreover, because of the structure of the bloc and the growing dependence of politics on economics, there were precious few ways out of the economic problems of state socialism. These systems could either pretend that they had no problems (for instance, the Brezhnev solution) and thereby mortgage future growth for political stability in the present, or they could pretend that they were reforming their economies—a policy having similar effects in the long run (for example, Kadar's approach) (see Kornai, 1989).

By the late seventies, these difficulties led to an actual decline in the standard of living in Poland, Hungary, Romania and Yugoslavia (see Mencinger, 1989). This occurred primarily because the decision made in the 1970s to join the global economy ended up making matters worse. Exposure to the global economy was not joined with genuine economic reform; instead, it was used to plug up the holes, economic and political, of these systems. Moreover, the party was too divided and the public too pressing to allow for the economic liberalization that was sorely needed if these economies were to benefit from integration with the global economy and to become more efficient and more productive (see, for instance, Poznanski, 1986; Linden, 1986).

This crisis worked to exaggerate the process, already in motion, of redistributing power from the party to the society. For the party, this meant divisions over economic reform, more conflicts as a result of less surplus, growing corruption and rising fears that a divided party and a resentful public would, as in the past, lead necessarily to domestic upheaval. For the society, the economic crisis forced publics to hive off in order to maximize their economic interests and generated a great deal of anger targeted, of course, at the party (see *Marksistichka Misao*, 1989).

These problems meant, in turn, that the party could not do what it had to do; that is, implement economic austerity measures and a genuine liberalization of the economy. To do so would be to put the party out of business—either indirectly by producing massive protests given violation of the social compact, or directly by breaking up the party's economic and therefore political monopoly. While economic liberalization was the only solution, then, it was a politically impossible solution, particularly in Eastern Europe. In this sense, the party and the public saw eye to eye, with their short-term economic interests being precisely the same.

The Eastern European regimes, of course, passed on the costs of their economic and "governability" crises (Hankiss, 1988) to the Soviets (see Bunce, 1985; Ash 1988). What this meant by the mid-1980s was that the Soviet Union was paying enormous costs for two-tiered Stalinism. The debt crisis in Eastern Europe disrupted intrabloc trade, closed the Soviets out of Western markets and increased the demands the Eastern

Europeans made on the Soviets to bail them out of their domestic political and economic difficulties. At the same time, the Soviets were paying for Stalinism at home, including the mounting costs of their own social compact.

Liberalization, Decolonization. With resources redistributed at home and within the bloc, the stage was set for systemic transformation (Bunce, 1989b). All that was needed, as analysts of protest and reform remind us (see Tarrow, 1991), was a change in opportunity structure. This was provided by the new Soviet leadership that in less than five years in office dismantled the Soviet bloc and the Soviet Union itself and, with that, destroyed the postwar international order as well (see Bunce, 1991). And all this happened in a surprisingly peaceful way, for "new" regimes are usually born in bloodshed—as the Russian Revolution of 1917, for example, testifies—and so are "new" international orders. This, for instance, was much of what the First and Second World Wars were about.

These dramatic changes have led many to assume that the prime mover in all this was the new leadership. However, new policies—in particular, deregulation of politics and economics—were rather the result of a long-term historical process. The leadership's specific contribution was not just that it adopted radical policies, which is rare enough, but also, even more rare, that it adopted rational policies—it saw the handwriting on the wall and responded accordingly.

The Soviet leadership realized that state socialism was in crisis at home and in the bloc, which placed it in jeopardy and, more to the point, placed the Soviet Union itself in jeopardy (see Bogomolov, 1989, 1987; Gorbachev 1989, 1988a, 1988b, 1988c). The regime, therefore, saw but two choices: either allow the Soviet Union and Eastern Europe to slide in status and become unstable and poor countries, much like Third, not Second World states, or try to save socialism in at least one country by embarking on revolutionary reform. The leadership rationally opted for major reform, which was high risk/high return, and not for lesser reform, which was higher risk/no return (Bunce 1989a, 1991).

The Soviet regime decided that the whole of the system had to be dismantled, since as the long history of reforming Stalinism had shown, no revision of the system could solve the problem (see, for instance, Gati, 1989; Kornai, 1989). What Gorbachev did was to recognize that he had the power to change the system as a whole. The Soviet party, after all, functioned as a dual monopoly controlling both the Soviet Union and Eastern Europe, and he was head of that party.

The structure of the bloc, geographical proximity and the considerable similarities among these states in terms of regime structure, regime assets and regime liabilities together guaranteed that every state would respond in similar fashion to the opportunities for change provided by Gorbachev. Moreover, the structure of the bloc, the economic crisis and the long-term and informal redistribution of power from the party to the society guaranteed that these parties would collapse, that these societies would be able to seize power without bloodshed (except in Romania) and that the result would be the creation in all cases of regimes committed to economic and political liberalization (on the events of 1989, see Ash, 1989; Brown, 1991; Glenny, 1991, Bunce and Chong, 1990).

Down the Road

There is no way of being certain about the future directions the newly emerging regimes will take. Political and economic liberalization, after all, carry no guarantees. For example, regimes can liberalize their political systems and this can produce, alternatively, dictatorship, revolution or liberal democracy—in other words, the full gamut of political outcomes now existing in the world. Moreover, we cannot be sure that liberalization will evolve into capitalism and liberal democracy until we see how far liberalization goes and whether it is institutionalized. These regimes are too new and too "unformed" to assess either of the above (see Csanadi and Bunce, 1991).

The usual argument, of course, is that the Stalinist pasts of these countries will function as obstacles in the struggle for market capitalism and liberal democracy (see, for instance, Brown, 1989). The essential point here is that what distinguishes Stalinism is the certainty it provides in terms of economic and political outcomes—for example, guaranteed employment, subsidies to consumers, security for enterprises. This all goes against the logic of capitalism and liberal democracy.

But Stalinism cannot be understood simply as an obstacle to capitalism and democracy. Paradoxically, in fact, Stalinism made some contributions to at least the democratic side of the equation. Indeed, this is one reason why political liberalization has proceeded far faster than economic. What Stalinism did, in particular, was to create—by virtue of development, growing weakness of the party, and societal homogeneity—a resourceful and autonomous society—a necessary, but by no means sufficient, condition for liberal democracy.

In a way, Stalinism also made a smooth transfer of economic and political power possible. The peculiar process by which power was transferred from the old to the new regimes in these countries bodes very well for the future of liberal democracy. Such a process has created a strong consensus not just among leaders but also among their many followers. Revolutions, by contrast, tend to leave in their wake diverse values and searing political divisions. While this consensus will, of course, break down once the politics of values is replaced by the politics of interests, it will nonetheless provide a welcome cushion for regimes committed to democratization.

One more peculiar advantage is the degree to which the process of slow transfer of political power functioned as a school for democracy. What we saw in 1989 in what we once called Eastern Europe, for example, was mass (and massive) political participation, bargaining as *the* means by which political conflict was mediated and commitment on all sides to sticking by the agreements forged in the roundtables and in the streets. This was not just a heady and empowering experience; it was also a very democratic experience.

Stalinism, therefore, did not just produce an economic and thus a political crisis; it also, mostly by accident, made some important contributions to the development of liberal democracy, in particular in Eastern Europe. This does not mean, of course, that Stalinism is an irrefutable asset in the struggle for liberal democracy. It was a nasty system and it left nasty residues. However, it is to argue that the way Stalinism died and the reasons Stalinism died speak well, if imperfectly, for the future of democracy in these liberalizing regimes.

Conclusion

The dramatic changes of late in what we used to call the Soviet bloc can be seen as a consequence of the structure of Stalinism—as a domestic and as a regional political economy—and its many unintended consequences over time. The essential point is that Stalinism was self-destructive, but it was also constructive. It was Stalinism that created the basis for a new economic and political order and, with that, a new international order. What strikes one, therefore, is the power of Stalinism. It remade the world twice—first in its own image and then, irony of ironies, in the image of its arch nemesis, the West.

Notes

1. This has been by design (that is, through regional organizations and meetings) and by accident (that is, as a consequence of similar domestic political-economic arrangements).

2. The observation of an American political scientist is relevant here:

"Especially in times of political crisis, a very important part of the people deciding who they are is to decide who their enemies are." (Barrington Moore (1977, p.16).

3. Of course, there was also the burden of military competition with the West. These costs were extraordinarily high since the Soviets lacked both the West's economic strength and the West's reliable allies.

Bibliography

Ash, T. 1989. "Refolution: The Springtime of Two Nations." *New York Review of Books*, 36 (June 15), pp. 3–10.

_____. 1988. "The Empire in Decay." *New York Review of Books*, 35 (Sept. 29), pp. 53–60.

Bogomolov, O. 1989. "Meniaiushchiitsiia oblik sotsializma." *Kommunist*, 11 July, pp. 33–42.

_____. 1987. "Sotsialisticheskie strany na perelomnon etape mirovo ekonomicheskogo razvitiia." *Kommunist*, 10 (July), pp. 31–44.

_____. 1985. "Soglasovanie ekonomicheskikh interesov i politiki pri sotsializme." *Kommunist*, 10 (July), pp. 82–93.

Brown, A. 1989. "Political Change in the Soviet Union." *World Policy Journal*, 6, Summer, pp. 469–502.

Brown, J.F. 1991. *Surge to Freedom*. Durham: Duke University Press.

Brus, W. 1983. "Political Pluralism and Markets." In S. Solomon, ed., *Pluralism in the Soviet Union*, p. 108–130. New York: St. Martin's.

_____. 1980. "Political System and Economic Efficiency: The East European Context." *Journal of Comparative Economics* vol. 4, pp. 40–55.

Bruszt, L. and T. Reti. 1989. "The Rise and Expected Fall of Functional Corruption: A Hungarian Case Study."

Bunce, V. 1991. "The Soviet Union under Gorbachev: Ending Stalinism and Ending the Cold War." *International Journal*, 46 (Spring), pp. 220–241.

_____. 1990. "Stalinism and the Management of Uncertainty." Paper presented at the American-Hungarian Roundtable in Political Science in San Francisco, Sept. 1.

_____. 1989a. "Decline of a Regional Hegemon: The Gorbachev Regime and Reform in Eastern Europe." *Eastern European Politics and Societies*, 3 (Spring), pp. 235–267.

_____. 1989b. "Economic and Political Liberalization in the Soviet Union." Paper presented at the Conference on "Shifting Boundaries between State and Society" in Ljubljana, Yugoslavia, June 3.

_____. 1989c. "The Polish Crisis of 1980–1981 and Theories of Revolution." In T. Boswell, ed. *Revolution and the World System*. Boulder, Co.: Westview Press.

_____. 1985. "The Empire Strikes Back." *International Organization*, 39 Winter, pp. 1–46.

_____. 1981. *Do New Leaders Make a Difference: Executive Succession and Public Policy Under Capitalism and Socialism*. Princeton: Princeton University Press.

Bunce, V. and D. Chong. 1990. "The Party's Over: 1989 in Eastern Europe."

Paper presented at the annual meeting of the American Political Science Association in San Francisco, Sept. 2.

Cohen, S. 1985. *Rethinking the Soviet Experience*. Oxford: Oxford University Press.

Csanadi, M. 1989. "Party-State Interlocking Directorates: Economic and Political Decision-Making in Hungary." Unpublished manuscript.

Csanadi, M. and V. Bunce. 1991. "A Systematic Analysis of a Non-System: Post-Communism in Hungary." Paper presented at the Hungarian-American roundtable in Budapest, Dec. 17.

Dawisha, Karen. 1988. *Eastern Europe, Gorbachev and Reform*. Cambridge: Cambridge University Press.

Gati, C. 1989. "Reforming Communist Systems: Lessons From the Hungarian Case." In W. Griffith, ed. *Central Eastern Europe and the Current Crisis*, pp. 218–240. Praeger.

Glenny, Misha. 1990. *The Rebirth of History*. London: Penguin.

Golubovic, Zagorka. 1988. *Kriza identiteta savremenog jugoslavenskog drustva*. Belgrade: Filip Visnjic.

Gorbachev, M. 1989. "Doklad general'nogo sekretaria Ts.k. KPSS M.S. Gorbacheva". Pravda, April 26: 1.

_____. 1988a. "K polnovlastiiu sovetov iz sozdaniiu sotsialisticheskogo pravovogo gosudarstva." *Pravda*, November 30, pp. 1–3.

_____. 1988b. "Na osnove polnogo ravnopraviia, samostoiatel'nosti, vzaimnogo uvazheniia." *Izvestiia*, March 118, pp. 1–2.

_____. 1988c. "Revoliutsionnoi perestroike—ideologiiu obnovlenniia." *Pravda*, Feb. 19, pp. 1–3.

Hankiss, E. 1988. *Eastern European Alternatives: Are There Any?*, Parts One and Two. Unpublished book manuscript.

Harding, N. 1984. "Socialism, Society and the Organic Labour State." In Neil Harding, ed. *The State In Socialist Society*, 1–50. Albany, New York: SUNY Press.

Hirszowicz, M. 1986. *Coercion and Control in Communist Society: The Visible Hand in a Command Economy*. New York: St. Martin's Press.

Horvat, B. 1984. "Pravno-formalna: drustveno-ekonomska dimenzija vlasnistva." *Nase teme*, 32, pp. 2922–2926.

Jowitt, K. 1971. *Revolutionary Breakthroughs and National Development: The Case of Romania, 1944–1965*. Berkeley: University of California Press.

Kelliher, D. 1989. *The Chinese State and Peasant Society*. Unpublished book manuscript.

Kornai, J. 1989. In D. Stark and V. Nee, eds. *Remaking the Economic Institutions of Socialism: Lessons from the Hungarian and Chinese Cases*. Stanford University Press.

_____. 1980. *The Economics of Shortage*. Amsterdam: North Holland.

Lapidus, G. 1989. "State and Society: Towards the Emergence of a Civil Society in the Soviet Union." In S. Bialer, ed. *Inside Gorbachev's Russia*. Boulder, Co.: Westview Press.

Lewin, M. 1988. *The Gorbachev Phenomenon*. Berkeley: University of California Press.

Lindblom, C. 1977. *Politics and Markets*. New York: Basic Books.

Linden, R. 1986. "Socialist Parties and the Global Economy: The Case of Romania." *International Organization*, 40 (Spring), pp. 171–204.

Link, P. 1989. "The Chinese Intellectuals and Revolt." *New York Review of Books*, June 29, pp. 38–41.

Loriaux, Michael. 1991. *France After Hegemony: International Change and Financial Reform*. Ithaca: Cornell University Press.

Mann, M. 1986. "The Autonomous Power of the State: Its Origins, Mechanisms and Results." In J. Hall, ed. *States in History*, pp. 109–136. London: Basil Blackwell.

Marksistichka Misao. 1989. Special Issue on "Reforma Politichkog sistema moguchnost novikh projekata sotsializma kako nas drugi vide: Jugoslavia u krizi." (June).

Mencinger, J. 1989. "The Yugoslav Economy: Systemic Change, 1945–1986." Pittsburgh, Pa.: The Carl Beck Papers.

Moore, Barrington. 1977. *Injustice: The Social Bases of Obedience and Revolt*. White Plains, New York: M.E. Sharpe.

Nove, A. 1980a. "Socialism, Centralised Planning and the One-Party State." In T. Rigby, et al., ed. *Power and Policy in the USSR*, pp. 77–97. New York: St. Martin's.

_____. 1980b. "The Soviet Economy: Problems and Prospects." *New Left Review*, 119, pp. 1–18.

Olson, Mancur. 1987. *The Rise and Decline of Nations*. New Haven: Yale University Press.

Poznanski, K. 1986. "Economic Adjustment and Political Forces: Poland Since 1970." *International Organization*, 40 (Spring), pp. 455–489.

Pravda, A. 1981. "East-West Interdependence and the Future of Eastern Europe." In M. Bornstein, Z. Gitelman and W. Zimmerman, eds. *East-West Relations and the Future of Eastern Europe*, pp. 162–190. London: Allen and Unwin.

Przeworski, A. 1986. "Some Problems in the Study of the Transition to Democracy." In G. O'Donnell, P. Schmitter and L. Whitehead, eds., *Transitions from Authoritarian Rule: Comparative Perspectives*, pp. 47–63. Baltimore: Johns Hopkins.

Schopflin, G., R. Tokes and I. Volyges. "Leadership Change and Crisis in Hungary." *Problms of Communism*, 37 (September–October), pp. 23–46.

Scott, James. 1985. *Weapons of the Weak: Everyday Forms of Peasant Resistance*. New Haven: Yale University Press.

Szelenyi, I. 1989. "Eastern Europe in an Epoch of Transition: Toward a Socialist Mixed Economy?" In D. Stark and V. Nee, eds. *Remaking the Economic Institutions of Socialism. China and Eastern Europe*, pp. 208–232. Stanford: Stanford University Press.

Tarrow, Sidney. 1991. *Struggle, Politics and Reform: Collective Action, Social Movements and Cycles of Protest*. Ithaca: Cornell University Western Societies Paper, No. 21.

Vanous, Jan. 1982. "East European Economic Slowdown." *Problems of Communism*, 31 (July–August), pp. 1–19.

Whyte, M. 1989. "Who Hates Bureaucracy? A Chinese Puzzle." In D. Stark and V. Nee, eds., *Remaking the Economic Institutions of Socialism: China and Eastern Europe*, p. 233–254. Stanford: Stanford University.

3

Political Economy of the Eastern European–Soviet Trade: Rethinking the Past and Searching for the Future

Jozef C. Brada

The combination of great opportunities for the exercise of political power by the Soviet Union in the design and operation of its trading bloc with Eastern Europe (i.e., CMEA) and a lack of objective economic mechanisms to act as a counterweight to such power constitutes to many observers strong prima facie evidence that the bloc was an organization whose genesis and outcomes reflected primarily political rather than economic forces and that in this political process the Soviet Union and its interests were the dominant factors. This view of the bloc was supported by a number of studies claiming to provide evidence of the exploitation of the smaller members by the Soviet Union or of the inequitable distribution of the gains from integration in a way reflective of Soviet political objectives.

Since the trade bloc was perceived primarily as having been a political creature of the Soviet Union, providing few genuine benefits of integration to its members, it is not surprising that relaxation of Soviet hegemony over Eastern Europe was likely to lead to the bloc's demise unless an economic rationale was developed to replace political judgments, but it was not. In fact, the CMEA was abandoned in its existing form in 1991 and it remains uncertain whether any alternative integration scheme—other than some consultative body—will fill the vacuum.

This chapter examines the evidence on the political and economic determinants of the integration in the former bloc. From this evidence the trade integration emerges as having fulfilled a useful economic function for its members in the past, namely, the provision of a regime for the conduct of foreign trade. This bureaucratic regime was, of necessity, both unique and flawed, but as demonstrated below, it not only allowed for a rapid expansion of trade volume but also assured that the specialization pattern was at least in general consistent with the structure of endowments. Thus, it may be in the interests of the former members to attempt some regional integration scheme to provide them with the full benefits of trade specialization.

The Nature of the Bloc

Like any other regional economic integration scheme, the one in question was partly an economic organization and partly a political one. Regional economic integration schemes are economic in that they seek to generate gains in trade to raise both the level and the growth of incomes of their members. They are political in that their formation requires an unusual degree of trust and cooperation among would-be members who face the prospect of yielding some sovereignty over the integration scheme. Moreover, within each integration scheme, rules for operating the scheme and for the sharing of costs and benefits of integration require the existence of some political means for policy decisions.

Basic Asymmetry. The analysis of the organization of CMEA trade has tended to stress its political aspects rather than economic factors. There are several reasons for that, including the overwhelming role played by the Soviet Union, contrasting with other integration schemes characterize by diversity in member size and political leverage. Moreover, Soviet predominance encompassed virtually all aspects of relations among members, including ideological leadership in formulating the objectives of socialism. The Soviet Union also played a major role in the defense of the member countries by generally carrying a higher share of the bloc's defense burden. Its economic preeminence was reflected in the fact that the Soviet Union was the largest single trade partner for each of the Eastern European members, all critically dependent on the Soviet Union for its supplies of energy and raw materials and purchase of industrial goods that were difficult to sell in western markets.

The evolution of the bloc as an institution also seems to support the hypothesis that politics rather than economics was the basis for its structure and operation. The organization was founded in 1949, the height of Stalin's political control over Eastern Europe and a period of

Soviet economic exploitation of Eastern Europe.[1] Only under Khrushchev when the informal, Stalinist means of control and exploitation began to be dismantled did the bloc's institutions begin to be strengthened, in large part on Soviet initiative. It is appealing to view the expansion of the bloc's role as a bureaucratic substitute for Stalin's autocratic means of strengthening the Soviet economy at the expense of its partners.

Another reason for stressing the political nature of the trade bloc is the nontransparency of its mechanism. The means by which trade among market economies was promoted is relatively easy to understand: When tariffs are reduced, relative prices change, thus increasing trade and leading to factor movements. In trade among centrally planned economies the comparison of domestic and foreign prices was not the motive force behind trade flows; there appears to have been no autonomous, purely economic mechanism that could be used to promote intra-bloc trade. Rather, trade was promoted by means of plan coordination among member countries, specialization agreements, complex programs and other bureaucratic measures. These measures had one common feature: they were all political, as their implementation required the conscious effort of authorities in each member country to comply with the agreements.

Major Criticisms. To the extent that the bloc has been viewed as an economic organization, the assessments of its success have been distinctly negative.[2] The members are alleged to have had economic endowments that differed excessively so that integration led to trade diversion, with the importers of manufactures turning from low-cost developed-economy producers to higher-cost suppliers within the bloc. Moreover, a lack of similarity in endowments precluded opportunities for intra-industry trade and competition, thus limiting the opportunities for integration to promote competition and specialization.[3]

These structural barriers to trade were augmented by the economic systems of the member countries and by the integration mechanism. The system of central planning vitiated the competition- and efficiency-stimulating effects of integration-induced trade in two ways. First, because prices did not influence input or output decisions, trade could not displace inefficient domestic production or direct resources toward efficient export industries. Second, planners tended to be trade averse and disinclined to depend on supplies from producers beyond their control, and enterprises tended to be vertically integrated in order to protect themselves from shortages in, and the poor quality of, input supplies.

These tendencies limited the volume of trade and the ability to trade parts and components in addition to finished products. Distortions in pricing and inconvertibility of national currencies further constricted trade by forcing bilateral balancing of both aggregate trade as well as trade in various categories of hard and soft goods.[4] Finally, integration was limited to traditional commodity trade, particularly of finished products. There was no real movement of capital and of labor and particularly of technology and firm-specific knowledge among members.

The Evidence for a Political Nature

If the bloc was a creature of the Soviet Union, designed largely to achieve Soviet political and economic objectives at the expense of Eastern Europe, then the evidence must be sought in the distribution of gains between the Soviet Union and the other members. The first attempt to provide such evidence was undertaken by Horst Mendershausen (1959, 1960), who examined Soviet foreign trade data for 1955–59 and discovered that the Soviet Union charged its Eastern European partners prices 15 percent higher than those charged Western European importers of the same goods. Similarly the Soviets were found to pay, on average, 15 percent less to importers of similar goods from Eastern Europe than they paid Western European exporters.

Mendershausen interpreted the above findings as evidence that the Soviet Union was able to exploit its Eastern European partners by virtue of its large size and the monopoly and monopsony power derived therefrom.[5] In this interpretation, the political objective behind the integration was the maximization of Soviet economic benefits at the expense of Eastern Europe. This view was strongly challenged by Franklyn Holzman (1962, 1965), who examined not only Soviet trade with Eastern Europe and the West but also the trade of the other Eastern European countries. He found that the Soviet pricing pattern uncovered by Mendershausen held true for these countries also, so the Soviet Union did not exploit its Eastern European trading partners through the intra-bloc pricing mechanism any more than they exploited the Soviet Union.

The perception of exploitation resulted, according to Holzman, from two phenomena. The first was that the West discriminated against Eastern Europe and the Soviet Union. Thus, in order to sell to the West, these countries had to discount their exports below the prices obtained within the bloc and they also had to pay more for imports from the West. Second, and more important to Holzman's view, was the fact that the trade regime should be viewed as a special kind of customs union, and therefore intra-bloc trade prices did not need to approach world market prices and the appearance, but not the reality, of exploitation was created.

Implicit Subsidies. A methodologically similar approach was employed by Michael Marrese and Jan Vanous (1983, 1988) to show that, in the 1970s and 1980s, it was the Soviet Union that provided subsidies to—or was, in effect, exploited by—its partners in Eastern Europe. The basis of the Marrese-Vanous estimates of the Soviet subsidy rests on well-known features of intra-bloc prices. For most of the period under discussion, these prices were based on an average of past world market prices and were fixed at this level for several years at a time, so systematic differences between contemporaneous intra-bloc and world market prices evolved. Specifically, a country exporting fuels and raw materials to the members obtained lower prices than could be obtained on world markets, while if it imported manufactures from its partners, it paid more for them than their value on the world market.

If the commodity composition of trade for all member countries were roughly similar, such a distortion in prices would have had no great implications. However, in intra-bloc trade the Soviet Union was by far the largest, if not the only, net exporter of fuels and raw materials and net importer of manufactured goods. Thus, the Soviet Union was exploited by Eastern Europe both because it sold its raw materials at prices below those available on world markets and because it paid world market prices for low-quality Eastern European manufacturers that could be replaced either with higher-quality western goods or with goods of Eastern European quality purchased from the West at prices lower than those paid to Eastern European exporters. The exploitation of the Soviet Union was estimated by Marrese and Vanous to be in excess of $5 billion annually in the late 1970s.

This finding that the Soviet Union was subsidizing Eastern Europe is paradoxical if one accepts Mendershausen's results or at least the implicit logic behind them, that the Soviet Union's political and economic power vis à vis its smaller and weaker partners should have enabled it to exploit them. Marrese and Vanous attempt to resolve this paradox by arguing that rather than being exploited by its smaller and weaker partners, the Soviet Union designed the pricing mechanism so as to disguise from its own citizens and from the citizens of the other members the fact that the Soviet Union was paying subsidies to the Eastern European countries.

The objective of these subsidies was to purchase from these countries a range of intangible geopolitical goods and services (e.g., military security, support for expansion in the Third World, and ideological conformity). The proof for this view of the bloc as a political creature designed to further promote Soviet aims is the way these subsidies were distributed among members. Loyal countries bordering on the west, such as Czechoslovakia and East Germany, received the largest subsidies on a per capita basis while less subservient and less strategically located members, such as Poland and Romania, were provided with smaller subsidies. Thus, the more the Soviets paid, the greater the geopolitical benefits they received.

This view of the trade regime as a mechanism for distributing political payoffs among its members has been challenged on both technical and conceptual grounds. Among the technical critiques are those by Paul Marer (1984) and Kazimierz Poznanski (1988), who argue that assuming more realistic values for discounts on Eastern European manufactures would have either sharply reduced the magnitude of Soviet subsidies to Eastern Europe or eliminated them altogether. While such critiques may well be correct, or at least equally plausible from a methodological standpoint, the prevailing perception was that the phenomenon in question did, indeed, exist, and it was this perception more than any scholarly work that drove the geopolitical behavior of the countries involved.

This is not to say that Eastern European or western observers agree that the Eastern Europeans' belief in the existence of these subsidies did, in fact, induce them to reciprocate with political and military benefits. Holzman (1987, Ch. 10), for example, argues that Soviet subsidies were a form of compensation to Eastern Europe for the welfare losses these countries were made to bear by being forced to trade too much within the bloc. This view that Eastern Europe suffered static losses from overtrading within the bloc has a dynamic counterpart in the arguments of Köves (1983) and Marer (1984), who claim that Eastern Europe's excessive reliance on the undemanding Soviet market stifled its development and caused technological stagnation.

Other Views. The view that subsidies measured by Marrese and Vanous were a conscious or unconscious form of reparations for the economic damage done by the Soviet Union has, in turn, been subject to criticism (Brada, 1985, 1988). The argument for the existence of static losses rests on the impressionistic assumption that the member countries overtraded with each other; in the following section evidence is presented that casts doubt on this belief. The argument for dynamic losses assumes that it was trade with the Soviet Union that led to the low quality and lack of innovation that characterized Eastern European industrial output. The reality, however, is that these defects are a function of the economic system that existed in these countries.

The cited defects in goods designed for export to the Soviet Union or to other members of the bloc are equally evident in goods destined for domestic consumption or for nonbloc markets. This line of argumentation thus reduces to the claim that the Soviets were paying reparations for the damage wrought by the imposition of their economic and political system on the countries of Eastern Europe. Although "new thinking" in the Soviet Union may well have led to this realization in recent years, it is most unlikely that the previous Soviet leadership would have viewed the imposition of Soviet-style communism on Eastern Europe as anything other than a boon for which the Soviet Union ought to reap thanks rather than make amends.

A more fundamental critique of the conception of the integration scheme as a predominantly political scheme focuses on weaknesses in the political economy of the Marrese and Vanous approach (see: Brada, 1985, 1988). A key shortcoming is that the way in which the subsidies were allocated is not clearly explained by Marrese and Vanous, though the explanation they do offer tends to change over time, presenting critics with something of a moving target.[6] At times it is claimed that subsidies were the outcome of Soviet welfare maximization, at other times that a rather ill-specified bargaining process where Soviet behavior was rather naive and Eastern European interests were articulated in a one-dimensional way prevented any strategic behavior in negotiations over the supply of benefits to the Soviet Union and certainly did not link the economic demand of these countries for subsidies to a willingness to provide geopolitical benefits to the Soviet Union.

Although Marrese and Vanous attribute to the Soviet Union the ability to allocate subsidies to the members with considerable precision by selecting the net volume of raw materials and fuels exports and manufactured good imports, the total volume of subsidies was hardly controllable. Indeed, they divide total subsidies into intended and unintended, the latter resulting from unanticipated movements in world market prices. However, undesired subsidies tended to be greater than desired ones, a curious outcome in view of the precision in the allocation of subsidies among the members, and total subsidies increased steadily in the 1970s, implying that Soviet demand for geopolitical benefits was unaffected either by détente or by increasing economic difficulties in the Soviet economy.[7]

Finally, the subsidy theory assumes rather than demonstrates that the payment of subsidies brought forth a supply of geopolitical benefits. Since the entire objective of pricing was to hide the subsidies from the populations of the recipient countries, it was then difficult to understand how the political attitudes and behavior of these populations were to be influenced.[8] If the populations were not the objects of the subsidies, then the subsidies must have been directed to the leadership of the respective countries, and here an analysis of their geopolitical interests that goes beyond subsidy maximization is needed but not provided.

The Evidence for an Economic Nature

Thus to view the bloc solely as a political mechanism whose design and operation were geared primarily to the political and strategic objectives of the Soviet Union cannot be established solely on the purported existence of the kind of exploitation and subsidies. What is also needed is proof that the economic benefits of the trade integration were minor. If, on the other hand, its economic benefits were significant, then it is correct to view the trade regime as having been primarily an economic organization that provided useful trade benefits to members, and thus an organization that, after fundamental reform, should be able to survive a major change in political relations between Eastern Europe and the Soviet Union. Thus, the economic basis for the existence of the regime must be sought in a quantification of these effects and their comparison with the effects of other integration schemes that are generally accepted as having been successful.

Static Gains. Among the first efforts to measure the ability of the CMEA to increase trade among its members was that of Ed Hewett (1976). Hewett estimated a so-called gravity equation, a general equilibrium model of bilateral trade among countries. The model posits that exports from one country to another can be determined as a function of these countries' national incomes, populations, and the distance between them. It is generally assumed that countries with higher incomes will trade more, that larger countries are more self-sufficient, and that distance is a barrier to international trade. The effects of a customs union are estimated by adding a dummy variable that takes on a value greater than the one when the two countries being observed belong to the union but is equal to zero otherwise.

Hewett estimated this equation using 1970 data for the members of the CMEA, the European Economic Community (EC) and the European Free Trade Area (EFTA). He found that the Soviet Union and Eastern Europe did, indeed, increase inter-member trade to the extent that intra-bloc trade volumes were somewhere between the level of trade expected between two western countries that do not belong to the same integration scheme and that expected between two western countries that belong to an integration scheme such as the EC or the EFTA.

Jozef Brada and Jose Mendez (1985, 1988) undertook a similar study for 1977 data using a modified form of the gravity equation, including as variables the level of development and distance between the integrating countries. The bloc's potential for increasing inter-member trade was found to be less than that of the EC, in part because of the lower level of development of the Soviet Union and Eastern European countries and in part because of greater inter-member distances. On the other hand, the bloc's potential was about that of the EFTA, with the bloc's lower level of development offset by EFTA's greater inter-member distances.

Potential for increasing inter-member trade can, of course, never be fully realized. The Brada and Mendez (ibid.) study demonstrated that the effectiveness of integration policy was no worse than that of the EC, with each scheme achieving about 60 percent of the potential increase in inter-member trade. Thus if increases in trade among members—trade creation—is a useful measure of the economic benefits of integration, then the policies of the Soviet Union and Eastern Europe achieved as much of the potential for increasing trade among members as did the policies of the EC for its members.

A frequent criticism raised against the use of trade creation as a measure of the economic benefits to its members is that much of the increase in intra-bloc trade represented trade diversion (Holzman [1976] Ch. 3). That is, by favoring inefficient intra-bloc suppliers at the expense of efficient western or developing country suppliers, integration caused its members to overtrade with each other and to undertrade with the rest of the world. One argument is that prior to the formation of the trade system, its members tended to trade very little with each other and therefore the increases in trade observed were the result of the diversion of trade from normal pre–World War II patterns. However, those patterns can hardly be viewed as normal, both because of the effects of the depression on international trade and, more important, because of the extensive system of barriers to intra–Eastern European trade that existed in the inter-war period (see Montias, 1966).

Another argument for the existence of overtrading among the Soviet Union and Eastern European countries is that the volume of intra-bloc trade was too high primarily at the expense of East-West trade. However, it is evident from the actual trade behavior that the member countries appeared to be only marginally more inclined to import from each other than from outside sources than were the EC countries. Moreover, it must be kept in mind that the low volume of East-West trade often offered as evidence of the CMEA's trade diverting effect may more properly be ascribed to Western trade policy discrimination against the Soviet Union and Eastern Europe in its early years and to the difficulties experienced by those countries in exporting their manufactures to western markets.

Customs Union. Given the underlying concept of the integration, it proceeds not by the lowering of tariff and other barriers but rather by means of a web of administrative agreements (see Lavigne, 1988) mirroring the domestic economic mechanisms of its members. Negotiations over trade flows and prices were facilitated and regularized by the trade bureaucracy, thus providing members with an international regime that reduced the costs of reaching such agreements and thus promoted specialization among members (Brada, 1988).

The price-setting mechanism, although cumbersome, was an important component of the integration mechanism. It encouraged inter-member trade by providing price stability, a valuable characteristic for central planners and, more important, an objective rule for setting prices. The latter was particularly valuable because bilateral trade negotiations between two members were, in fact, negotiations between bilateral monopolists. In such a situation, equilibrium prices were difficult to settle, and the existence of an agreed-to starting point clearly must have facilitated agreement and thus reduced the costs of trade.

This benefit came, of course, at a cost. Fixed prices set to world market levels with little account for quality differences did, in fact, lead precisely to the kind of subsidies discussed earlier. In part these subsidies arose because by the very construction of intra-bloc prices, there were differences between them and continually changing world market prices. Moreover, as in any customs union, there were differences between inter-member and world market prices reflecting differences in tastes and factor endowments between members and the rest of the world. Within the bloc, capital was scarce and the demand for capital-intensive products high relative to the rest of the world. Thus, it is no surprise that countries like Czechoslovakia and East Germany, which were more abundantly endowed with capital, the scarce and highly demanded factor, benefited most from the difference between intra-bloc and world market prices.

The trade regime had other shortcomings as well, but these reflected not so much flaws in the design of the integration mechanism itself as limitations imposed on integration by the economic systems of the integrating countries. For example, the monetary arrangements were unsatisfactory largely because there was no universally acceptable means of settling trade imbalances between countries. Thus, such imbalances were minimized and settled on a bilateral basis, imposing limits on both the volume of trade and on capital flows among countries. However, it is difficult to see how, under the classical system of central planning, the "commodity inconvertibility" of national currencies could have been overcome in a practical way.

Another failure of integration was that it did not allow for the activities of bloc-based multinational firms. The lack of such firms limited integration to commodity trade and prevented the exploitation of the many sources of competitive advantage to be found in unique and firm-specific advantages. The uniqueness of such advantages made it difficult for their owners to sell them to outsiders, and thus multinational firms arose to exploit them in other countries by establishing operations abroad. In many cases these firm-specific advantages arose in nontradable products such as services rather than in tradables, and it was especially in such cases that integration was powerless.

Finally, integration was based more on political than on economic competition. Specialization, and the ability to capture export markets within the bloc, was based much more on a political calculus of give and take than on the legitimate competitive potential of each country's producers. Thus, there was an allocation of competitive positions followed by extensive development of production facilities, but little objective verification that specialization positions were effectively developed to a competitive standard and surely even less elimination of wasteful and inefficient capacity.

The Future of the Regional Trade

Overall Environment. Granting all the shortcomings in socialist integration, it is conceivable that if the economic mechanisms of the members were reformed, these negative aspects of integration could also be reduced or eliminated while at the same time a number of the positive benefits that the integration mechanism used to provide could be retained. The type of reform that might be implemented would depend critically on domestic reforms undertaken by the bloc's members and, at the same time, would have to reflect the possibilities and incentives for member countries' interactions with the rest of the world.

The pace of domestic economic reform has accelerated in all member countries, but, nevertheless, important differences remain both in the conception of reform measures and in their implementation. The most advanced reform measures have been undertaken in Poland, Hungary and less by Czechoslovakia, all explicitly calling for rapid marketization and privatization. Nevertheless, it would be quite wrong to assume that progress toward these objectives will be as rapid as the reform blueprints at times suggest.

Poland, facilitated by a long period of high rates of inflation, has to a large extent freed prices and eliminated or reduced many producer and consumer subsidies. In Czechoslovakia and Hungary the drive for price reform is less intense, from fear of an uncontrollable inflationary spiral that would negatively affect low-income individuals who spend much of their incomes on food, cause unemployment and require a restructuring of production that would entail enormous short-run dislocations.

In even these more reformist countries, prices are likely to remain distorted for at least eight to ten years, thus making such prices of dubious value in guiding foreign trade decisions without the aid of an elaborate system of tariffs, subsidies and other ad hoc levies. In the Soviet Union or its successor states, Romania and Bulgaria, the liberalization of prices is unlikely at this time, so liberalization will take even longer. In the Soviet Union, the so-called ruble overhang, the pent-up purchasing power in the hands of the population, represents an important barrier to the freeing of prices as do concerns over the effect of food-price increases. Moreover, in none of these countries is the conception of reform such as to make extensive price liberalization or price reform necessary.[9]

Except for Czechoslovakia, all countries where privatization has been considered have eschewed wholesale privatization through national distribution of ownership rights to the population. Instead, incrementalist schemes—such as sale or leasing—have been viewed as more appropriate. Given the virtual nonexistence of credit markets, the only domestic resources available for the purchase of assets from the state are private savings. Since these are in most countries a fraction of the value of the state assets, then in privatization, progress will be gradual.

Western Dimension. An important factor in the reform of the system is the terms under which its members can engage in trade with nonmembers, particularly the European Community. There is a feeling among Eastern European countries that unless they act decisively now, they may be shut out of Western European economic and political integration for ever. Czechoslovakia, Hungary, and Poland, for instance, have all indicated a desire for more intimate associate status with the European Community, with a view toward eventual full membership, and have engaged in lengthy and difficult negotiations with the EC toward that end.

While there is no doubt that economic contracts will increase, it is also evident that reformers in Eastern Europe (and the Soviet Union) are engaging in a good bit of self-delusion by believing that such an expansion will be a panacea for their economic problems. Many of these countries are in deep disequilibrium in their relations with the West, a disequilibrium characterized by extensive hard currency debts. Moreover, their trade structure is inclined toward a more rapid growth of imports than of exports,[10] and many of these countries continue to express a preference for an industrial structure that may be at odds with what can be realized in economic competition with the West.

There are also likely to be some reservations on the part of the European Community, which will, of course, seek to increase its economic contacts with the Soviet Union and Eastern Europe but which may well wish to stop short of moving toward an intimate relationship, in part on political grounds. While amorphous national coalitions that replaced the Communist Party have given way to more focussed political parties, it is premature to predict that viable multiparty democracies will emerge in due course. Until a solid record of political stability can be established in Eastern Europe, a process that will take at least ten years and perhaps even more in some countries, it is unlikely that the European Community will be willing to extend full membership to any member.

In addition, economic obstacles to an intimate relationship will exist for many years.[11] As the European Community becomes more integrated, the problem of incorporating new members will grow since the Soviet Union and Eastern European countries would find it more difficult to conform to mechanisms existing among the current European community members. The addition of Eastern European members would be a drain on community funds, both to support the large agricultural sectors of these countries and to assist their backward regions. Finally, the addition of Eastern European countries with their hypertrophied smokestack industrial sectors would only exacerbate structural adjustment and unemployment problems in Western Europe's iron and steel, mining and metalworking industries. The agricultural surpluses that appeared in Czechoslovakia, Hungary, and Poland after the elimination of subsidies for food consumption also played an important role in the collapse of Polish-EC negotiations over an association agreement.

Thus the centrifugal forces acting on Eastern Europe and the Soviet Union are likely to diminish as East and West reach a more realistic assessment of the possibilities while the centripetal forces may increasingly assert themselves as these countries turn from the dismantling of communism toward the more practical problem of creating functioning economic systems on the ruins of central economic planning. In terms of their international trade, it is quite clear that the basing of trade among the former members of CMEA on dollar clearing and world market prices eliminates any means of promoting integration or above-average levels of trade among these countries. If some trade regime is to be created to facilitate intra-regional exchanges, it must reflect its external environment and the evolving economic systems of its members. In the next section, we consider several alternatives that have been proposed as potential models for a new order.

Options Available for Reform

Dollarization, Marketization. One model of reform, that employed in CMEA trade since January, 1991, is to undertake trade at world market prices and pay for it in hard currencies. Such a reform of the CMEA seemed appealing for several reasons, including that by setting prices equal to world market prices it avoids the distorting effects that existing differences between intra-bloc and world market prices now create. Moreover, by paying for imports and exports in dollars, trade surpluses could be utilized in trade with other countries.

There are, nevertheless, some shortcomings to this approach, in part because it has represented a tremendous gain for the Soviet Union, since at world market prices, Soviet trade with the rest of the bloc showed a surplus of $11 billion rather than a deficit of $4 billion. In addition, the payment for imports and exports in dollars has generated both an increase in the transactions demand for foreign exchange in each country as well as a greater reserve demand as the volume of hard currency denominated trade increases. A further implication is that precisely by placing internal trade on a par with trade with non-members, the integrating effects of the bloc have been effectively eliminated. This, coupled with the inability of the Soviet Union to provide foreign exchange to its enterprises and with the collapse of the Soviet economy, led to a very steep decline in Soviet–Eastern European trade as well as in intra–Eastern European exchanges in 1990 and 1991.

The proposal also suffers from a number of practical problems, not the least of these being the determination of world market prices for Eastern European manufactures. It is easy to argue that low quality Eastern European goods are over-priced in intra-bloc trade, but there is no objective way of determining what the world market price for such goods might be. Indeed, unless trade is conducted on the basis of cumbersome efforts to document the world market prices of Eastern

European manufactures, intra-bloc prices must continue to be based entirely on bilateral negotiations. Such a practice is more time consuming and cumbersome than the existing system, thus serving as a disincentive to intra-bloc trade.

Finally, although the former Soviet Union stands to gain through an improvement in its terms of trade, such an improvement would, in fact, militate for a shift in productive resources from industry, the import competing sector, to natural resources, the export sector. Indeed, in a dollarized world-market priced trade, the resource rich reconstituted Soviet Union's industry would be the victim of a particularly virulent form of Dutch disease. In fact, exports of manufactures to Eastern Europe, a priority of the Soviet leadership, have declined sharply.

In sum, the dollarization and marketization of the bloc trade has been proceeding very slowly, with hard currency payments reserved for a small fraction of total trade. Supplementing the rather small volume of dollar-cleared trade in the region is a new form of barter trade that is most evident in the bilateral trade agreements negotiated between individual Eastern European countries and various parts of the Soviet Union or more recently with the individual republics. These very much reflect the old intra-CMEA exchanges of fixed lists of goods, but they clearly lack the institutional background of CMEA price rules, suggesting that they are a costly, and therefore limited, substitute for the institutionalized barter system of the CMEA.

Alternative Schemes. If the bloc cannot be turned into a marketized/dollarized customs union quickly, it is worthwhile examining proposals for reforming the bloc—after its resurrection—that move toward this goal in a more gradual, evolutionary way that is more consistent with the pattern of reform in the member countries. One such proposal has been put forward by Jozef van Brabant (1988), who suggests a mechanism reminiscent of the European Payments Union (EPU) for promoting a form of intra-bloc convertibility and thus increasing both the volume and the economic efficiency of trade among members. Van Brabant proposes to expand the idea, already approved by most members, of direct inter-enterprise relations between enterprises in two or more countries, with clearing to take place through a special facility.

Such a scheme would be a critical improvement over the existing system where balances are settled bilaterally, leading to various forms of log-rolling over trade and prices, and over one where the hard currency contribution is simply absorbed by those countries who are able to run a surplus in the beginning. This limited form of convertibility can be expanded as the range and scope of interfirm operations expands. Thus the scheme not only strengthens the degree of integration by giving it an economic basis but also provides the benefit of an increasingly convertible currency for member countries.

For such a reform of the trade mechanism to succeed, not only a dismantling of the state's monopoly over foreign trade is required, but at the same time, members would have to equilibrate their goods markets and set realistic prices that reflect real costs. In the near future, however, even the most reformed economy will continue to display tremendous distortions in prices. The consumption of agricultural products will continue to be heavily subsidized, as will fuels and raw materials and capital goods. Importantly, this pattern of subsidization will continue to vary widely from one member to another. An example of the effect of such differences on trade in the region is the fate of a proposal by Hungary at the meeting of the heads of state at Vysegrad, Hungary, in the spring of 1991. The Hungarians proposed a free trade area be established among the three countries. The Czechoslovak response was to complain about Poles buying subsidized food products in Czechoslovakia's border regions and thus disrupting supply. Needless to say, the Hungarian proposal received little consideration.

Because of these distortions, the most feasible, yet far-reaching, reform might be to marketize trade in some commodities while maintaining the former system for trade in other commodities, among them food, fuels and raw materials, because it is unlikely that the importing countries would be willing to yield decisions over such strategic inputs to enterprise-to-enterprise contacts. Moreover, to make the importation of such commodities profitable to firms would require either massive subsidization of importers, with its attendant inefficiencies, or an increase in the domestic prices of fuels and raw materials and the consequent inflation of all prices.

Agricultural products fall in the same category since both the desire to maintain adequate supplies for domestic consumption and the subsidization of the consumption of food argue against dismantling the former system of state-to-state trade. Since producer prices are higher than consumer prices for many staple items in all these countries, few would be willing to import food purchased at the wholesale prices of another member if it were to be sold at the retail prices of the importing country. On the other hand, no country would be willing to export many agricultural products if foreign enterprises were to purchase them at retail prices, since sales at these prices are highly subsidized.

While for the above "fixed-price" goods, the former arrangements are simply too costly to dismantle at this time, consumer manufactures and capital goods would make up the so-called free-price goods that could be traded by enterprises at negotiated prices. Consumer goods could thus be imported either by retail establishments for sale to the general public or by producing enterprises for sale to their own workers. In this way the effort to develop a functioning internal market and to stimulate competition on national markets that are often monopolized or oligopolized would be materially aided by the foreign trade sector. Moreover, competition from enterprises in other countries would be "fairer" and more equal competition than that provided by imports of western goods where the preferences of the buyers would be overwhelmingly for the western good.

One key prerequisite for such enterprise-to-enterprise trade on a large scale, rather than on the very limited scale now being attempted, is the creation of internal markets for these "free price" goods. This would be complicated by the presence of a significant excess demand for consumer goods in all these countries. Nevertheless, a large part of this excess demand makes itself felt on the markets for foodstuffs, housing, services, and certain consumer durables such as automobiles, while clothing, footwear and some consumer durables are in adequate if not excess supply. Thus with foodstuffs, a fixed-price good, and housing and services not traded, the creation of a genuine domestic market for consumer manufactures may be quite feasible. For those consumer manufactures such as automobiles that are in short supply, tariffs could limit the volume of imports.

To implement such a trade scheme a different monetary regime is required too. Enterprises in each country participating in this scheme should be permitted to buy and sell free-price goods in any other member country. The foreign exchange, that is, the domestic currency of other countries earned through the export of free-price goods, could be converted into domestic currency by the national bank of the exporter's country. Similarly, enterprises seeking to import free price goods could do so either by offering to pay in the importing country's currency or by purchasing the exporter's currency from the importer's national bank. If one country found itself with an undesirable surplus or deficit in a particular currency it could eliminate it either through a currency swap with another central bank or it could change the exchange rate.[12]

Trade in fixed-price goods would be carried out much as before, so each two countries would negotiate a bilateral trade agreement specifying quantities and prices. In the country with the reformed trading system a trading company would be charged with buying the appropriate amounts of free-price exports, competing with other buyers on the domestic market for such goods. Similarly the trading company would have to sell the planned imports on domestic markets for whatever prices could be obtained. In this way domestic markets would retain their allocative function without forcing all members to adopt the new trading regime.[13] Such a mechanism could serve not only to restore Eastern European trade with the former Soviet Union but also as a framework to liberalize and marketize trade among the former Republics of the USSR.

Conclusion

While the Eastern European members tend to put all their efforts into improving their economic relations with the West, their trade flows will not change much in the near future. Eastern Europe will continue to require imports of fuels and raw materials, and if Russian or Ukrainian exports of these commodities are redirected toward western markets, then these or the identical goods from other suppliers will find their way to Eastern Europe. Similarly, the former Soviet Union will continue to import manufactured goods, and it is not conceivable that all her imports will be replaced by Western supplies. Consequently, past links will maintain a large part of Eastern European trade flows with what is now called the Commonwealth of Independent States, or whatever emerges from it intact.

There are a number of ways to upgrade the now formally abandoned scheme—in tune with the overall transition to market competition—but the fundamental difficulty with all these reforms is that they require concerted effort to make them function. Given the current political climate in the region—with what was once called the Soviet Union turning inward to deal with its own breakup into semi-independent states and adopting a policy of benign neglect toward Eastern Europe and Eastern Europe viewing a turn to the West as a panacea for many of its problems and trade with the former Soviet Union largely as a source of problems—there seems to be little impetus for serious efforts to salvage even those elements of integration that could be retained without much additional effort.

Notes

1. Marer (1974) provides a useful survey of the measures employed and economic costs involved in Soviet exploitation during the late 1940s and early 1950s. At the same time, it cannot be argued that the creation of the trade bloc in 1949 either facilitated or increased this exploitation. Indeed, neither western nor

socialist specialists are able to offer compelling explanations for the establishment of the trade regime (Kaser [1973], ch. 2, van Brabant [1980] Ch. 1). The original objectives of the organization, exchanges of experience among members, extending technical aid and rendering mutual assistance, were surpassed in their modesty only by the concrete results achieved in this period.

2. For a good summary of western views, see Holzman (1976), who sums up the consensus among western observers by asserting that ". . . it is safe to infer that CMEA is a losing proposition in economic terms." (p.59) For a candid assessment from the Soviet standpoint, see Institute of the Economics of the World Socialist System (1988), which sums up the new Soviet view of the trade system this way: "Integration in CMEA took an administrative-bureaucratic route. Instead of working for a true economic partnership . . ., spurious and pretentious measures and projects were substituted by the higher . . . echelons. The process of integration was reduced to one of bureaucratic organization of economic interaction among the state systems of self-contained . . . countries which were separated from one another by . . . financial, economic, legal, and other barriers."

3. The low volume of pre-socialist trade among member countries is often cited as evidence that it does not constitute an appropriate integration scheme. Montias (1966), however, points out that policy barriers rather than resource endowments or economic structures may explain this low volume of intraregional in Eastern Europe.

4. For some estimates of the costs of such bilateralism, see van Brabant (1973).

5. Moreover, the political power of the Soviet Union may have induced Eastern European trade officials to adopt a "soft" approach to negotiations over prices with the Soviet Union. That one of the charges leveled against Rudolf Slansky during the Czechsolvak show trails was that he was a hard bargainer in trade negotiations with the Soviets may have been instructive for trade officials in other countries. On the other hand, if this change against Slansky had any validity, then it is evident that market power may not have been on the Soviet Union's side.

6. Compare, for example, Marrese and Vanous (1985) Ch. 8, Marrese (1986) and Marrese and Vanous (1988) for rather different views of the subsidy setting process and the way in which political payoffs are generated.

7. In the early 1980s, on the other hand, subsidies decreased despite the collapse of detente and increasing super power tension and a competitive arms buildup by the U.S. and Soviet Union.

8. In addition, the per capita amount of the subsidies was rather unimpressive. See Brada (1985, p.87; and 1988, p. 643).

9. I do not discuss the reforms of East Germany, it being reunited with West Germany along the lines of the latter's economic system. Nevertheless, given the strong East German economic ties with the Soviet Union, there may develop strong bilateral relations between the two nations based on a mix of market and nonmarket mechanisms. Such mechanisms may serve as useful models for the eventual marketization and monetization of relations as well.

10. In particular, Eastern European exports to the West tend to be income inelastic and subject to successful competition from newly industrializing countries, see Poznanski (1986), while their imports from the European community tend to be more income elastic.

11. The experience of German reunification serves as an interesting dress rehearsal for the affiliation of other Eastern European and Soviet economies with the European Community, with the important difference that the Eastern European countries could devalue their currencies to make their exports competitive in the West, thus avoiding the unemployment experienced in former East Germany.

12. The use of inter-bank swaps of currencies at the going exchange rate would avoid the problem of bilateral balancing of trade between members. The ability to change the exchange rate effectively prevents those countries that suffer most from repressed inflation from "exporting" it to other participants by running large trade deficits. Instead, the currencies of such countries would depreciate while the currencies of countries that have achieved equilibrium in their domestic markets would appreciate.

13. The bloc could also develop—in line with the above discussed measures—new institutions to make the reformed trading system function more smoothly, including an agency to soften the impact of changing terms of trade, organized along the lines of the European Community's Common Agricultural Policy. Another device would be an auction where central banks could sell and purchase the currencies of other members according to their reserve needs (so that the commodity inconvertibility that plagues the transferable ruble would be avoided). Such additions seem feasible in that they can be adopted under the "interested countries" principle, avoiding the need to have reform of the trade scheme tied to the pace of its least reform-minded members.

Bibliography

van Brabant, J. 1973. *Bilateralism and Structural Bilateralism in Intra-CMEA Trade.* Rotterdam: Rotterdam University Press.

_____. 1980. *Socialist Economic Integration.* Cambridge: Cambridge University Press.

_____. 1988. "Regional Integration, Economic Reforms and Convertibility." *Jahrbuch der Wirtschaft Osteuropus.* Bonn: Olzog.

Brada, J. 1988. "Soviet Subsidization of Eastern Europe: The Primary of Economics over Politics?" *Journal of Comparative Economics*, vol. 9, no. 1 (March), pp. 80–92.

_____. 1988. "Interpreting the Soviet Subsidization of Eastern Europe." *International Organization*, vol. 42, no. 4 (Autumn), pp. 639–658.

Brada, J. and J. Méndez. 1985. "Economic Integration among Developed, Developing and Centrally Planned Economies: A Comparative Analysis." *Review of Economics and Statistics*, vol. 67, no. 4 (November), pp. 549–556.

_____. 1988. "How Effective is the CMEA? An International Comparison." In J.

Brada and I. Dobozi, eds. *The Hungarian Economy in the 1980's*. Greenwich: JAI Press.

Hewett, E. 1976. "A Gravity Model of CMEA Trade." In J. Brada, ed. *Quantitative and Analytical Studies in East-West Economic Relations*. Bloomington: International Development Research Center.

Holzman, F. 1962. "Soviet Foreign Trade Pricing and the Question of Discrimination." *Review of Economics and Statistics*, vol. 44, no. 2 (May), pp. 134–147.

_____. 1965. "More on Soviet Bloc Trade Discrimination." *Soviet Studies*, vol. 17, no. 1 (July), pp. 44–65.

_____. 1976. *International Trade Under Communism*. New York: Basic Books.

_____. 1987. *The Economics of Soviet Bloc Trade and Finance*. Boulder: Westview Press.

Institute of the Economics of the World Socialist System. 1988. "East West Relations and Eastern Europe: The Soviet Perspective." *Problems of Communism*. (May–August).

Kaser, M. 1967. *Comecon*. London: Oxford University Press.

Köves, A. 1983. "Implicit Subsidies and Some Issues of Economic Relations within CMEA." *Acta Oeconomica*, vol. 31, no. 1–2, pp. 125–136.

Lavigne, M. 1988. "The Evolution of CMEA Institutions and Policies and the Need for Structural Adjustment." In J. Brada, E. Hewett and T. Wolf, eds. *Economic Adjustment and Reform in Eastern Europe and the Soviet Union*. Durham: Duke University Press.

Marer, P. 1974. "Soviet Economic Policy in Eastern Europe." In Joint Economic Committee, U.S. Congress, *Reorientation and Commercial Relations of the Economies of Eastern Europe*. Washington: U.S. Government Printing Office.

_____. 1984. "The Political Economy of Soviet Relations with Eastern Europe." In S. Terry, ed. *Soviet Policy in Eastern Europe*. New Haven: Yale University Press.

Marrese, M. 1986. "CMEA: Cumbersome but Effective Political Economy." *International Organization*, vol. 40, no. 1 (Spring), pp. 111–151.

Marrese, M. and J. Vanous. 1983. *Soviet Subsidization of Trade with Eastern Europe: A Soviet Perspective*. Berkeley: University of California Institute of International Studies.

_____. 1988. "The Content and Controversy of Soviet Trade Relations with the Eastern Europe, 1970–84." In J. Brada, E. Hewett and T. Wolf, eds. *Economic Adjustment and Reform in Eastern Europe and the Soviet Union*. Durham: Duke University Press.

Mendershausen, H. 1960. "The Terms of Soviet Satellite Trade." *Review of Economics and Statistics*, vol. 42, no. 2 (May), pp. 152–163.

_____. 1959. "Terms of Trade Between the Soviet Union and Smaller Communist Countries." *Review of Economics and Statistics*, vol. 41, no. 2 (May), pp. 106–118.

Montias, M. 1966. "Economic Nationalism in Eastern Europe: Forty Years of Continuity and Change." *Journal of International Affairs*, vol. XX, no. 1, pp. 45–71.

Poznanski, K. 1986. "Competition Between Eastern Europe and Developing Countries in the Western Market for Manufactured Goods." In Joint Economic Committee, U.S. Congress, *East European Economics: Slow Growth in the 1980's*, vol. 2. Washington: U.S. Government Printing Office.

———. 1988. "Opportunity Cost in Soviet Trade with Eastern Europe: Discussion of Methodology and New Evidence." *Soviet Studies*, vol. LX, no. 2 (April).

PART TWO

Reconstruction of Markets

4

Property Rights Perspective on Evolution of Communist-Type Economies

Kazimierz Z. Poznanski

The abrupt phasing out of Communism in Eastern Europe and the former Soviet Union is a phenomenon of historical proportions. Many expected capitalism to collapse—from failures, such as alienation, as stressed by Karl Polanyi (1944), or from successes, as Joseph Schumpeter (1942) predicted—and then to be replaced with some form of socialism. Now, when socialism is collapsing and capitalism seems to be moving in, one would like to know what forces brought down the Communist system and how it will be replaced.

This chapter offers a property rights perspective on the institutional changes in Eastern Europe and the now disintegrated Soviet Union. This particular approach links evolution in economic institutions—particularly property rights—to resource scarcity and recognizes that property forms affect the allocation of resources and the efficiency of their use. In this approach, it is further assumed that to operate, institutions of property rights need state enforcement and ideological sanction for such coercive actions.

My main argument here is that Eastern Europe and what used to be called the Soviet Union have been forced to radically reform their economies because the traditional property regime—public ownership and state allocation—became completely ineffective given the drastic increase in scarcity of productive factors. In fact, public ownership and bureaucratic allocation contributed to the rapid depletion of resources. This incompatibility was aggravated by the fact that the undermining of the Communist parties—related to their fading ideology—left the state without the ability to enforce public ownership.

A logical response for the region is to increase the incentive for efficient use of resources by replacing public rights with private ones. This change will have to be combined with the establishment of a democratic state and a liberal ideology. The conclusion of this chapter is that a complex set of factors, some rooted in the pre-communist past, make a quick, smooth movement in that direction by these countries unlikely. One should rather expect slow progress, with some hybrid forms and sudden reversals. Moreover, particular countries may follow an independent track of change.

Factor Scarcity and Property Rights

No society can escape from the scarcity problem, and to solve it, its members have to develop an order that ensures the proper incentives to economize on resources. In the property rights tradition, the essential element of such an order is ownership, i.e., customary or legal rules on who decides on the transfer of a given resource. Such rules specify the transition costs or relationship between individual returns from specific actions and their social returns and therefore determine the incentives to economize on scarce resources.

Threat of Increasing Scarcity. The property rights theory states that the strength of the incentive structure increases with property rights becoming more specific or exclusionary. This is because with such rights more specified, transaction costs consisting of costs of measuring value of what is being exchanged (North, 1990, p. 27) are reduced. In other words, more exclusionary rights allow owners to appropriate a larger share of the benefits that their actions bring about or, to phrase it differently, to move individual and social returns closer together (Pejovich, 1989). Since in practice property rights are never perfectly specified, these respective returns are never equated. However, what societies need is just incentives that are sufficient given the level of resource scarcity.

It follows from the above theorem that whenever a given type of resource—land, labor, or capital—becomes markedly scarcer or if the balance between available resources and societal needs changes in a critical way, the necessity arises for a modification of property rights (well stated in a historical account of modern development in North and Thomas, 1973). Specifically, if the gap between needs and resource endowments widens, society has to further specify property rights, and if it fails to do so, economic performance will deteriorate.

The historical record demonstrates that societies most often fail to create appropriate ownership structures and that a perverse response, when growing scarcity is met with despecification of property rules, is not uncommon either. This is why economic stagnation or regression periods in development have been more frequent historically than those of sustained growth in production (see North, 1981). Institutional inefficiency also explains why only a segment of the contemporary world economy enjoys affluence while the rest remains at a subsistence level.

The introduction of the Stalinist system first in the Soviet Union and later in Eastern Europe represented a total assault on private property. Since private ownership, in view of the property rights theory, is superior to collective, at least as a basic organizing principle in modern societies, this change must be seen as an example of regressive reform. What made this system appear particularly regressive is that ownership of the most scarce resources—capital and land—was turned over to the state.

That Eastern Europe and the Soviet Union grew very fast during the first decades of the Stalinist system does not invalidate the above claim as to the regressive nature of that design. The reason is that this fast growth in physical outputs was due mostly to the mobilization of labor (e.g., through the elimination of urban unemployment and absorption of manpower surplus in agriculture). Given the abundance of labor, the need for strong incentives to economize on labor resources was not then so critical. Moreover, while certain state limits were put on mobility, labor remained more in the domain of private agents—workers—than did other inputs.

In addition, these high rates of growth obscured the notorious waste that ensued with the nationalization of capital and land. From the beginning, it took more of these resources for Eastern Europe and the Soviet Union to generate one unit of production than in comparable countries with private ownership (see Bergson, 1978). As long as excess labor was available and economies grew fast, the waste could be tolerated. In Eastern Europe, favorable conditions for economic growth had been exhausted by the late fifties. By that time much of the surplus labor was absorbed and the waste of resources, including labor itself, became more painful.

Waste was particularly detrimental to the nonrenewable resource—land (raw materials, energy, water, soil). The initial response by these countries was not to strengthen incentives for economical use of land but to pour more capital in. For instance, in Poland, Gomulka devoted much of his tenure to the expansion of the raw material and energy sector, while Khrushchev in the Soviet Union tried to lessen food problems by opening new areas for cultivation (e.g., in Kazakhstan). The policy quickly failed, however, since these economies could not provide sufficient amounts of capital to support gigantic and, for the most part, poorly prepared projects.

In the late sixties, the Communist leaders decided to attack the capital barrier by tapping foreign credit. This was a departure from the Communist dogma, but the party found borrowing more tolerable than the radical reforms needed to restructure incentives. So while accepting credit helped to temporarily accelerate production, the waste was such that those countries who did so ended up with excessive debts. They made continuation of rapid growth impossible, since payments drained domestic sources of capital. Moreover, during the years of extensive borrowing, Eastern Europe, and to a lesser degree the Soviet Union, allowed much of that money to be spent on consumption as part of the social compact (see Poznanski, 1986). As a result, expectations by workers, as well as wage pressures, increased tremendously; a case in point was Poland under Gierek. Communist leaders lost much of their ability to siphon resources from the consumer sector to capital goods industries (cf. Kornai, 1986).

Thus, the Communist system left Eastern Europe and the Soviet Union with depleted land and, more important, an extreme shortage of capital. Radical reforms in the ownership structure thus became unavoidable, and some moves in that direction were made by a few Communist parties, for instance, in 1976 in Hungary (see Commisso and Marer, 1986). However, only with the collapse of the communist parties in 1989, as in Poland, or the metamorphosis of former communists into social democrats, as in Bulgaria, has such a transformation become really possible.

All the countries in the region are now involved in reforming property rights, but other than a decrease in the scope of state ownership, the results are hard to predict. No clear pattern of proprietary reforms has yet emerged in any of the countries, and there is even less certainty about the type of transformation that will dominate in the region. State leaders (and other social groups) are quickly learning that there are a number of options available for establishing a market for capital (Poznanski, 1989).

Types of Ownership Reforms. The first, most conservative variant of departure from the existing order is to make the changes that the Communist parties, particularly during their final years, considered necessary but were afraid to risk introducing. The bottom line here is not to change ownership but to replace direct orders by the state with truly aggressive incentives borrowed from the market system but operated in a nonmarket fashion. This is the case of a *real simulation* of the market, with the state closely monitoring each enterprise (see Kornai, 1986).

The authorities may try a number of such incentives, including laws allowing the state to initiate bankruptcy proceedings against deficit enterprises (as done before the end of Communist rule in Hungary and Poland). Open unemployment, with the state deciding which workers are going to be released, is another possibility (tried first by the Communists in Hungary, and later in Poland). Finally, the authorities can encourage efficiency by permitting people to accumulate nonfinancial wealth (e.g., to buy real estate).

Important improvements are possible in the sphere of capital allocation, including replacement of the old-fashioned mono-bank system with a diversified network of banks (e.g., started a few years ago in Hungary and Poland, following much earlier reforms by Yugoslavia) (see Tyson, 1981). Another device is a secondary allocation—the stock market—primarily or exclusively for state-owned enterprises, experimented with shortly before their departure by the Communists in Hungary (and on a growing scale in still-communist China). Moreover, new financial instruments to attract private savings can be introduced (e.g., bonds offered since 1988 to the public in Hungary).

A second, alternative variant of ownership reform, here called *dual-track*, is to expand the private sector, not in order to put an end to the dominant state sector but in order to strengthen it. Thus, the private sector is provided only selectively with access to production, for instance, in those activities where authorities find it difficult to put together a viable state-owned operation and/or in those that can scarcely pose a competitive threat to existing state capital. Such partial privatization can take various forms with different implications for efficiency.

The dual-track reform can be accomplished through the offering of state-owned capital to private individuals (including those organized in a cooperative-type collective) for temporary control. Here contracts are signed for a fixed period between the state (represented by any level of administration, including the management of enterprises) and private parties, allowing the latter to have use rights for specified assets. These use rights, or leases, are offered for a price so that they can, for instance, be auctioned off to the highest bidder. If properly conducted, such auctioning should ensure that state assets are efficiently applied.

The strategy of dual-track reform can also be forwarded by allowing privately owned capital to expand. Private ownership of capital was never completely erased by the Eastern European Communists, or even in the Soviet Union or China (including by the most anticapitalistic actions taken during the Cultural Revolution). By now, in all these countries, there is at least some limited private ownership of land (with most agriculture being private in Poland), as well as industry (e.g., in former East Germany and in Hungary). Thus, there is a basis for the authorities to build upon.

Finally, there is the third, most radical type of ownership reform, namely, *full-scale termination* of the state sector. Among the ways of resurrecting the market for capital is the profit-oriented custodian model. The idea (as put forth, for example, by Tardos, 1986) is to create holding institutions run by state officials as sort of custodians of public assets. The function of these holdings will be to allocate funds through credit or stock operations in state-owned enterprises. The holdings will be free to choose location of funds without state intervention (e.g., criteria or priorities for selection). To encourage rational allocation, the managers of these holdings will be rewarded according to the performance of their portfolio.

In what I would call the institutional ownership model, control over capital allocation is entrusted to various financial institutions such as insurance companies, savings banks, or retirement plans. If relieved of the state intervention that typifies the old-time system, these institutions can be expected to act as proprietary agents (i.e., to be driven by the profit-maximizing motive). All these institutions would rely on contributions (i.e., premiums, deposits, retirement payments) from households or enterprises, and they would be given a free hand in allocating their money, but there should be enough pressure on these institutions to find the best way for allocating funds.

Under the next option, labor-management model, use of capital is turned over, as in postwar Yugoslavia, to the workers (i.e., worker councils). The Yugoslav model is just one possible arrangement, by which all capital assets belong to the state. However, it is theoretically possible to have a labor-managed system in which workers not only use but also own their enterprise (i.e., as long as they stay with a given enterprise; they may even be allowed to transfer their stocks to another enterprise when changing jobs).

In what I call a "corrupt" (or "political") market, control over capital is put in private hands, with the majority of assets made available to the Communist authorities, the party, and/or the state (see discussion by Tardos, 1986). In the transfer, private owners are forced into a patron-client relationship with the political leadership. As a consequence, both access to and exit from production are made conditional on loyalty to the political establishment. At the same time, this support for the "super-structure" becomes essential to private owners for securing access to capital means.

Another version is a dependent market where the allocation of capital is primarily in the hands of foreign agents, either private or public (though the latter is less likely given that state-owned enterprises rarely go international). Under this variant state assets could be turned over to foreign agents rather than to domestic private actors. As foreigners, these capital owners would be subject to stricter state controls than would domestic agents of comparable financial status. This control over foreigners is tighter, of course, when foreign and state ownership are mixed, as in joint venture arrangements.

Finally, there is a variant of termination called the universal market, which, unlike the corrupt market, is not based on political privilege, though, of course, in the real world, politics always interferes with economics. Here access to capital is determined by an individual's ability to raise the required minimum funds, as is also the case with exit (i.e., bankruptcy or merge-in). The relative level of this minimum is the single most critical factor distinguishing various forms of the universal market (i.e., from perfect competition to full monopoly).

Prevailing Trends. It is very difficult to determine which variant of ownership change is most likely to prevail. Among the high probability options is the corrupt market, in part because most of the market operations allowed by the Communist parties before their departure fall into that category. Such operations were promoted primarily to extend party members' privileges from the political to the economic sphere, or at least to substitute the latter for the former. In both cases, it was political influence that guaranteed acquisition of property rights, as in Hungary and Poland (more, see Poznanski, 1990).

The transfer of power to non-Communist governments, as in Hungary and Poland again, has increased political opposition to acquisitions by former nomenklatura. However, many of them have retained positions of power by joining new parties or assuming the status of independents. While rejecting on moral grounds the transfer of assets to nomenklatura, the new authorities will find it difficult to depoliticize the privatization process. In all these countries, the state apparatus is reassessing its authority, which puts the post-Communist establishment in a position to make disposition of assets part of the reward or co-option system.

Development of such a market will also be helped by great complications in the valuation of state capital. Even the most relaxed Stalinist economies, such as that of Hungary, have, at best, left behind only very imperfect capital markets and obscure accounting. Creating, or recreating, markets for capital will be time-consuming. With this comes the opportunity for the post-Communist state to provide capital at great discounts that would hardly be detected by the general public (particularly because the state can drive down the value by obstructing an enterprise targeted for sale).

The region is likely, however, to move in a different direction—towards a dependent market. The original Communist system was designed, at least in part, to prevent dependence on the more advanced, capitalist countries. This was done partly out of contempt for capitalism but also out of a desire to maximize state power, not to mention a naive hope that isolation would cure many economic problems without creating other, possibly more severe, ones. The decay of communism brought down this design, opening the door to foreign economic influence, or dependence.

The movement towards a dependent market was started by many late Communist regimes, particularly in Hungary. Selling state assets to foreigners was seen as an attractive solution since generally it is less controversial than transfer of assets to domestic actors. This variant is also relatively simple financially since foreign sources of money are more abundant than domestic. Finally, though such sales do not necessarily bring new capital into the country, they bring other benefits, particularly links to foreign markets. The post-Communist regimes may be even more tempted to accommodate foreigners because of their interest in quick mergers with advanced market economies. If foreign ownership goes up to forty or fifty percent of total capital assets, this won't represent a departure from regional historical patterns. Before the installation of the Communist system, foreign ownership in many Eastern European countries was not far from that mark (e.g., in Romania or Hungary). Eastern Europe was then a periphery of Europe, which explains its high dependence on external—mostly German—capital. Eastern Europe is again entering Europe as a periphery, and recreation of the historical pattern may come with it.

State Power and Property Enforcement

For property rights to provide an incentive, they have to be enforceable. Rights of those to whom specific resources are assigned must be protected in some way, for arbitrary seizures of benefits from rightful owners act as disincentives. Individuals or groups may try enforcement on their own but the costs are necessarily very high, often prohibitive. It is the state that has to provide enforcement of property rights, since its key comparative advantage is in coercion (see Levi, 1988). Thus, the state must not only specify property rights but also protect them.

Crisis of State. For any Stalinist economy to operate effectively, public ownership needs to be protected, as does private ownership in the market system, and in both cases this has to be done by the state. The difference between the two orders is that to ensure respect for property in the Communist economy, the use of state coercion must be more extensive, since there are hardly any resource users to make the customary efforts to protect the value of assets. In addition, the state here has to be more cohesive and unified, since only when those in a position of allocating resources share common political interests will an effort be made to protect public assets.

When the Stalinist order was introduced, the above two conditions could easily have been met. The early political regimes were not only eager to apply repressive measures but the societies, after emerging from the horrors of war, were, in a way, accustomed to coercion (see Gross, 1988). These regimes were basically dictatorial, with a single person, the party secretary, controlling the state and thus being the ultimate "owner" of the national wealth and personally interested in its protection.

It is certainly difficult to determine how much of the terror of these early years was driven by purely political concerns and how much by the interests of the ultimate owner, the ruler. Theoretically, they can be separated, but not empirically. Still one must be impressed with the number of imprisonments, deportations, and executions of individuals accused of real or unreal economic failures to protect the value of assets (e.g., missing state production targets, unreported revenues, illegal transactions).

With the tide of terror over in the late fifties, the Communist regimes gradually increased their tolerance for abuses of state property. As Joseph Berliner (1952) correctly pointed out, for instance, petty theft by workers eventually became an integral, accepted part of the economic system. Thus, the opportunities for appropriation of state property came to be viewed by those offering positions and those seeking them as part of the package to be negotiated.

The state apparatus, practically identical with the Communist party, by then also began losing its cohesiveness. The interests of the party, which were identified with the views of the tyrant, were eventually replaced by diversity of interests. In many cases, this differentiation resulted in severe internal competition and growing insecurity by its members. Under the circumstances, common interest by the state in the value of productive assets was emerging, almost exclusively, in the face of an economic crisis.

The increased tolerance and splits within the party eventually had to shift the balance of power from the state to society, putting these economies further in a position impossible to sustain, i.e., unenforceable property rights. Clearly, the Polish economy arrived at that juncture first despite the desperate effort by the party to turn the balance in its favor during martial law (involving military commissariats in state enterprises, increased financial control, harsher punishment for "destruction" of public property).

The most obvious evidence of a state's weakness is usually its inability to avoid huge budgetary deficits, as they indicate that the state is poor in collecting taxes and failing to provide services expected by the public (see Levi, 1988). Runaway budgetary deficits characterized the Communist regimes of, say, Poland during the last few years of their tenure and were plaguing the former Soviet regime more recently (since cities failed to make payments to republican authorities and the latter refused to contribute to the federal budget).

The collapse of the Communist political economy—combining state allocation and party monopoly—has left a vacuum that has to be filled. In addition to the overhaul of the property structure, new political economies have to be created, i.e., combinations of markets and states. There are a number of options or variants available. The few major alternatives to "real" socialism of the past are outlined below (for a more detailed discussion, see Poznanski, 1989).

Political Economies. One option is *reformed communism,* in which the Communist countries stop short of dismantling state economies but absorb many market-type features. In the economic realm, this could be achieved either through "simulated" markets, as discussed earlier, and/or with the help of dual-track reforms in the economic system. The end product of such changes is a system with extensive central controls over state-owned enterprises but also with strong competitive pressures coming from within the public and/or private sectors.

The key to the success of that model is a new approach by the state to economic intervention. It is essential that this control be more indirect, not individualized and based on a set of fixed rules, something that the reformists in Eastern Europe and the former Soviet Union have long advocated. But even more important is that the state aggressively enforce good economic performance. So, even though subsidies to producers and protection for workers won't be discontinued, they will have to be offered more on the basis of efficiency than they used to be (earlier they were provided almost unconditionally).

In the political sphere, such reformed communism responds to demands for participation by citizens, though without challenging the political monopoly of the party. The obvious option is for the party to reform itself (see Lewin, 1988) and/or to allow the state, as opposed to the party, to voice opinions of the nonparty majority. Such a solution could be helped by the revival of the office of the presidency and parliament (as tried by Mikhail Gorbachev in the Soviet Union, where the strong presidency was expected to protect the party from dissolution while the weak parliament was expected to provide an effective forum for opposition views).

A more radical option, here called *communist capitalism*, involves replacement of state allocation with the private market, possibly a "corrupt" version but without demonopolization of politics. This is a hybrid, combining a generally repressive, Communist superstructure with a capitalist economic basis. These two are usually seen as incompatible, even though private markets—the essence of the capitalist mode of production—seem to be able to work within a number of political structures, not only within a textbook parliamentary democracy, as claimed by early liberal philosophers, but within single party systems, too.

It is obvious that for any Communist party to work within it, this model must be even further modified than in the reformed variant discussed earlier. Specifically, allowing some space for legal political opposition may be needed and the party must abandon much of its ideology, but very carefully. Allowing for an ideological vacuum does not seem practical, so there is a need in this variant for a substitute ideology that will not only help the party to preserve its corporate structure—centralized leadership, hierarchical order, and exclusive membership—but will also make it credible in the eyes of the public (see Jowitt, 1978).

Interestingly, during the final years of the system, many Communist apparatchiks, including those in China, convinced themselves that such a change would be similar to the maneuver of Roosevelt's New Deal, when the state made an assault on the market only to save it from self-destruction (i.e., recurrent depressions and class polarization). In the case of the Communist system, a New Deal in reverse, or a market assault on the state, appealed to some party members as the only way to prevent the system from destroying itself.

A partial dissolution of "real" socialism (instead of opening the gate to capitalism) could, alternatively, provide workers with an opportunity to return to the original radical dream—another variant of political economy—*the workers' state.* For this model to materialize, workers will have to succeed in forcing the Communist leadership to surrender its power and put themselves in control of the allocation of resources, as in the labor-managed model. What specific political shape such a system of total workers' control would take if not confined to the enterprise or sectoral level, as in Yugoslavia today, is open to speculation.

Economists are generally skeptical of the efficiency of a labor-managed economy, mostly because such a system is seen as conducive to monopolistic practices (i.e., lowering of outputs for the sake of higher prices). Such a model is also viewed as leading to impaired mobility of labor, as already hired workers are unwilling to admit new workers (Tyson, 1981).[1] In addition, few political scientists picture the workers' state as an ideal model of politics, in part because factory workers typically tend to stay away from politics and mobilize themselves only in crisis situations.[2]

There is evidence that there are strong popular pressures by workers in some countries to increase their powers. The rapid erosion of the political authority of Yugoslavia's party in the last years has benefited workers, including successful efforts to take advantage of the recently relaxed regulations on enterprises and purchase of their assets. In Poland, there are constant demands by the workers, at least for the moment the key political force, particularly their radical elements, to acquire stocks in their enterprises as a protection against the job losses that are more likely if ownership is passed to private, particularly foreign, hands.

Finally, there is the variant of radical transition in which the countries return to the political economy of *liberal capitalism,* combining the universal, generalized market and democratic pluralism. This transformation cannot be the same as the process that transformed the feudal system into capitalism, as "real communism" is an aberration in historical evolution. Many institutions of the capitalist economy were already present in a reduced, limited form in feudal society and the transition to capitalism helped to accelerate their development. As a deviation, "real communism" does not seem to have such a strong pre- or proto-capitalist background.

One wonders whether, for instance, the safety net existing in feudal societies was as developed as that under the old-time Communist system. Here the whole superstructure is designed to perform paternalistic functions, for example, by letting real prices of labor for enterprises go below their value. Further, providing security for people was probably not as central a part of feudal ideology as it has been in "real communism." Thus, breaking away from paternalism for the sake of markets may be more difficult in post-Communist economies.

All these aberrations might be seen as a result of the misinterpretation of Marx by the practicing Communists in the Soviet Union and Eastern Europe, at least on the following important account. According to Marx, economic conditions determine the political superstructure, though it, if obsolete, may hamper progress in production. However, under practical Communism, the dictates of political needs are the norm. While many changes were made in the postrevolutionary Soviet Union in the name of economic requirements, the primary motivation was political, be it the need to insulate its quasi-sacred identity (Jowitt, 1987, p. 306) or to save the multiethnic empire.

The paradox of the situation is that the increasing centralization that was expected by Marx to destroy the capitalist economy has not undermined that system but has turned out to undercut, rather than facilitate, the communist economy. While Polanyi (1944) predicted that the capitalist system would collapse because of the ever-expanding state protection for workers that limited market competition, this has not happened. The same phenomenon has immobilized the countries of "real socialism." This is a fascinating subject of study in itself.

Empowering State. It is difficult to establish what combination of economics and politics will dominate in Eastern Europe and the former Soviet Union in the near future. A look at the economic conditions and social structure of those countries suggests that those political economies mentioned above that involve a strong activist state as a dominant player seem more appropriate, and thus more likely. What this means is that after fundamentally weakening the state, an inevitable by-product of undermining the Communist party, these societies have to rebuild it.[3] A strong state is needed, most of all, because the economic crisis discussed above comes at a time when there is still a long distance for these countries to go in achieving the economic standards of the most advanced capitalist societies. By now, it is obvious that the leaders of both Eastern Europe and the Soviet Union had a false sense of catching up with the capitalist world. Even if there was some convergence, it stopped more than a decade ago, with these countries frozen in an extensive "equilibrium gap."[4]

To make things worse, at this point, these economies are dominated by smokestack industries way above their needs, and some of them continued to expand these capacities until very recently. Thus, while struggling to close the gap with the capitalist world, these countries must rid themselves of much of their production capacities, which will force a large number of workers out of jobs (the majority of them from sectors that represent the core of the political basis for some key new parties in Eastern Europe). Again, a strong state is needed to execute such a restructuring at an acceptable social cost (see Kornai, 1990).

Also relevant here is the fact that these countries have an under-developed social structure. "Real" socialism left behind what some economic historians of the region call an incomplete society (Berend, 1986). Unlike typical modern societies, these countries lack a strong middle class. While Marx predicted that the capitalist nations would squeeze this group out, the Communist system has, in fact, proved best at doing so. This incompleteness makes these societies potentially un-stable, thus inviting a strong state.

While the middle class, which has proved to enhance the politics of compromise, is very weak, the two dominant segments—bureaucracy and workers—are in deep disagreement. They have not shared identical interests under party dictatorship, and they cannot be expected to quickly reconcile their differences after its collapse. Poland's conflict between Tadeusz Mazowiecki and Lech Walesa during 1989–1990 is a case in point, and it has continued since, as demonstrated by the out-come of the 1991 parliamentary elections.

The conflict mentioned above could be aggravated by the workers of Eastern Europe having greater economic expectations than they had during the early stages of industrialization fashioned after the Stalinist model. They are now more interested in consumption than savings and tend to withdraw to their private lives. At the same time, the status of manual jobs has been diminished and the ethic of hard work has nearly vanished as well. Mobilizing such a group for another industrialization, undoing the failures of the past, will be particularly difficult for the authorities—which is not unusual when an economy is out of step with its society.

Thus, it seems there is hardly any other means available to the bu-reaucratic class, if they choose to promote the private market, than to do so through some sort of coercion. Overcoming the natural opposition of the workers (with the exception of maybe a few highly skilled groups in the modern sectors) to the private market might take what could be called a terror of reforms. It took such a terror for the preexisting Communist party to replace capitalism with state allocation and it may take equally forceful measures for its successors to restore private markets. In fact, even an extreme version of authoritarianism, military rule, might be necessary in some cases to assure political stability, at least in some post-Communist Eastern European countries (similar to measures taken by the late Communist rulers in Poland). These remarks are consistent with the prediction by Barrington Moore (1954) that the system will either become extinct or will mutate in such a way that political control of the Communist party is replaced by either industrial managers or the traditionally nationalistic military elite (see remarks on Moore's speculations in Janos, 1986, pp. 108–9).

Transaction Costs and the Dominant Ideology

Sheer coercion is too costly under most, or possibly all, circumstances, so societies have to imprint on their members some degree of restraint from pursuing their selfish objectives. Instilling such restraints is the function of ideologies—or worldviews. By articulating a common set of moral commandments and norms of behavior, ideologies help to make particular actors in the economic scene comply with a compatible state. The stronger the legitimacy of the state provided by a given ideology, the lower the costs of enforcement of property rights or other economic institutions.

Ideologies come and go depending on whether their content helps societies to organize production in an efficient way. Ideologies that are rigid or sterile lose more quickly in competition with worldviews that are open and subject to corrections. The more ideology departs from reality, the more utopian it is, the greater the likelihood that it won't last. This competition between ideologies is, however, very slow, in part or mostly because once individuals absorb them, they become second nature.

State Legitimacy. Even in its very early version, the Communist system, despite its enormous resourcefulness in coercion, needed ideology to reduce the number of instances when state intervention was required. It was the role of the Communist ideology to convince people that they were a unity and that state property was actually their own, meaning that yield from productive resources was to be equally and unconditionally distributed. In fact, this claim that "the state is us" was believed by a sufficient number of people in the early days of Communist rule to greatly reduce the need for coercion.[5]

The above perception was first shaken during the de-Stalinization by Khrushchev when segments of these societies realized that the results of their efforts were channeled by the state almost exclusively to the further expansion of the capital stock rather than to their personal wealth. Moreover, as the Communist rulers had already accumulated great privileges (Carrere d'Encausse, 1980), it became clear to many workers that joint ownership did not translate into equality.

Not surprisingly, the Communist leaders of that time put great effort into relegitimizing the state by departing from certain practices of the past. Economic reforms initiated at that period were made mostly in the name of strengthening incentives for the productive use of resources with a new set of instruments, but another underlying motive was to increase workers' confidence in the state as custodian of their assets. These were as much economic reforms as ideological redressing needed to strengthen the party/state in its role as a property enforcer.

The essence of that redressing was the concept of self-management, or labor-managed enterprises endowed with state resources. Revisionist thinkers revived this specific idea (e.g., by looking at earlier works of Marx) first in Yugoslavia, then labor-management gained popularity elsewhere in Eastern Europe. Only Yugoslavia fully adopted the concept and went into a cycle of reforms meant to reassure workers, mostly in the face of periodically emerging economic adversities, that they were the actual, though not legal, owners of the capital assets. Outside of Yugoslavia, the efforts to socialize state ownership did not go beyond creating worker councils with little authority over production decisions. Afraid of giving too much power to the workers, the state chose in the late sixties to enter into a Communist social compact in which workers were expected to trade their acceptance of party monopoly for uninterrupted improvements in consumption. Hungary tried first to legitimate state control of capital in that way under Janos Kadar, and Edward Gierek's strategy in Poland was another important case here (see Poznanski 1986).

While the original Communist ideology was difficult to test empirically and thus very useful, the social compact was not. As long as real consumption kept growing in the early seventies, largely fueled by imported capital, the state seemed to be delivering. With the economic downturn at the end of the decade, society found the agreement invalid and responded with political demands to limit the party's monopoly (the clearest example being the show of disobedience in Poland during 1980–1981, as Poland was the Eastern European country worst hurt by the recession). With the social compact broken down the Communist party was forced to search for a substitute ideology and found it in "political realism." The party/state started justifying its monopoly on the grounds that loss of its power would provoke foreign intervention (i.e., Soviet in the case of Eastern Europe) or lead the country into chaos. When the Polish regime invaded its own territory in 1981, the first part of this claim was discredited; the second was invalidated when military rule produced only an illusory recovery (Poznanski, 1986).

Great Transformation. Now, with power having been transferred to the non-communist opposition or shifted within the previous party/state elite (as has happened in most parts of the former Soviet Union), the practical question facing the leadership in the region is not only how to legitimize the dispersal of public capital but also how to ensure that private property is socially acceptable. This might seem to be a rather trivial problem since one could assume that after decades of trying to subvert the state and carve something for their own, the people of this area would be ready to embrace a system based upon private ownership. If this were true, it should just take the introduction of some missing capitalist institutions—stock market, legally enforceable contracts or bankruptcy law—to bring private property back.

The assumption that institution building is sufficient for the restoration of markets based on private property is consistent with or reflective of the simplistic theory of capitalist markets that minimize the role of human behavior. Many contemporary economists believe that people are so adaptable that the mere establishment of market structures would suffice to eradicate any remnants of anti-capitalist prejudice left from a pre-capitalist past. This is seen to be the case especially with respect to the building of free-choice capitalist orders, since these orders are assumed to concur with "natural" predispositions, or deepest instincts of all human beings.

Many economists who believe that free markets are "natural" forget that the market economy consists of two elements—a set of specific institutions and, inseparably, a state of mind. When classical economists speak about the market, they assume not only the existence of basic economic institutions such as private ownership but also the presence of so-called rational agents. However, they not only falsely presume the same level of rationality to be an attribute of all beings but they also forget that it takes more than merely thinking in terms of costs/benefits and personal gain maximization to form a necessary market-facilitating mentality (Blinder, 1987, pp. 26–27).

For any economic institution such as the market to work effectively, those who operate within it have to exhibit certain dispositions. Any state could push through with systemic reforms without concern for the frame of mind of those who would "use" the new institutions that would result from these reforms. If, however, these state alterations were well-directed, but also well-measured, agents would be able to learn how to act accordingly. If the changes were too drastic, then these agents would most likely resist and thus make new institutions ineffective.

It follows then that the process of creating working capitalism, with private property as its centerpiece, should be viewed as a "great transformation," or a complex social change affecting the basic fiber of these societies.[6] Since implementing institutional change alone is not sufficient to resurrect the market, the region must develop some ideological formula that would facilitate the emergence of a market-type mentality. This would have to be accomplished under very peculiar circumstances, since populations of Eastern Europe and the former Soviet Union have just rejected one ideology, i.e., Soviet communism, and thus generally tend to be suspicious of any ideology.

To be sure, what exists in the Eastern European countries is still more in the category of markets than a market society as defined by Polanyi. Markets are a transactional mode that has existed in a confined form (as a by-product of political or religious structures) throughout history in various societies, including communist Eastern Europe. The market society, however, in which people are organized by contract rather than status—where the economic dominates the social—is a unique contemporary phenomenon, still somewhat ahead of Eastern Europe.

One of the outcomes of Communist rule is the destruction of the market agents, and with them of the market ethos. The most extreme case of undercutting the market mentality is that of the Soviet Union, where shortly after the revolution of 1917, the Communist leadership began eliminating "class enemies," most of them rich peasants, retail people, and industrialists. At the same time, the market institutions were quickly replaced with central control, which turned people into wage earners hired by one employer, the state. The economic reforms undertaken since the mid-fifties have not much changed the situation.

Clearly, the Communist system has operated in Eastern Europe for a much shorter period, only since 1946–48. In addition, these countries did not go through such a massive elimination of class enemies by the newly installed Communist regimes (though many of them suffered severe losses during the Nazi occupation, particularly because of the extermination of Jews). Also, unlike the former Soviet Union, the systems in Eastern Europe have been challenged on a number of occasions (e.g., at least four times in Poland). Still, the damage to the market ethos in the region has been deep enough to make a difference.

Among the missing ingredients is a basic understanding of profit-oriented activities and a tolerance for income so obtained. Most often, these activities are seen as profiteering or speculation. Moreover, there is very little appreciation of individualism, while the majority of people retain a strong expectation that the state will provide a number of economic safeguards, some of which we've mentioned above. What also makes the existing state of mind not conducive to market-type reforms is that the majority of people do not believe that a hierarchical order and economic inequality are "natural." This is why, for instance, interparty purges on the grounds of corruption always won popular support.

Also by and large missing is respect for or attachment to private property. Wartime expropriations by the Nazis (e.g., Jews' property) and then forceful acquisitions of capital assets by postwar Communist regimes seriously undermined peoples' trust in the sanctity of private ownership, a trust further shaken by the vague laws that followed. In addition, despite severe sanctions, the state sector has become the scene of widespread theft, ranging from large-scale scams involving higher-ups to petty stealing. A related element that is basically lacking is a sense of legalism in general, the product of years of arbitrary judgments and loose legal rules inviting abuse by the authorities (see Lewin, 1988).

Substitute Ideologies. With the death of traditional Communist ideology, many post-communist political forces of Eastern Europe have instinctively embraced the philosophy of liberalism. The liberal doctrine of freedom is favored since it appears to many people as the most decisive departure from the discredited ideology of Communism. Moreover, the ideas of liberalism appear most consistent with the recent efforts to quickly rebuild a capitalist economy and its foundations— private ownership and freedom of enterprise. However, the progress of liberalism may be complicated due to both some historical forces and the peculiar nature of a transition to capitalism itself.

One very critical obstacle to societal embracement of liberalism is that liberalism itself is the "natural" ideology of the bourgeoisie in its struggle against the political monopoly of unproductive strata and a "prohibitive" state apparatus. In Eastern Europe, the bourgeoisie has been historically weak despite the partially successful, predominantly state-sponsored industrializations throughout this region that were initiated around the turn of the century and continued through the interwar period. The Communist postwar project resulted, as indicated earlier, in reducing the strength of the previous bourgeoisie expansion, not only numerically but also in terms of class self-esteem.

In the virtual absence of the class whose interests liberalism is supposed to express, the promotion of this doctrine would therefore have to depend on backing by other segments of these societies. Thus, one finds in post-communist Eastern Europe examples of state bureaucracies engaging in the propagation of liberal ideas (e.g., the former government of Bielecki in Poland or the first cabinet formed by Yeltsin after the declaration of independence by Russia). All these forces face a difficult dilemma, as political capital may not be easily accumulated by sponsoring the interests of the bourgeoisie, the weakest, or in some cases the most absent, social group (a lesson learned by Bielecki's party in the 1991 parliamentary elections).

Interestingly, ideas of liberalism have also been supported by some elements in organized labor, as in Poland, where many labor leaders, including the former head of the independent unions, Walesa, have openly endorsed the ideology of aggressive capitalism. This move generated similar political risks to those facing some post-communist bureaucracies, Poland again being a good example. The rapid decline in popularity of independent unions could be partially attributed to the sudden change of preferences by many labor leaders from "third road" solutions, which call for control of capital assets by workers, to a vision of genuine capitalism with private property.

While liberal language could spread rather quickly throughout the region, diffusion of a deeper understanding of modern political pluralism—with its inherent type of institutions and requirements—might suffer from a lack of bourgeoisie and its substitution by the state or other actors (i.e., "substitute class," from the German, "Ersatzklasse"; for an excellent historical account of Eastern European modernization, see Berend, 1986, pp. 163–168). Specifically, there is a risk that ideas of liberalism, when not emanating from their natural social base, may be misinterpreted and thus acquire meanings having little relation to the original concepts, concepts that were formulated by countries having a long tradition of liberalism.

Liberalism prescribes more than one specific way of organizing societies in accordance with the general requirement of ensuring maximum freedoms for individuals and political representation. There have always been two main traditions in the liberal movement, laissez-faire, or conservative liberalism, which seems to ignore the issue of equality, and "embedded" liberalism, which propagates social welfare as a remedy for inequality. The laissez-faire version of liberalism assumes that free markets provide for the necessary cooperation between individuals, while the "embedded" liberalism openly calls for the state to ensure sufficient elements of harmony by correcting various market "imperfections."

The difference between these two modes of liberalism—conservative and embedded—is not that one is unconcerned for the weak and the other is compassionate, but rather it is in selection of the means to take care of society's unfortunates (i.e., philanthropic versus state aid). One should remember that Adam Smith, who formulated the core of laissez-faire doctrine, assumed that people are motivated by self-interest and moral restraint (i.e., "fellow feeling"), an assumption consistent with his religious background. Moreover, it was Smith's understanding that not only do both these motives express themselves through the market but that they are also strengthened by the market (see Janos, 1986, pp. 9–11).

The above two versions of liberalism are both truly liberal doctrines whose incorporation leads to a working pluralism, which is in contrast to the "perverse" liberalism that is a recipe for political and economic anarchy (see Comisso, 1976). Such a "perverse" interpretation of liberal philsophy in post-communist Eastern Europe and the former Soviet Union is more than just a theoretical possiblity. In fact, there is already growing evidence that liberalism has often been reduced in the region by many of its most devoted "disciples" to a few principles totally unrelated to the mainstream liberal doctrine. It is largely deprived of its traditional concern for universal well-being and instead praises "jungle" struggle for survival (or "private warfare").

The liberal philosophy has been greatly twisted by its many proponents not only because most often the ideas of freedom have not been experienced in their own lives but also in part, as one could suggest, because the whole doctrine has been interpreted through the daily experience of people who face great uncertainty. In the post-Communist Eastern Europe, where most of the traditional ways of enhancing personal security, including the mega-welfare state, have idled or been eliminated, there is a tendency for individuals to forget about their commitments to the community of people they are part of, hence they bend the message of liberalism accordingly.

This may be another moment in the history of Eastern Europe and Russia/the Soviet Union when their societies, in seeking to catch up with the more advanced "frontier" countries like those found in Western Europe, and while attempting to swiftly endorse their political doctrines, misinterpret these doctrines and inflict difficulties on themselves. This misinterpretation would not be easy to avoid, since the ideas or worldviews being replicated are often absorbed without an understanding of their original social context (see Janos, 1989). In fact, not long ago, Bolshevik Russia rejected one western-born doctrine, liberalism, for another, i.e., communism, only to twist the latter doctrine to the point where its original form had become hardly recognizable (mostly by instilling it with Russia's tradition of despotism).

Even further, one might doubt whether conservative liberalism, in its true version, is really most suitable as a basic doctrine for the ongoing transition to modern capitalism. Specifically, while this form of liberalism would seem to complement the expansion of the private sector, the economies of Eastern Europe would for many years come to be dominated, as correctly stressed by Kornai (1990), by the public sector. The post-communist state would find it difficult to manage the large public sector effectively without some ideology that could justify its extensive interventions in production. Laissez-faire philosophy, which calls for a "minimum-state" intervention, does not seem to be the answer.

Conservative liberalism might not only be a rather impractical solution for the mixed economy, a model that most of the post-Communist countries will most likely resemble for more than a decade, but it might also be quite unsuitable for the divestment of public assets by these states. Laissez-faire liberalism pronouncements for "equal" opportunity (or lack of so-called barriers to entry) could easily be interpreted as an invitation to simply disperse public assets at no cost to whoever wishes to get involved in the "market game" while letting competition decide who stays in the game. In fact, this is how many proponents of capitalist markets have adapted the liberal doctrine.

With the notable exception of Hungary (and former East Germany, which is a special case where the society has been basically excluded from designing its future model), all countries of Eastern Europe have endorsed the idea of free-of-charge distribution of a large portion of public assets, a system known as "popular capitalism." While this is quite consistent with liberal philosophy, and while in fact it has been receiving its strongest support from many ultra-liberal factions, like those found in Poland, this particular approach to privatization might easily prevent the formation of working capital markets, as correctly stressed by some economists (e.g., Kornai, 1990, Poznanski, 1992).

Providing equal access to public capital, which represents most of the existing wealth of capital in these countries, might upset the transition to capitalism by favoring passive owners, i.e., those that are separated from the decisions on the productive allocation of assets. Such an approach might also induce speculation by those interested in a quick resale of their stakes rather than enhance the value of their capital, which they have received free of charge. Moreover, since only a limited number of owners would be in a position to acquire sufficient knowledge to invest in capital markets, the popularization of stocks could also lead to excessive volatility when poorly prepared "players" overreact.

Embedded liberalism, which legitimizes state activism, might be a more practical response to the needs of ongoing transition, both with respect to managing the remaining public sector and to controlling access to the privatized assets. For the reasons mentioned above, an ideology even more pro-state than embedded liberalism could be more appropriate for the process of transition. Such an ideology could be populism, which calls for an organic symbiosis (or "corporatist" relations) between an emerging capital-based class and a deeply reconstituted labor-based class. The state would then behave as a powerful arbiter, ensuring that the basic needs of workers are satisfied and that those who appropriate capital act "responsibly" (see Staniszkis, 1990).

Conclusion

Great economic failures contributed significantly to the decay of the Communist system. Massive waste of resources—capital, land, but also labor—left the Communist economies with extreme shortages, and no prospects for resumption of rapid growth. The only viable way out of this economic crisis had been to relax the political structure and change property rights so that strong social groups interested in economizing on resources were reintroduced. There are a number of theoretical options for changing politics and reforming these rights, i.e., the incentive structure, but no late Communist regime had the courage to fully try them.

The decay of the Communist system does not mean its immediate worldwide extinction as prematurely heralded by some writers (see Fukuyama, 1989). In most of Eastern Europe, this process is almost irreversible, but at least in parts of the reconfigured Soviet Union (particularly in Central Asia), and even more in China, the Communist parties continue to enjoy political monopoly. Everywhere, however, these parties have been demythologizing private markets and allowing them to expand. If liberalism is triumphing, it is more in the economic realm and less in the political one.

Possibly the worst part of the post-Communist reality is what was left unchanged, in particular the fact that the region has remained on the periphery or semiperiphery, at least within the European sphere. With that status comes a tremendous gap between social expectations that are driven by the demonstration effect and the possibility of meeting them in an equitable way. Under such conditions, the democratization of political life now being pursued and the substitution of public with private property rights will necessarily be complicated and even explosive.

Construction of genuine capitalism following the destruction of Soviet-type Communism promises to be a lengthy process in which the property regimes and political styles that come closest to the desired final product of transition are not necessarily the ones that would be most suitable as interim, transitory solutions. The task before post-Communist Eastern Europe is to adopt the least costly methods of rebuilding capitalism even if they do not meet the standards of the ultimate system. Allowing illusions that the end product is in sight to override the transition process is one of the greatest threats to the region's recent effort to establish effective incentives and stable politics.

Notes

1. In fact, there is ample evidence that the Yugoslav economy is characterized by underutilized capital, inflationary pressure, and very high entry barriers for those joining the labor force (see Svejnar and Prasnikar, 1988).

2. Stojanovich (1989) holds that it is doubtful ". . . that workers will emerge as a "ruling" class. . . . Being an economic class . . . workers . . . cannot become a ruling class. . . . The crucial question is whether the working class is capable of creating organizations and institutions that are sufficiently powerful to prevail over the tendency of the new state apparatus to become independent and even constitute itself into a new ruling class." (p.52).

3. The conventional measures show Eastern Europe and the Soviet Union way behind the advanced capitalist countries in labor productivity, particularly if corrected for the lower quality of goods making up their national product (see Marer, 1985). This was in part or largely due to pervasive overmanning and chronic underutilization of capital equipment. Another critical reason was inferior technology (estimated by Gomulka, 1986, to have been in 1985 around a dozen years behind the frontier technology in the capitalist world).

4. Latin American authoritarianism seems to offer a solution to political instability, with societies wanting to actively participate but lacking workable procedures for reaching a consensus. So that while authoritarianism is here constantly challenged, it periodically takes the foreground to correct the excesses of interparty or intergroup politics (see: Croan, 1970).

5. As North (1981, p. 11) stated: ". . . the Marxist simply ignores the free rider problem and makes the immense leap of faith that people will set aside their own individual self-interest to act in the interests of a class, even at considerable personal sacrifice. The best evidence that this is not standard behavior comes from Marxist activists themselves who devote enormous energies to attempting to convince the proletariat to behave like a class."

6. As Polanyi (1944, p. 41) phrased it: "Transformation implies change in the motive of action on the part of the members of society: for the motive of subsistence, the gain must be substituted."

7. This substitution of universal values for a revolutionary program seemed to offer some help in maintaining Soviet leadership in the Communist world, but such a world no longer exists. Neither nationalism nor populism could have helped the Soviet Union to preserve its role of a cult place for the movement, the source of symbols and validation for other Communist parties or countries (Jowitt, 1987). Nationalism is by its nature divisive so that while it helps to mobilize a given society, it offends or hurts other societies. Populism is also self-centered, though not necessarily as aggressive outside.

Bibliography

Berend, I., 1986. "The Historical Evolution of Eastern Europe as a Region," *International Organization*, vol. 40, no. 2.

Bergson, A. 1978. *Productivity and the Social System: The USSR and the West.* Cambridge, Mass: Harvard University Press.

Berliner, J. 1952. "The Informal Organization of the Soviet Firm." *Quarterly Journal of Economics* (August).

Blinder, A. 1987. *Hard Heads, Soft Hearts, Tough-Minded Economics for a Just Society.* Reading: Addison-Wesley, Inc.

Bunce, V. 1989. "Decline of a Regional Hegemon: The Gorbachev Regime and Reform in Eastern Europe." *Eastern European Politics and Societies*, vol. 3, no. 1.

Carrere d'Encausse, H. 1980. *Confiscated Power, How Soviet Russia Really Works.* New York: Harper & Row.

Comisso, E., 1986. "Introduction: State Structures, Political Processes, and Collective Choice in CMEA States," *International Organization*, vol. 40, no. 2.

_____ and Marer, P. 1986. "The Economics and Politics of Reform in Hungary," *International Organization*, vol. 40 no. 2.

Croan, M. 1970. "Is Mexico the Future of East Europe?: Institutional Adaptability and Political Change in Comparative Perspective." In S. Huntington and C.H. Moore, eds. *Authoritarian Politics in Modern Society.* New York: Basic Books.

Fukuyama, F. 1989. "The End of History." *National Interest* (February).

Gomulka, S. 1986. *Growth, Innovation and Reforms in Eastern Europe.* Madison: University of Wisconsin Press.

Gross, J. 1989. "Social Consequences of War: Preliminaries to the Study of Communist Regimes in East Central Europe," *Eastern European Politics and Societies*, vol. 3, no. 2 (Spring).

Hirschman, A. 1988. "Rival Interpretations of Market Society." *Journal of Economic Literature.*

Janos, A. 1986. *Politics and Paradigms: Changing Theories of Change in Social Science.* Stanford: Stanford University Press.

_____. 1989. "The Politics of Backwardness in Continental Europe: 1780–1945," *World Politics*, vol. XLI, no. 3.

Jowitt, K. 1987. "Moscow 'Centre.'" *Eastern European Politics and Societies*, vol. 1, no. 3 (Fall).

_____. 1978. "Soviet Neo-Traditionalism: The Political Concept of a Leninist Regime." *Soviet Studies*, vol. 35 (July).

Kornai, J. 1990. *The Road to a Free Economy.* New York: Norton Press

_____. 1986. "The Hungarian Reform Process: Visions, Hopes and Reality." *Journal of Economic Literature* (December).

Levi, M. 1988. *Of Rule and Revenue,* Berkeley: University of California Press.

Lewin, M. 1988. *The Gorbachev Phenomenon.* Berkeley and Los Angeles: University of California Press.

Marer, P. 1985. *Dollar GNPs of the U.S.S.R. and Eastern Europe*, Baltimore: Johns Hopkins University Press.

Moore, B. 1954. *Terror and Progress, USSR: Some Sources of Change and Stability in the Soviet Dictatorship*. Cambridge, Mass.

North, D. 1981. *Structure and Change in Economic History*. New York: W.W. Norton.

_____. 1990. *Institutions, Institutional Change and Economic Performance*. Cambridge: Cambridge University Press.

_____ and R. Thomas. 1973. *The Rise of the Western World: A New Economic History*. Cambridge: Cambridge University Press.

Pejovich, S. 1989. "Liberty, Property Rights and Innovation in Eastern Europe," *The Cato Journal*, no. 1.

Polanyi, K. 1944. *The Great Transformation: The Political and Economic Origins of Our Time*. Boston: Beacon Press.

_____. 1968. *Primitive, Archaic and Modern Economies*. Garden City, N.Y.: Anchor Books.

Poznanski, K. 1986. "Economic Adjustment and Political Forces: Poland Since 1970," *International Organization*, vol. 40 no. 2.

_____. 1987. "Technology Competition and the Soviet Bloc in the World Market." Berkeley: Institute of Institutional Studies of University of California-Berkeley.

_____. 1989. "The Evolution of 'Real' Socialism in Eastern Europe and the Soviet Union." Jackson School of International Studies, University of Washington (mimeo).

_____. 1992. "Privatization of the Polish Industry: A Study in Transition." *Soviet Studies*, vol. 44, no. 4.

Schumpeter, J. 1942. *Capitalism, Socialism and Democracy*. Cambridge, Mass: Harvard University Press.

Staniszkis, J. 1990. "Patterns of Change in Eastern Europe." *Eastern European Politics and Societies*, vol. 4, no. 1.

Stojanovic, S. 1989. *Perestroika from Marxism and Bolshevism to Gorbachev*, Buffalo: Prometheus Books.

Svejnar, J. and J. Prasnikar. 1988. "Economic Behavior of Yugoslav Enterprises." *Advances in Economic Analysis of Participatory and Labor-Managed Firms*, vol. 3.

Tardos, M. 1986. "The Conditions of Developing a Regulated Market," *Acta Oeconomica*, vol. 36, nos. 1–2.

Tyson, L. 1981. "Aggregate Economic Difficulties and Workers." In J. Triska and C. Gati, eds. *Blue Collar Workers in Eastern Europe*. London: George Allen & Unwin.

5

The Affinity Between Ownership and Coordination Mechanisms: The Common Experience of Reform in Socialist Countries

Janos Kornai

The world witnesses a great upheaval in real socialist countries, where dramatic events have been happening since 1988. The present chapter concentrates on evaluating past experience in the hope that a correct understanding of the past will help in devising sound policies for the future. Of course, the number of socialist countries that have engaged in reform in the past is small, and the situation in all socialist or formerly socialist countries is still very unsettled. What can be attempted is nothing more than an outline of a few preliminary conjectures that will have to be tested against future historical developments.

The issues to be discussed in this chapter have many political ramifications. Decisions concerning ownership and coordination mechanisms are, of course, strongly linked to questions concerning power, political institutions and ideology. Apart from a few short hints, this chapter does not elaborate on the political aspects of these topics.

Classical Versus Reform Socialism, Reform Versus Revolution

Some conceptual clarification is needed. In the following, I distinguish two prototypes of real socialism. The first one is classical socialism, i.e., the form of socialism that prevailed under Stalin, Mao Zedong, and their disciples in other countries. The second one is reform socialism, i.e., the new form of socialism that evolved, for instance (in chrono-logical order), under Tito in Yugoslavia, Kadar in Hungary, Deng Xiaoping in China, and Gorbachev in the USSR; some further countries could be named as well. The reform socialist countries made some steps toward liberalization in the political sphere, somewhat decentralized the control of their state sector, and allowed a somewhat larger scope for the private sector. At the same time, these countries still maintained the fundamental attributes of a socialist system: the Communist party did not share power with any other political force, the state sector still played a dominant role in the economy, and the main coordinator of economic activities was the centralized bureaucracy, even though coordination was effected with the aid of less rigid instruments.

A distinction should also be made between reform and revolution. The former aims at major changes in the existing socialist system but preserves its basic characteristics. The latter starts a transformation that ultimately shifts the country in question away from socialism. Thus, the difference between reform and revolution does not lie in the method of transformation—violent versus nonviolent change, nor in the speed—slow process versus sudden explosion. The distinguishing criterion is whether the transformation abolishes the power monopoly of the Communist party. In this sense, in 1989, a revolution began (in temporal order) in Hungary, Poland, East Germany, Czechoslovakia, and Ruma-nia.[1] East Germany and Czechoslovakia avoided the reform stage and took a leap, by jumping from classical socialism directly to systemic transformation.

In this chapter, I am concerned with reform socialism and do not discuss the problems of "post-socialist" systemic transformation.[2] At the time of my writing the final version of the chapter, reform socialism is still the regime ruling over the largest country, China, and also a few smaller ones like Cuba or Vietnam. For Eastern Europe it is history, yet still so close to the present that it has an extremely strong impact not only on the initial economic conditions of the transformation process but also on political thought and intellectual debates. Therefore, the subject of the chapter, common lessons of reform socialism, should be more than timely as it might provide some orientation in the midst of the breath-taking changes in the socialist world.

Transformation Without a Strategy

If we look at the history of the socialist reform countries, we find that without exception, reform blueprints or programs were in circulation before the actual period of the reform. For the first example of such a proposal for reform within socialism one can go back as far as Oscar Lange's famous proposal for market socialism and to the debate to which his idea gave rise in the 1930s. Some blueprints and reform programs were also prepared by the leadership in charge. There were also instances of programs published illegally or semi-legally by dissidents and scholars.

While all these reform proposals became interesting historical documents, and while some of them had a certain influence on the course of events, reality in the reforming countries never corresponded to any of the blueprints. Of course, history stands witness to other cases of discrepancies between intent and outcome: the fate of the French Revolution reflected little of the ideas encyclopédistes, along with Rousseau, discussed in their works, and the Soviet Union in the 1930s turned out to be a country quite different from the one Marx or the participants of the revolutions of 1917 had imagined.

It is ironic to note, nevertheless, that major changes in centrally planned economies never took place according to a "central plan." There is a Chinese adage that talks of "crossing the river by touching the stone." The reform process in socialist economies conformed exactly to this image: whole societies proceeded to cross the deep water without accurate knowledge about the final destination by a process of moving from one stone to another.

The reality of reform in socialist countries was characterized by historical compromises, by movements backward as well as by movements forward, by periods of euphoria and of optimism alternating with periods of lost illusions and of frustrations. It also often turned out that, in spite of great efforts, some changes could not be preserved.[3] People often learned the limits of reformability by, figuratively speaking, running against a stone wall, i.e., the limits to changes imposed by the undivided power of the Communist party and the taboos maintained by the official ideology.

Under such circumstances it becomes extremely important to recognize what evolved spontaneously in the reform process. Marx used the German term "naturwüchsig," (as grown in nature) to characterize spontaneous historical processes. These are phenomena that appear not as a consequence of governmental orders or of administrative pressure but of the free will of certain social groups, reflecting their voluntary decisions and revealed preferences. The study of "naturally grown" changes—ignored to date—is all the more important since individual freedom of choice typically increased as a consequence of reform. Spontaneous changes thus reflected the voluntary decisions and revealed preferences of various social groups.

Exactly this approach distinguishes the present chapter from many other studies. Most of the earlier works on reform in socialist systems discussed the intentions and actions of the leadership and the apparatus. This chapter would like to draw attention to another, not less important aspect, namely spontaneous developments in the reform countries, developments that did not occur in response to leadership actions and maybe even contravened their intentions.

The Evolution of the Private Sector

In this endeavor, we should at first focus on the evolution of the private sector. When, for example,the author first began to participate in the beginning of Eastern European discussions on reform in 1954–1956, all scholars who took part in the debate were almost exclusively concerned with questions of reform in the state-owned sector. Initially, it was discussed how to give more autonomy and stronger profit-based incentives to state-owned firms and how to decentralize economic administration while at the same time maintaining state ownership in all but the most marginal sectors of the economy. As the reformers came to realize the inadequacy of these proposals, they envisaged larger and larger scope for market coordination in the economy. Yet they still clung to the notion of the dominance of state ownership.[4]

History took quite a different course from the one outlined in these blueprints. In all socialist economies where reforms had time to develop, and especially in Hungary, Poland, and China, the emergence of a significant private sector was the most important result of the reform in the economy.[5]

The most important inroad of private activity in socialist economies occurred through private farming.[6] Private agricultural production took different forms. In some reform socialist countries, the land was reprivatized *de facto*, as, for example, under the Chinese "family responsibility system." In others, private farming was never abolished and survived all kinds of political changes, as, for example, in Yugoslavia and in Poland. Other forms of private or semiprivate agricultural activity also evolved, for instance, an increased role for household plots and auxiliary agricultural production in Hungary.

A significant formal, i.e., legal, private sector emerged in various branches of the service, transport and construction industry, but, to a lesser extent, private business was allowed to operate in manufacturing as well.[7] In addition to the formal private sector, various types of informal "moonlighting" appeared; unlicensed, and perhaps illegal, but nonetheless tolerated activities proliferated in the service, commerce, transport, and construction sectors.[8]

Reform economies also experienced a significant increase in elaborate do-it-yourself activities such as the building of one's own house with the help of one or two professionals and that of some friends.[9] There appeared different forms of income derived from private property, for example, from the renting out of private homes in cities or from privately owned second homes in recreational areas.

In some countries, and in some sectors such as housing, services, and agriculture, it even happened that property owned by the state or by some other social organization was sold or leased to individuals in the reform period. The idea of genuine privatization in the British way, that is to say, the idea of the sale of the stock of state companies to the public, came up in debates in the reform economies even before the more recent discussions in the context of revolutionary transformation. In practice, however, the larger part of the growth of the private sector took place as a result of entrepreneurial initiative, partly based on private savings but for the most part on the labor input of the individual. Indeed, private firms were mostly very small-scale.[10]

It must be stressed that the government typically did not have to convince its citizens to enter the private sector by a propaganda campaign. Usually, after certain prohibitions on private activity were lifted, the private sector began to grow quite spontaneously with individual enterprises sprouting up like mushrooms in a forest after rainfall.[11] This increase in private activity was all the more notable as it often followed a period of brutal repression of any form of private ventures. People did not have to be cajoled or coerced in order to choose this way of life. In fact, they were immediately attracted by the higher earnings, by the more direct linkage between effort and reward, and by the greater autonomy and freedom that the private sector offered.[12]

Private activities in reform socialist economies generated relatively high income because they were able to meet demand left unsatisfied by the state-owned sector. A craftsman, the owner of a corner grocery store or of a small restaurant would typically be in the middle income group in a private enterprise economy. But in the environment of what was still a chronic shortage economy, the same activities catapulted these people into the highest income group, not because they were particularly smart or greedy but because of the rarity of the service that they provided. The price they got for their output was just the market clearing price in the small segment of the economy where a genuine market operated. They could be grateful to the state-owned sector and to the fiscal and monetary systems that created supply and demand conditions leading to free market prices significantly higher than the official prices in the state-owned sector.

The dimensions of this growth of private economic activity are even more noteworthy if one takes into account the fact that private business had to adjust to the hostile environment of the halfheartedly reforming socialist economy. Despite some improvements, the daily life of private businesses in reforming countries was still characterized by a multitude of bureaucratic interventions and restrictions. Access to materials and credit and foreign exchange was limited and often had to be acquired in illegal and semi-legal ways.

A further element in the hostile environment was the jealousy of people who were suspicious of growing income differentials. Envy of individuals who suddenly come to earn more than others, while it occurs in all systems, is likely to be all the more divisive in a society in which people have been brought up to consider equality to be a major social desideratum.

Finally, halfhearted reform caused further difficulties due to the absence of legal institutions for the consistent protection of private property and for the enforcement of private contracts, as well as the repression of political movements and associations devoted to the artic-ulation of the private sector's interests. And that leads to the ideological aspects of the issue.

Can one justifiably assume that this small scale private activity in re-form socialism inevitably leads to capitalism? Many advocates of reform in socialist countries are tempted to simply answer "no." Nevertheless, if we want to be objective, it is not possible to dismiss this question so easily.

Using now the terminology of Marxian political economy, we may classify the overwhelming part of private sector activities in socialist economies as small commodity production. Roughly speaking, the decisive distinction between small commodity production and genuine capitalism in the Marxian sense is that the former uses only the labor input of one individual, together perhaps with that of his family mem-bers, whereas the latter uses hired labor regularly and thus becomes exploitative as it seeks to extract the surplus from the employee.

In this context, the ideology and practice of classical socialism sup-pressing not only full-blown capitalism but small-scale private produc-tion as well has been very much influenced by Lenin's frequently quoted dictum that ". . . small production engenders capitalism and the bourgeoisie continuously, daily, hourly, spontaneously, and on a mass scale."[13] In the author's opinion, Lenin was absolutely right. If a society allows for the existence of a large number of small commodity producers, and if it permits them to accumulate capital and to grow over time, a genuine group of capitalists will sooner or later emerge. To appreciate this fact, the reader is asked to imagine for a moment what would happen if private producers had the same access to credit and to all kinds of inputs as the state-owned enterprise in a socialist economy and, moreover, were treated equally by the tax and subsidy system. Without any doubt, the more successful private businesses would begin to accumulate and grow.

Thus, the negative answer of some reformers to the question of whether small commodity production breeds capitalism is already predicated on the assumption that the government will not allow private business to grow beyond a certain critical threshold. Indeed, the growth of the private sector in reform socialist economies was not only hampered by the excessive red tape of an ubiquitous and omnipotent bureaucracy; the sustained growth of private businesses also ran counter to the ideological premises of the system and was therefore held in check by the ruling Communist party and the government, which were not willing to tolerate a significant capitalist sector.

There have been different ways of imposing constraints on the private sector's ability to grow in a socialist economy. Sometimes, these constraints simply took the form of legal restrictions such as, for example, an upper bound on the number of people that a legal private enterprise was allowed to employ, or of a limit on the amount of capital that it was allowed to invest in private business. Obstacles to growth were also incorporated in the tax system. The extent of taxation of a particular activity at a given point in time could vary quite substantially, thus providing the authorities with an additional tool for keeping the private sector under control. Private craftsmen and private traders could point to the exact level of taxation up to which they would be able to uphold the private venture, and beyond which they would have to abandon it and return to work in the state-owned sector. The most powerful upper limit on accumulation was uncertainty and the fear of future nationalization and confiscation. Memories of past repression were alive, and the individual might well have been scared that he and his children might one day be stigmatized as "bourgeois" or "kulak."

In this situation, limits on capital accumulation made it difficult to achieve economies of scale. It might be individually more rational in a given political and ideological climate to waste one's profits rather than to put them to productive use. In historical accounts of capitalist economies, we are used to reading about the parsimony of the founders of family businesses who endeavor to bequeath their wealth to future generations. In accordance with the picture painted in Thomas Mann's novel "Buddenbrooks," we begin to associate wastefulness only with the second and subsequent generations of a family line of capitalists. By contrast, wasteful consumption in family businesses in socialist reform countries often began on the very first day of their existence given that it was quite uncertain whether the venture would have a prolonged existence even within the individual founder's own lifetime.

The social environment of the private sector also resulted in myopic behavior. The private firm was typically not interested in building up solid good will with its customers for its products or services because its owners felt that they might not be in business the following year. And they were not forced to treat their buyers well given the seller's market. The private firms could afford to cheat so as to reap the largest possible amount of one-time profit.

To the extent that consumers were used to the queues and to the shortages in the state-owned sector, it was generally easy for the private firm to keep its customers even though its employees might hardly be more forthcoming and polite than the employees of its counterpart in the state-owned sector. Instead of raising the overall standards of service of the sellers under state ownership in the direction of those of a buyers' market, the standards of a new small private venture often dropped downward to those of sellers in a chronic shortage economy.

In all reform economies, private ventures also had to adapt to the use of bribery in the acquisition of the necessary inputs. Cheating was needed not only in order to acquire inputs but also in order to defend the business against the state. There are many stories about Soviet cooperatives and small private businessmen in other countries having to bribe local officials in order to obtain a license. Many individuals joining the private sector were not entrepreneurs but adventurers. Such was the natural selection process under the given conditions.

These circumstances set the trap for the social position of the private sector. Daily experience supplied arguments for "anti-capitalist" demagoguery and for popular slogans against profiteering, greediness and cheating. It is ironic that some politicians and journalists in the reform and even in the "post-socialist" countries (sometimes even in the "new left" circles within oppositional groups) argue against high prices and profiteering on moral grounds.

It is not recognized that it is inconsistent to declare the desirability of a market and at the same time to refuse the legitimacy of a price generated by the very same market mechanism. Such propaganda fuels restrictions and interventions leading to further deterioration—to capitalism at its worst. We therefore face a vicious cycle. The contemporary socialist system needs the active contribution of a private sector, otherwise it is not able to deliver the goods to the people. Socialism arrived at a stage in history when it was unable to survive in its pure, strictly noncapitalist fashion and had to co-exist with its self-acknowledged arch-enemy not only worldwide but within its own borders as well.

The Persistence of Bureaucracy

As far as the state-owned sector is concerned, the central idea of the original reform blueprints had been the abolition of the command economy, that is the elimination of mandatory output targets and mandatory input quotas. Among the reform socialist countries, Yugoslavia and Hungary were the only countries that more or less consistently implemented these proposals before the recent wave of accelerated changes.

When the reform process began in the 1950s and 1960s, the initial expectation was that once the administrative system was abolished, there would be a momentary vacuum that would then be filled by the market mechanism. In other words, bureaucratic commands would be instantaneously replaced by market signals. The underlying assumption was that of a simple complementarity between the two mechanisms of coordination, namely bureaucratic and market coordination.[14] However, this expectation, which was shared by the author in 1955–56, has turned out to be naive. The vacuum left by the elimination of administrative commands, and thus by the elimination of direct bureaucratic coordination, was filled not by the market but by other, indirect tools of bureaucratic coordination.[15]

Although the role of the market, of course, increased in the wake of the reform, the role of the bureaucracy continued to remain pervasive. For instance, the role of the bureaucracy was still paramount in the selection and in the promotion of managers, and in the decision-making power with regard to the entry and the exit of firms. And while the bureaucracy had reduced or completely relinquished direct administrative control over the quantities of output and input of state firms, it could still control them through formal state orders and informal requests, through administrative price setting as well as through the extremely strong financial dependence of the firm on its superior organs, i.e., the ministries in charge of production, the foreign-trade authorities, the price control office, the financial bodies, the police, and so on. Party organizations also frequently intervened in the affairs of the firms. A change took place in the form but not in the intensity of dependence.

In our description of the private sector, we have used the terms "spontaneous" or "naturally grown." Here we shall emphasize that the persistence of a huge bureaucracy is a spontaneous and natural outgrowth of the socialist economy as well. The Central Committee or the Politburo of the Communist party did not have to decide to maintain as much of the bureaucracy as possible during the process of reform. On the contrary, the bureaucracy grew despite sincere attempts to reduce it, and in the face of dramatic campaigns to get rid of it such as the one that took place during the cultural revolution in China. The Soviet *perestroika* initially again set as its goal a reduction in the size of the bureaucracy; yet the experience up to 1990 did not provide much ground for maintaining the belief in the possibility of checking the natural growth of the bureaucracy by reform alone.

A self-reproduction of bureaucracy could be observed in the sense that if it was eliminated at some place in one particular form, it reappeared at another place in some other form. The bureaucracy ruled the socialist economy, both in its classical and reformed forms. This permanent restoration of bureaucratic control is to a large extent explained by certain strong incentives of the bureaucrats. One is, of course, all the material advantages associated with bureaucratic positions, namely financial benefits, privileges and access to goods and services in short supply. Even more important is the attraction of power. And here we arrive at a highly political issue again. The relative shares of the role played by bureaucratic and market coordination are not simply a matter of finding the most efficient division of labor between two neutral mechanisms. Allowing the genuine functioning of the market means the voluntary surrender of an important part of the power of the bureaucracy.

The most important consequences of this situation were the limits imposed on the reformability of the state-owned sector by the systemic tendency of self-reproduction of the bureaucracy. We might be able to appreciate this point more clearly by considering the question of the constituency for reform. On the one hand, in the case of the private sector, this constituency was large and well-defined. It consisted of all citizens of a socialist country who chose to or at least would have liked to have the option to work in the private sector, as entrepreneurs or as employees.

On the other hand, nobody would have been an unqualified winner in the far-reaching decentralization of the state-owned sector. Every person involved in the state-owned sector would have gained as well as lost as a result of decentralization. Each member of the bureaucratic apparatus might have gained autonomy vis-à-vis his superiors but at the same time might have lost power over his subordinates. Reduction in paternalism and a concomitant hardening of the budget constraint[16] would have entailed advantages as well as disadvantages both for managers and workers of a state-owned firm. They would have gained in autonomy but at the same time lost in protection. Every individual working in the state-owned sector had schizophrenic feelings with respect to the soft budget constraint, paternalism, and protection. While high taxes were disliked, subsidies, even if the firm was not receiving them, might have come in handy in the future and could therefore not be opposed quite firmly. Shortages, while they inconvenienced the firm as a buyer, suited it as a seller.

Thus, it turned out that neither the bureaucrats, nor the managers, nor indeed the workers were enthusiastic adherents of competition or of the marketization of the state-owned sector. Some enlightened government officials and intellectuals may have come to the conclusion that a hardening of the budget constraint and a decrease in paternalism was needed so as to improve the performance of the economy. However, there were no strikes or street demonstrations in favor of increasing economic efficiency at the expense of state protection. There did not exist a grass-roots movement for the decentralization of the state sector. Since on the one hand there was a strong inducement to maintain the bureaucratic positions, and on the other hand there was no unambiguous constituency against their maintenance, the final result was the permanent reproduction of bureaucratic coordination.

Weak and Strong Linkages:
The Weakness of Market Socialism

After discussing the private and state sectors and looking at the bureaucracy and market in a prototype reforming socialist economy, we will now approach the theme of this chapter from a somewhat more general point of view.

Two strong linkages between the ownership form and the coordination mechanism exist.[17] Thus, it is common to encounter classical, pre-reform socialist economies that combined state ownership with bureaucratic coordination and classical capitalist economies that combined private ownership with market coordination. These two simple cases might be looked upon as historical benchmark models.

By contrast, we can observe that in the reform socialist economies, the private sector, while mainly controlled by the market, was also subject to bureaucratic control. Yet this attempt to impose bureaucratic control on private activities does not and cannot work smoothly due to the basic incongruity of this pair. In addition, there exist other, generally also inconsistent, attempts to coordinate the state-owned sector via market coordination. This idea was the center of the blueprint of market socialism. However, it turned out not to be possible to decrease the dominant influence of the bureaucracy.

To sum up: the relationship between the latter two pairs, namely the relationship between state ownership and market coordination and between private ownership and bureaucratic coordination, can be characterized as weak linkages.

The notion of "strong" and "weak" linkages does not imply a value judgement but is purely descriptive. In accordance with the general philosophy of this analysis, a linkage between an ownership form and a type of coordination is strong if it emerges spontaneously and prevails in spite of resistance and countermeasures. It is based on a natural affinity and cohesion between certain types of ownership and certain types of coordination mechanisms. The adjective "weak" refers to linkages that are to some extent artificial and not sufficiently strong to resist the impact of the stronger linkage. Weak linkages are pushed aside by the strong ones time and again, whether the intellectual and political leaders of the reform like it or not.[18]

The observation that the linkage between state ownership and the market is weak should be seriously taken into account in the ongoing debate on whether it is possible to find a Third Way between old-style Stalinist, classical socialism and contemporary capitalism.[19] There is a large number of visions of such a Third Way, market socialism being just one in this vast array of blueprints and system engineering proposals. It is an appealing ideology in the eyes of people who attach intrinsic value to the abolition of private property mainly on political and moral grounds but who at the same time recognize the inefficiency of bureaucratic coordination. This paper does not argue against the desirability of a market socialist system, but against its feasibility. Indeed, its weakness and inner inconsistency are sufficient reasons to reject this idea.

The Weakness of Other "Third Forms"

Aside from market socialism, other Third Way doctrines abound in socialist (and formerly socialist) countries. Without aiming at a complete classification, I observe the following characteristics. As for ownership, many adherents of Third Way ideologies are attracted to configurations of property rights that exclude both strict state ownership and conventional private ownership. Various "substitute forms" are advocated: cooperative ownership, communes, labor management, etc.

As for coordination mechanisms, again the emphasis is on the negative element: exclusion of both bureaucratic control and the market. Let us introduce as a convenient shorthand for all these "third" coordination mechanisms the term "associative coordination," which includes self-governance, free association, reciprocity, altruism, and mutual voluntary adjustment.

The early literature on socialism is rich in proposals suggesting that a socialist society should be based on cooperative ownership, and on nonmarket, nonbureaucratic associative coordination. In referring to this tradition of thought Marx coined the somewhat derogatory term "Utopian Socialism." Early representatives of this line of thinking have been Proudhon, Fourier (to some extent), Owen, and others.

The more recent literature does not always couple genuine cooperatives and labor management with associative coordination. Some authors place the emphasis on cooperatives and labor management, others on associative coordination, while in some cases the two are considered together. Of course, cooperative ownership can be linked not only to associative coordination but to the market as well. Ideas of this kind frequently came up in the reform discussions in socialist countries.

Yugoslavia, for example, experimented with a coupling of labor management with both market and "associative" coordination. Large segments of the economy were coordinated in the usual way by the market mechanism. At the same time, so-called "social compacts" were arranged to establish direct contacts between the representatives of producers and consumers; they were expected to voluntarily make mutual adjustments. While the official policy alternated in the emphasis given to the market and associative coordination, in fact bureaucratic coordination prevailed all the time and was in a latent fashion the dominant force.

The Chinese cultural revolution may be looked upon as another attempt to smash the bureaucracy and to proceed to a nonbureaucratic socialism without the introduction of market elements. But neither the Yugoslav nor the Chinese experiment led to conclusive results. In both cases, the changes were forced upon society by the political leadership. Although at the beginning the initiative from the top had enthusiastic support among at least a part of the population, changes were subsequently institutionalized and forced through without countenancing any deviation from the central party line. Therefore, the fact that something resembling cooperative ownership and labor management was and still is the dominant ownership form in Yugoslavia or that the rhetoric of Mao's Cultural Revolution reasserted principles similar to associative coordination is not enough to draw conclusions concerning the true strength of these forms.

Let us apply instead the criterion proposed previously and look at whether cooperative ownership and associative coordination grow spontaneously and naturally during the reform process. This question is meaningful because the establishment of genuine voluntary cooperatives, voluntary adjustments, and other forms of associative coordination are not prohibited in these countries. Small cooperatives are far more tolerated by the communist rulers than are more outright private economic activities, and altruism and noncommercialized reciprocity are of course legal in any system.

However, while third forms (cooperatives, labor management, and associative coordination) existed even at the peak of bureaucratic centralization, these forms did not experience a spectacular growth after the command system had been abolished. When forms other than centralized state ownership were permitted, private ownership gained ground rapidly. While the elimination of direct bureaucratic control left a momentary vacuum, this vacuum was filled mainly by indirect bureaucratic control, as well as by some form of market coordination. Cooperative ownership, labor management and associative coordination played only an auxiliary role at most.[20]

Let us sum up our arguments concerning the strengths or weaknesses of the forms of social organization. State ownership and private ownership are both robust, while the various third forms of ownership have relatively few followers. Similarly, while bureaucratic and market coordination both are widely applied, associative coordination operates only in a rather restricted area. There is an affinity between state ownership and market coordination and between private ownership and market coordination; all other potential linkages between forms of ownership and forms of coordination are weak and tend to be overridden by the two strong linkages.

With a view to the discussions about transformation now going on in socialist and formerly socialist countries, it must be admitted that the observations concerning the weakness of third forms are drawn from a small sample observed over a brief period. Perhaps twenty or thirty years from now, researchers will be able to observe that this tendency was stopped and that history took an alternative route. History is always unpredictable. But as long as no contrary evidence is provided by experience, it is worthwhile to keep in mind these preliminary observations concerning the strength and weakness of the alternative ownership forms and coordination mechanisms and linkages between them.

It is fully understandable that various social groups and intellectual currents advocate a wider role for third forms. These efforts may have beneficial effects, but it would be intellectually dishonest to hide the evidence concerning the weakness of third forms.

About Normative Implications

No search for third forms of ownership and coordination mechanisms allows one to evade the real tough choices. We really have to decide what the relative importance of the two robust forms of ownership—state and private—should be. Closely related to this is the choice concerning the relative shares of the two robust coordination mechanisms, i.e., bureaucratic and market coordination.

We are not faced with an "either-or" type of binary choice between mutually exclusive forms: either state ownership cum bureaucratic coordination, or private ownership cum market coordination. The ideas presented here, however, entail the following. State and private ownership can coexist within the same society. Yet in the political, social and ideological environment of reform socialist countries, this is an uneasy symbiosis loaded with many grave dysfunctional features. The decision concerning the actual shares of state and private ownership, and the associated decision concerning the combination of bureaucratic and market coordination, are both dependent on the ultimate value judgements of those participating in the choice.

This chapter does not comment on these value judgements, or on the political and ethical criteria underlying the choice. It offers some conditional predictions based on conjectures about the strengths and weaknesses of various possible linkages between ownership and coordination mechanisms. History warns us not to have illusions and false expectations. Once one arrives at a large share for state ownership, one gets a "package deal" that inevitably contains a large dose of bureaucratic coordination.

Another warning is also needed: if one really wants a larger share for market coordination, one must ipso facto accept a larger share for private ownership and for individual activities. But a desired coordination mechanism (say market) does not come about without a significant backing of the appropriate ownership form (for instance, private ownership). Likewise, one cannot get the desired ownership form (say, public) without getting its associated form of coordination (such as bureaucratic coordination). Such has been the Realpolitik of reforms.

The usual slogans dominating the published economic literature in the reform countries demanding state ownership cum market entailed a misunderstanding or engendered naive, false hopes for a Third Way that are clearly disproved by the bitter track record of experimentation with half-reforms. But then, must these countries tread the painful path of gradual disenchantment? Is it really hopeless to expect that the late-comers to the reform process might learn from the disappointments of the pioneers in reform?

Those who sincerely want a larger role for the market must allow more room for fully legal private activities, for free entry and for exit, for competition, for individual entrepreneurship and for private property. The author is strongly in favor of this course of action.[21] Only a radical extension of the private sector creates favorable conditions for the marketization of the whole economy, including more effective market signals and more powerful profit incentives for state-owned firms. Movement in that direction, namely in the direction of the extension of the private sector, is the most important yardstick of economic transformation.

Notes

This chapter opened in its original form in "Economic Perspectives," vol. 4, no. 3, 1990. Its earlier version was presented at the Roundtable Conference on "Market Forces in Planned Economies" in Moscow, March 28–30, 1989. I should like to express my thanks to the participants of the Roundtable and to the editors of "Economic Perspectives," Carl Shapiro, Joseph Stiglitz, and Timothy Taylor for their valuable comments. I am especially grateful to my closest collaborators, Maria Kovacs and Carla Kruger for their devoted help in the revision of the paper. The paper is a by-product of my ongoing research on the political economy of socialism, supported by the Hungarian Academy of Sciences, Harvard University, the Sloan Foundation, and WIDER, the World Institute for Development Economic Research; the help of these institutions is gratefully acknowledged.

1. At the time of completing this chapter, in March 1990, it was not yet clear where Bulgaria and Yugoslavia fit in this classification.

2. The author's views on revolutionary transformation are discussed in his recent book (1990).

3. To give just one telling example, early on in the Soviet perestroika, it was envisaged to replace plan targets with state orders covering not much more than 30 percent of output. Under conditions of shortage, fixed supplier-customer relations, and bureaucratic intervention, they ended up covering over 90 percent of output. An 1989 amendment to the Soviet enterprise law then stipulated that state orders were no longer allowed to cover 100 percent (sic) of output. (See text of the amendment in *Pravda*, August 11, 1989.)

4. See, for example, the following sample of the earliest papers advocating a decentralization based reform in Eastern Europe: B. Kidric (see his papers from the fifties in the (1985) volume) for Yugoslavia, Gy. Péter (1954a,b, 1956) and J. Kornai [1957] (1959) for Hungary, W. Brus [1961] (1972) for Poland, E. Liberman [1962] (1972) for the USSR and Sun Yefang [1958–1961] (1982) for China.

5. About the formal and informal private sector, see G. Grossman (1977), I. R. Gábor (1985), C. M. Davis (1988), S. Pomorski (1988) and B. Dallago (1989).

6. The spectacular increase in the size of the private sector is well captured by data on total yearly work-hours spent by the population in the different sectors. In Hungary, total work-time spent in private agricultural activity was more than one-third of that spent in the socialist sector in the mid-1980s. All the data reported here and in Footnotes 7 and 8 to describe the Hungarian private sector are from J. Timár (1988), pp. 225, 229–245.

7. Taking the example of Hungary, total work-hours in the nonagricultural, formal, i.e., legal, private sector increased 2.4 times from 1967 to 1985, and 1.6 times from 1980 to 1985. Private business partnerships, owned and operated by a group of people belonging to the private sector, along with business owned and operated by single individuals or by a family. In the Soviet Union such partnerships are called "cooperative," although everybody knows that they are in fact private business partnerships.

8. Referring back to the Hungarian example, work-time in this informal private sector increased by 5.6 times from 1977 to 1986. Work-time spent in this sector was 1.5 times higher than that spent in the formal private sector.

9. For instance, in 1988, 65% of new residential construction in Hungary was organized by private owners (see in Central Statistical Office, 1989, p. 250).

10. For instance, in Poland, before the revolution of 1989, there were one million private enterprises employing two million people. (Source: Lecture by Jeffrey Sachs, Harvard University, February 8, 1990).

11. For instance, from 1987 when the Soviet government first gave its blessing to the small-scale cooperatives to 1989, the number of full-time cooperative members jumped from about 15,000 to over 2,000,000, with a multiple of this number in part-time and employee status.

12. For instance, in Hungary a lawyer in a state-owned enterprise decided to leave his job to open a small private restaurant—just so as to no longer have a boss tell him what to do. The same reason was given by former members of an agricultural cooperative who had chosen to quit and had opened a small regional food-processing plant.

13. V.I. Lenin [1920], (1966), p.8.

14. The term "bureaucratic coordination," here as in other works of the author is used in a value-free sense, without any negative connotation as in many Eastern European writings and speeches. It refers to certain types of controlling and coordinating activities. The main characteristics of this mechanism include the multi-level hierarchical organization of control, the dependence of the subordinate on the superior and the mandatory or even coercive character of the instructions of the superior.

15. The notions of direct and indirect control were firstly used by Kálmán Szabó, Tamás Nagy and Lászlá Antal.

16. The terms "soft" and "hard budget constraint" are discussed in the author's works (1980, 1986b). Basically, the notion of a hard budget constraint is a synonym of full financial self-reliance of the firm and a real threat of bankruptcy in the case of insolvency. The notion of a soft budget constraint refers to a situation where the state bureaucracy assists the state-owned firm in a variety of ways, through subsidies, tax exemptions, soft credits, negotiable administrative prices, etc., and where the firm is protected from financial failure. Thus survival and growth of the firm depends more on its relation to the bureaucracy than on success on the market.

17. The train of thought of this section was influenced by the literature on the theory of property rights in general—see, for instance, A.A. Alchian and H. Demsetz (1973), H. Demsetz (1967), E.G. Furubotn and S. Pejovich (1974)—and especially by those writings that discuss the question of property rights as regards the socialist system. Among the latter I would like to single out the classical work by L. von Mises [1920] (1935), as well as among the more recent works D. Lavoie (1985), and G. Schroeder (1988).

18. There are many other combinations of state and private ownership, and of market and bureaucratic coordination worth considering. For example, if the private sector of an economy is strong and stable, a certain segment of the economy can be state-owned and can be forced to operate according to the rules of the market.

19. Some politicians and scholars advocate a Third Way in the political sphere, different both from the Stalinist classical socialist political structure and from Western-type parliamentary democracy. According to the objectives of the paper, the discussion is limited to Third Way ideas concerning the economic sphere.

20. Third ownership forms and associative coordination are associated in many writings with certain political ideas such as administrative decentralization of government activities, the increased role of local governments, participatory democracy and self-governance, corporative ideas of various sorts and so on. Again, the discussion of these aspects is beyond the limits of the present paper.

21. For more details concerning my policy proposals, see Kornai (1990).

Bibliography

Afanas'ev, I., ed. 1988. *Inogo ne dano* (There is No Other Way). Moscow: Progress.

Alchian, A. and H. Demsetz. 1973. "The Property Rights Paradigm." *Journal of Economic History*, vol. 33 (March), p. 17.

Antal, L., L. Bokros, I. Csillag, L. Lengyel and G. Matolcsy. 1987. "Change and Reform." *Acta Oeconomica*, vol. 38, pp. 3–4, 187–213.

Brus, W. [1961], 1972. *The Market in a Socialist Economy*. London: Routledge and Kegan.

Burkett, J. 1989. "The Yugoslav Economy and Market Socialism." In M. Bornstein, ed. *Comparative Economic Systems: Models and Cases*, pp. 234–258. Homewood, IL and Boston, MA: Irwin.

Central Statistical Office. 1989. *Statisztikai évkönvv 1988* (Statistical Yearbook 1988.) Budapest: Statisztikai Kiadó.

Dallago, B. 1989. "The Underground Economy in the West and East: A Comparative Approach." In M. Bornstein, ed. *Comparative Economic Systems: Models and Cases*, pp. 463–484. Homewood, IL and Boston, MA: Irwin.

Davis, C. 1988. "The Second Economy in Disequilibrium and Shortage Models of Centrally Planned Economies," Berkeley-Duke Occasional Papers on the Second Economy in the USSR, no. 12 (July).

Demsetz, H. 1967. "Toward a Theory of Property Rights." *American Economic Review*, vol. 57 no. 2 (May), pp. 347–359.

Furubotn, E. and S. Pejovich, eds. 1974. *The Economics of Property Rights*. Cambridge, Mass.: Ballinger.

Gábor, I. "The Major Domains of the Second Economy." In P. Galasi and G. Sziráczky, eds. *Labour Market and Second Economy in Hungary*, pp. 133–178. Frankfurt and New York: Campus.

Grossman, G. 1977. "The 'Second Economy' of the USSR." *Problems of Communism*, vol. 26, no. 5, pp. 25–40.

Hewett, E. 1988. *Reforming the Soviet Economy: Equality versus Efficiency*. Washington, DC: The Brookings Institution.

Kidric, B. 1985. *Sabrana Dela* (Collected Works). Belgrad: Izdavacki Centar Komunist.

Kornai, J. [1957], 1959. *Overcentralization in Economic Administration*. London: Oxford University Press.

_____. 1980. *Economics of Shortage*. Amsterdam: North-Holland.

_____. 1984. "Bureaucratic and Market Coordination." *Osteuropa-Wirtschaft*, vol. 29, no. 4, pp. 306–319.

_____. 1986a. "The Hungarian Reform Process: Visions, Hopes and Reality." *Journal of Economic Literature*. vol. 24, no. 4 (Dec.), pp. 1687–1737.

_____. 1986b. "The Soft Budget Constraint." *Kyklos*, vol. 39, no. 1, pp. 3–30.

_____. 1990. The Road to a Free Economy. Shifting from a Socialist System: The Example of Hungary. New York: W. W. Norton and Company.

Lavoie, D. 1985. Rivalry and Central Planning: The Socialist Calculation Debate Reconsidered. Cambridge: Cambridge University Press.

Lenin, V. [1920], 1966. *Left-wing Communism: an Infantile Disorder*. Moscow: Progress Publishers.

Liberman, E. [1962], 1972. "The Plan, Profits and Bonuses." In A. Nove and D. Nuti, eds. *Socialist Economics: Selected Readings*, pp. 309–318. Middlesex: Penquin Books.

Mises, L. von. [1920], 1935. "Economic Calculation in the Socialist Commonwealth." In F. Hayek, ed. *Collectivist Economic Planning,* pp. 87–130. London: Routledge and Kegan .

Perkins, D. 1988. "Reforming China's Economic System." *Journal of Economic Literature,* vol. 26, no. 2 (June), pp. 601–645.

Péter, G. 1954a. "Az egyszemélyi felelös vezetésröl" (On Management Based on One-Man Responsibility). *Társadalmi Szemle,* vol. 9, no. 8–9 (Aug./ Sept.), pp. 109–124.

————. 1954b. "A gazdaságosság jelentöségéröl és szerepéröl a népgazdaság tervszeru irányitásában" (On the Importance and Role of Economic Efficiency in the Planned Control of the National Economy). *Közgazdasági Szemle.* vol. 1, no. 3 (Dec.), pp. 300–324.

————. 1956. "A gazdaságosság és a jövedelmezöség jelentösége a tervgazdaságban, I–II" (The Importance of Economic Efficiency and Profitability in Planned Economy I–II). *Közgazdasági Szemle,* vol. 3, no. 6 (June), pp. 695–711 and vol. 3, no. 7–8 (July/Aug.), pp. 851–869.

Pomorski, S. 1988. "Privatization of the Soviet Economy Under Gorbachev I: Notes on the 1986 Law on Individual Enterprise." Berkeley-Duke Occasional Papers on the Second Economy in the USSR, #13 (October).

Schroeder, G. 1987. "Anatomy of Gorbachev's Economic Reform." *Soviet Economy,* vol. 3, no. 3 (July/Sept.), pp. 219–241.

————. 1988. "Property Rights Issues in Economic Reforms in Socialist Countries." *Studies in Comparative Communism,* vol. 21, no.2 (Summer), pp. 175–188.

Shmelev, N. 1987. "Avansy i Dolgi" (Credits and Debts). *Novii Mir,* vol. 6 (June), pp. 142–58.

Timár, J. 1988. *Idö és munkaidö* (Time and Working Time). Budapest: Közgazdasági és Jogi Könyvkiadó.

Yefang, S. 1982. "Some Theoretical Issues in Theoretical Issues," originally published in the period 1958–1961. Edited and translated by K. Fung under title: *Social Needs versus Economic Efficiency in China.* Armonk: M.E. Sharpe.

6

Divestment of State Capital: Alternative Forms and Timetable

Jozef M. van Brabant

Markets are concerned with allocation and efficient exploitation of resources. Regarding inputs, the functions can be separated into the allocation of capital, labor, land, and other natural resources. As for outputs, the principal functions can be reduced to wholesale and retail trade of goods and services, the distribution of incomes between consumption and accumulation, and of time between leisure and work.

Whether "output" on the resource ledger can be negative or should be held nominally constant is a matter that society must decide, for otherwise the notorious short-range outlook of markets leads to failure. Note that markets do not necessarily prevent "unfair" distribution and possible abuses of ownership, in spite of the great emphasis placed on it by the neo-Austrian school.[1] To mitigate market failures, interference by government may be justified.

Eastern European—and, increasingly, Russian—policy makers see the need to entrust the entire wholesale and retail trade to operations other than the traditional material supply administration. In the case of wholesale trading, they recognize the necessity of allowing firms to interact on the basis of their own interests. Similarly, policy makers want retail trade to be handed over to firms seeking to maximize returns on their assets.

There is likewise little dispute about the choice between work and leisure, something for which there already has been considerable private sovereignty, subject, of course, to rules on shirking and idleness. Trading off leisure against labor income is largely up to the individual, certainly within institutional arrangements that can be flouted, for example, by becoming an independent operator—now a distinct possibility. Inasmuch as labor markets cannot be completely left to free-market operations, genuine trade unions are required.

The paramount issue involved in the establishment of a market, then, concerns capital assets,[2] namely, providing conditions for raising capital's net worth. Perhaps the most crucial question facing Eastern Europe and the Soviet Union is what to do with publicly owned capital now that the state has decided in principle to withdraw from exercising direct ownership functions.

The battle cry of the most liberal reformers has been for the quick and broad privatization of state assets by selling them off or giving them away. In some cases, this may be warranted. If capital services can be allocated at lesser cost, other things being equal, by internalizing the coordination process than through formal markets, obviously private property would be the answer. But it does not necessarily follow that privatization should be enacted quickly and below fair market value.

Ownership, Property Rights, and Privatization

Property Rights. In spite of claims lodged by the so-called property-rights school (see Alchian, 1987; Demsetz, 1967; Furubotn and Pejovich, 1972; Pejovich, 1990b; Ryan, 1987), there is no unanimity in the literature about what property rights mean. In what follows, I consider a property right to be a socially enforceable right to select uses of scarce goods. Any mutually agreed contractual terms are permissible, that is to say, ownership cannot be satisfactorily defined unless the right of property is the right of dealing with things in the most absolute fashion the law allows (Ryan, 1987, p. 1029). The crucial element, in Roman law, is the ius utendi, fruendi et abutendi, that is, the right of use to the fruits and the disposal of the object of ownership. The latter is very important, for, under some conditions, it can be separated from user rights as such.

An efficient property rights system can be established only by fulfilling at least three conditions (Comisso, 1989, pp. 214–5). First, property rights must be lodged in the hands of actors with purely economic responsibilities. In a market context, such rights would of necessity be attributes of the behavior of private agents. In Eastern Europe, however, a good part of the public capital stock for years to come will inevitably be used by state-owned enterprises.

Second, property rights must be enforced by a neutral party based on an effective judicial system and modern civil and commercial codes. This should aim not only at issuing a guarantee that the state has no intention to nationalize property, except perhaps under extraordinary circumstances (Kornai, 1990b, p. 11). It should also provide a guarantee about the framework—including the fiscal regime on the distribution and accumulation of income and wealth—in which property owners can augment their property. Above all, administrative institutions and political organizations must renounce their powers of direct supervision and restrictive regulation.

Finally, policy-making authority, including the ability to prescribe what kinds of activities the bearer of property rights can engage in, must be entrusted to institutions that themselves neither exercise nor enforce property rights. This is normally the role of the legislative branch of government in a system where there is a clear cut separation of powers.

Any distribution of property rights has consequences for allocative and productive efficiency. Social interaction among individuals, corporations, and government agencies is conditioned by limits on resources but also by rules or institutional arrangements that govern the choices of individual actors (Ickes, 1990; Kanel, 1974; Moser, 1989). Rules essentially define the framework within which these ordinary choices are made. Because they shape the structure of incentives, they bear on outcomes too.

The transfer of ownership, that is, the claim to the residual profits from operating an enterprise, from public to private sectors necessarily implies a change in the relationship between those responsible for the firm's decisions and the beneficiaries of its profits. In general, changing the allocation of property rights leads to a different structure of incentives for management and hence to modifications in both managerial behavior and company performance.

For the market coordination of economic decisions about production and distribution to work well in a society with diffused knowledge, economic agents must have secure, alienable private property rights in productive resources and products. These rights have to be tradeable at mutually agreed prices in reliable contractual transactions that can be negotiated at a fairly low cost.[3] The partitionability, separability, and alienability of private property rights enable the organization of cooperative productive activity in highly specialized economic units such as the complex corporation.[4]

Meaning of Privatization. Privatization is most often identified with divestment of state assets to entities other than with state and related government agencies. In cases where state ownership involves nonphysical assets, such as the right to airwaves or port management, privatization does, of course, refer to entrusting the exploitation of this sector to nonstate agents with at best some rent accruing to the state. This transfer, furthermore, involves all angles of property rights, including the alienation of assets: sale, destruction, inheritance, leasing, give-away, and others. Neither is necessary, however.

The outright identification of privatization with asset sales is misleading for several reasons. Perhaps least controversial is that outright sale need not be involved. Examples range from intangible assets such as the awarding of franchises for the running of public facilities (e.g., naval dockyards) to publicly maintained legal monopolies (e.g., broadcasting rights). As these examples demonstrate, privatization may simply divorce ownership from the exercise of some ownership rights. It is even possible to envisage privatization when no change in the ownership of tangible public assets takes place. An example would be the enjoinment of state-owned enterprises to emulate corporate firms (see Swann, 1988, pp. 3ff.). In that sense, though ownership does not change, privatization alters the balance of power between government as owner and private agents as executors so as to give the latter at least a larger, perhaps predominant, influence over the use of the underlying assets. Others include under privatization instances in which the government charges user fees for goods and services (Kent, 1987, p. 13).

Moreover, even if asset sale occurs, much of the impact of privatization may stem from decisions about regulation. The immediate effect of privatization is to substitute shareholder for governmental monitoring and control of state-owned enterprises. The impact of this change of monitor, therefore, depends very much on how well the new owners can motivate management to become more responsive to maximizing net asset values. The simple change in title does not necessarily produce a responsive chord.

Privatization, thus, can be taken to encompass a wide variety of changes in control over assets, some of which are concerned with alternative approaches to the supply and, indeed, financing of government services. As such, it is an umbrella term for widely differing policies that are loosely linked by the way in which they are taken to mean the strengthening of the market at the expense of the state. More specifically, I take privatization to mean the transfer from the public to the private sector of entitlements to residual profits from operating an enterprise, although there are other forms (Vickers and Wright, 1988, p. 3).

Socialization program. The original raison d'être of socialism was to overcome exploitation of labor by owners of the means of production without undermining economic efficiency. The Soviet Union and Eastern Europe tried to solve this dilemma peremptorily through full socialization based on state property. But far more than socialization is at stake. As János Kornai (1990a) so passionately emphasizes, public ownership has enabled an almighty bureaucracy with countless tentacles to reach throughout society into the life of virtually every citizen. Under the circumstances, sovereignty of the individual, exercise of private property, political freedoms, and the rule of law were all suppressed.

In postwar Eastern Europe, saving for capital-formation purposes was not actively promoted outside the narrow state and cooperative sectors. Assets available to individual households were essentially limited to savings accounts, involuntary bonds, lottery tickets, and cash; in some cases, wealth could be held also in the form of housing and perhaps even small service firms. But the bulk of capital assets was withheld from individual households. Similar was the case of enterprises: They were not encouraged to raise their net asset value, as central planners formulated capital formation priorities and financed investment according to their own criteria.

From a technical point of view, socialization is neither necessary nor sufficient for proper resource allocation. But neither am I aware of a sound technical argument that in all circumstances justifies privatization as offering a superior alternative to social ownership. Certainly, state ownership has a poor record in encouraging innovation and ensuring maintenance of assets, and it inhibits venture capitalism. For that there must, in principle, be the possibility for individuals to found their own firm and, hence, to assume the full risk of succeeding or failing with their own or borrowed capital.

There are unquestionably instances (such as housing, small retail outlets, or service firms) in which it is advisable to encourage private ownership, if only because of the high cost of ensuring proper allocation of user rights to state property. However, precepts on income and wealth distribution and access to a certain social dividend, as "scientific socialism" referred to it, may well counsel for rather than against maintaining state property in basic economic sectors. The same prevails in the case of market failure, notably natural monopoly and externality.[5] But that does not necessarily mean that the state should itself exert property rights or do so through central planning. The core question would be how to ensure that the service flow from such assets gets maximized as measured by some objective function.

The turn taken by reform socialism, entrusting assets essentially to the enterprise collective in some variant of worker self-management, has been a great disappointment. The highly monopolized structure of production in these economies led to economic rents that the firm itself captured rather than to the state as owner. But it also led all-too-easily to raising wages to ensure loyalty to management, which would not, of course, put at risk its own assets or jeopardize its entrenched position.

Markets cannot function well without competition, including for asset utilization, and thus require some measure of exit and entry motivated by economic incentives. Furthermore, this decentralization of ownership has left the legal basis of property rights ill-defined. Markets can function well only if rents or residual profit accrue to those having property rights—not necessarily the ultimate owners who may content themselves with a fixed rate of return or other measure of their opportunity cost.

There are several alternative organizational forms that allow governments to divest themselves without disturbing ownership structures. One is arranging leases of assets of state-owned enterprises to the highest bidder or to a party determined as the most appropriate in given circumstances; another option is the recognition of management contracts or franchising. The advantage is that the benefits of ownership are retained in the public sector but the operations are, in effect, privatized (Ramanadham, 1988, p. 9). It gives government time to decide on denationalization while securing the comparative advantage that the state-owned enterprises have in the public or private sector. Alternatively, government could simply declare that irrespective of its ownership, it undertakes not to interfere in the commercial decisions of the state enterprises so identified.

These alternatives presuppose that it is possible, without disturbing ownership and management structures, to devise criteria of managerial behavior as surrogates of markets that force a state-owned enterprise to operate as if it were a private corporation bound by market discipline in investment, costing, and pricing. Criteria would include, for example, a minimum required rate of return on capital; targets of overall and disaggregated net returns, unit costs and productivity; and the obligation to resort to commercial markets for funds. This leads to a paradox (Zeckhauser and Horn, 1989, pp. 55–56): Although privatization may seem most appropriate for state-owned enterprises operating in competitive markets, these are precisely the firms whose internal efficiency performance can be most readily improved by reforms in their public monitoring systems.

Dilemmas of Privatization

Balance Sheet. Since the early eighties, there has been a wholesale wave of privatization in market economies, most notably in France,

Italy, the United Kingdom, and the United States (Brabant, 1990b, 1991). Although privatization of public enterprises in Western Europe has been taking place in an environment that differs markedly from Eastern Europe's, some useful lessons could nonetheless be derived from this experience, especially when privatization was undertaken with explicit economic and wealth intentions. The most important outcome of privatization is a direct function of prevailing production structures.

Public ownership under conditions of monopoly suffers from a lack of product market competition and hence incurs productive inefficiency, just like a private monopoly. But public ownership need not imply state monopoly, just like private ownership need not forcibly foster competition (Vickers and Yarrow, 1988, p. 45). A public monopoly as a rule does not face the threat of bankruptcy as government is likely to bail out state enterprises in difficulty. A public monopoly is as a rule also eager to sacrifice cost minimization for political and trade-union reasons and can, therefore, be expected to have marginal costs exceeding the minimum attainable. But state enterprises operating under competitive conditions are able to reduce productive inefficiency, possibly mimic the level of efficiency attainable by private corporations in a competitive environment.

By contrast, a private monopoly, although also exhibiting productive inefficiency for lack of product competition, can be threatened with takeover, which will keep managers on their toes. But the disciplining role of potential takeovers is not very strong and declines with the size of the firm. A private monopoly, however, tends to exploit its market power, its price rising above cost with allocative inefficiency consequences. These need to be set off against any moderation in productive inefficiency, which suggests that private ownership might not be superior to public ownership under monopoly. Where the balance ultimately lies is an empirical matter that depends on the strength of conflicting influences.

For markets to function properly, competition is needed, which in turn requires, as Nuti (1990, pp. 18ff.) underlines, a sufficient number of autonomous and competitive firms subject to financial discipline and rewards, capable of responding to market incentives, and whose managers are chosen not for political merits but for their professional qualities. To attain this in Eastern Europe or the Soviet Union, the monopoly power of large-scale state enterprises must be removed or sharply curbed.

This requires not only physically breaking up many state-owned enterprises but also calls, in the case of a natural monopoly, for a sufficient regulatory framework, including on anti-trust and access to markets for new small and medium-sized enterprises. Above all, it necessitates breaking the link between government and state-owned enterprises as regards financing, managerial control, and incentives.

Finally, with private ownership and competition, one can expect full productive and allocative efficiency. The first will result because market competition is now being reinforced by the opportunity to challenge management for corporate control. Moreover, the firm faces the possibility of bankruptcy and its decisionmaking is not impeded by government interference. Competitive conditions will also tend to align prices with costs, hence yielding allocative efficiency.

Such demonopolization can be pursued by different means, one being privatization. But there are evidently other avenues. The elimination of the "petty tutelage" exercised by ministerial bureaucracies, including the central planning agency, should not lead to the dissipation of state ownership. In most of Eastern Europe, even after existing monopolies are broken up, it will be all but impossible to harness sufficient competition from within in the short run. Liberalization of the trade regime in conjunction with the explicit fostering of private enterprise from gross savings offers the only way in which sufficient competitive pressure can gradually be brought to bear on the performance of domestic industrial firms.

Market structures are, then, key ingredients of the decision to go ahead with privatization.[6] Changes in ownership in the absence of competition and an adequate regulationary environment (Helm and Yarrow, 1988) do not necessarily improve performance, an issue that is frequently overlooked in the confusion between ownership and competition and between deep cynicism and ignorance about the world of business presumed to prevail among civil servants and those acting under their supervision (Heald, 1988, pp. 33–35).

Divestment Issue. In order to ensure proper divestment in Eastern Europe, the real worth of assets must be assessed and be turned over to society, perhaps to reduce some of society's liabilities (such as amortizing external and domestic debts or offsetting claims to social services, pension rights, and so on). That is to say, a "proper" price needs to be established to avert a sell-out of existing firms, often through the intermediation of self-interested managers, who may engage in asset stripping and abuse insider information.

This is by no means an easy task for several reasons. To begin with, these assets have never been priced in a competitive environment, however constrained. Next, they cannot quickly be evaluated in that manner because prevailing prices are heavily distorted and their future path cannot be predicted. It is therefore all but impossible to estimate the discounted future stream of returns on assets. Finally, there is little experience with capital markets given that under central planning it was primarily the state budget that decided capital formation and that private asset accumulation was discouraged, if perhaps not interdicted altogether.

Under the circumstances, market evaluation can only begin once a certain volume of shares has been traded at competitive conditions. Arranging for such initial distribution is by no means straightforward given the starting conditions for reform in Eastern Europe. Particularly egregious has been the adoption of makeshift rules that have in fact allowed one group, usually the nomenklatura or Communist Party officials, to appropriate part of its specialized knowledge and transform it into a property stake. Certainly, not all such sales at bargain prices have been on account of malevolence on the part of those entrusted with privatization. They have also stemmed from incompetence and the intransparency inherent in these economies.

The absence of a capitalist class has repercussions for divestment as well. Most obvious is insufficient indigenous savings to purchase outright a sizable portion of state assets. In some cases, setting up proper financial institutions, such as independent pension funds, insurance schemes, commercial banks, and the like to whom state liabilities are transferred can assist in the intermediation, but this cannot be a panacea. Certainly, in some countries there is a substantial monetary overhang that could be mobilized for divestment of state assets. Unfortunately, this has been built up, notably in the former Soviet Union, through channels of questionable social merit.

This is not to say that citizens in these countries would be altogether risk aversive. But to turn their innate desires for wealth into managing state enterprises is something altogether different. Entrepreneurial abilities could certainly be unleashed by "petty" privatization, including of housing, small retail shops, repair firms, handicrafts, and plots of land, if necessary by making generous loans available from public savings (for instance, as in Dembinski, 1990, by rechanneling the cash flow of state enterprises). But it remains to be seen (Nuti, 1990) whether savers will willingly purchase such assets without there first being substantial other reforms, among them demonopolization of state enterprises.

Inasmuch as state assets belong to society, they should be distributed with a considerable degree of egalitarianism. This is particularly so because societies in Eastern Europe have a deeply engrained sentiment for income nivellation. Now, any incentive scheme that rewards enterprise management in accordance with its ability to maximize long-run profits, to encourage innovation and risk, and to penalize failure, perhaps through takeovers or outright bankruptcy, is bound to entail considerable disparity of individual incomes. Furthermore, to foster the proper allocation of incomes between consumption and savings, even if private property is not formally envisaged, it will lead eventually to disparate asset ownership, and hence disparities of inherited wealth (King, 1990, p. 15).

A wide distribution of assets would avoid future resentment about give-aways to a favored class, a danger in selling state enterprises to their managers at fire-sale prices. It would also ensure support for the temporarily painful measures needed to make those assets more productive by reforming monetary policy, freeing prices, and ending subsidies. Above all, it would support democracy by greatly reducing the power of the nomenklatura and would strengthen the economic power of the electorate.

The shortage of domestic capital could be overcome by allowing foreigners to acquire assets. This would also bring in badly needed managerial abilities, technology, marketing skills, access to foreign markets, and other beneficial aspects of foreign direct investment. In principle, it should not matter whether assets are sold to domestic economic agents or to foreigners. But one cannot completely ignore the issue of economic sovereignty, particularly in countries whose scope for autonomy was so narrowly circumscribed for so long by Soviet-type development and sociopolitical precepts. The question is probably less whether to sell assets to foreign owners as such than in what sectors, to what degree, and how foreign ownership will be regulated.

Operating assets. It is often assumed that new owners of privatized state assets will by definition allocate their services more efficiently than will state-appointed officials. There is no guarantee that they will automatically begin to maximize asset value, as few individuals in Eastern Europe have had experience in managing firms properly defined. An entrepreneurial and managerial culture will have to emerge through experience over time, in good measure through trial and error.

Related to this is the assumption that individuals, even when interested in holding some wealth in the form of shares, may be too apathetic or unsophisticated to monitor management. This is likely to be particularly acute when privatization involves a wide dispersal of ownership. Such dispersal would help foster a share-holding culture but not persuade the masses to monitor because of high participation costs, whether psychological or material. Giving away wealth is not likely to induce individuals to treat it with the proper attitude.

Management with a monopoly on information, perhaps because of widely dispersed shareholders, entails principal-agent problems that can potentially be quite serious. Monitoring is important in structuring incentives to make management behave according to the instructions of owners. The firm's monopoly on information must, therefore, be broken in part by regulating minimum accounting and disclosure practices. That, however, does not solve the problem of widespread ownership. If the intensity of monitoring is low, managers pursue their own objectives rather than maximizing the net worth of the firm's assets. That widespread ownership inevitably dilutes the monitoring role of owners and hence modifies the behavior of management is often ignored in the zealous advocacy of privatization (see Feige, 1990; Hemming and Mansoor, 1988; Leipold, 1983, 1988; Pejovich, 1990a, b; Schroeder, 1988).

It is all too facilely assumed that privatization will quickly foster fair competition in privatized markets. There is simply no guarantee that this will in fact emerge given the highly monopolized nature and small size of these economies. Substituting private for state monopolies will not necessarily enhance allocative efficiency or increase the net worth of the firm. For that, effective competition and regulation are required. The latter must be solved by countries individually. The former can be fostered through demonopolization, foreign competition, and rapid private capital formation. All these forms can be promoted without resorting to widespread and speedy privatization of state enterprises.

Moreover, two hundred years or so of experience with capitalism in the west has made it clear that there are numerous market imperfections. At the same time, experiments with other arrangements for allocating resources suggest that there is no alternative to embracing some form of market-type allocation if the economy is to progress steadily. To avoid the worst negative side effects, yet enhance the positive features of the market mechanism, a well-entrenched and adequate regulatory mechanism in the hands of an impartial body is required. Only then can private interests be harmonized with those of society as a whole, including those regarding monopolistic profits.

Finally, thriving competition must apply also to the acquisition and disposal of private assets. For that, it is necessary to have in place adequate capital markets with proper, transparent safeguards and regulatory mechanisms against abuses of stock-exchange provisions and the like. Functioning markets for goods and services require a transparent capital market. To attain it, firms must adhere to certain supervisory and accounting rules that foster competition among economic agents on the basis of expected returns on capital.

Alternative Forms of Privatization

Spontaneous Privatization. Privatization can take many forms, several of which have been explored in Eastern Europe. Of those, so-called spontaneous privatization has been most popular. Under this scheme, those entrusted with state assets take possession of the assets, for example by turning a state enterprise into a joint company, part of which can be transferred to clear owners. This was the route that Hungary and Poland initially—while still under Communist leadership—chose to take because decision makers did not wish—or dare—to renationalize assets. The experience with spontaneous privatization has not been a happy one because of economic, financial, political, and organizational problems (Lee and Nellis, 1990) other than insider trading and asset stripping.

Financially, spontaneous privatization allows former management and possibly workers to become owners without paying a fair price and thus deprives the government of needed revenues to offset its liabilities. Economically, there is no assurance that turning over assets to people who have run these facilities poorly under state control will measurably improve resource allocation. Although the incentives embedded in ownership could change the behavior of the old-style management, there is no guarantee that it will do better than other asset holders. Furthermore, free distribution may exacerbate already existing inflationary pressures on account of wealth effects (Nuti, 1990, p. 20).

Politically, the nomenklatura management in place should have been subjected to conflict of interest laws to prevent managers from laundering state assets through dummy corporations that they created in the private sector (Lipton and Sachs, 1990a,b). There is also bound to be an equity problem. Worker ownership might be fine for those employed in profitable or potentially profitable operations, but not for those in persistent loss-making operations. Of course, those not employed in state enterprises who nonetheless involuntarily contributed to asset formation would be excluded altogether.[7]

Free Distribution. Another form of privatization that Eastern Europe has considered is the free distribution of shares. The rationale is that state assets amassed either through nationalization or forced public savings belong to "society." Logically, then, societal property should be distributed free of charge (Hinds, 1990a,b). The most common format of free distribution has been worker management of state-owned enterprises.

The Yugoslav experience with the labor-managed firm[8] has amply shown that it encourages the maximization of income per worker rather than the long-run profit of the firm, in part because there is no capital market where the worker can voluntarily sell his share (that is, the right to participate in future profit earnings) at fair market value. That is to say, worker management is insufficient to ensure efficiency; ownership and a market in which such property can be traded are also required. This can function properly only if individuals with no connections to the firm are allowed to acquire shares. In other words, there must eventually be the possibility of capitalist ownership.

An alternative is to distribute property to workers on the grounds that firm assets should be transferred to those being employed there, who will then be requested to improve the firm's profitability. The key assumption is that property owners automatically improve allocation and thereby render the firm profitable. Such an assumption is fallacious and rather inequitable in any case. For one, the value of capital per worker in state firms varies a great deal for reasons that have nothing to do with the relative merits of the present labor force. Furthermore, free distribution of assets fails to provide revenue to offset some of the state's liabilities. Furthermore, it tends to favor reinvestment in existing types of activities under present management and to continue employment of the present labor force.

Whereas the labor-managed firm suffers from weak features, some employee share-ownership program is worth considering, particularly if it could be coupled with promises to limit demands for monetary compensation, to foster productivity, to change work rules and with other measures that would give workers a material stake in their enterprise. Note, however, that this can be done without outrightly privatizing the state enterprise. All it requires is that the employee-owned firm become a joint-stock company whose performance incentives include a share in the firm's capitalized value under some share ownership programs.

Several countries (especially Czechoslovakia but also Poland) are now contemplating the distribution of property to society at large, essentially for the egalitarian and equity reasons discussed earlier but also to buttress democracy and make the process irrevocable; it is also advocated in view of the inadequacies of capital markets and the shortage of domestic capital in Eastern Europe (Hinds, 1990b). Although free distribution of shares in state-owned enterprises is intuitively appealing, it has serious drawbacks apart from the wealth effects at a time of already significant inflationary pressures. It is divisive since there are potential losers as well as gainers. For example, the distribution of assets by states that are heavily indebted may diminish the prospects of repayment to creditors.[9]

Moreover, the fiscal base in most of Eastern Europe is precarious. In the absence of modern personal income and wealth tax systems, giving assets away further hampers the already inadequate revenue-raising ability of the government and deprives it of future returns on assets. Ideally, any such move should be accompanied by the retirement of state liabilities with financial implications. Giving assets away makes fiscal reform anchored to personal income taxation all the more necessary. Widespread ownership would also complicate the administration of shareholders, but mutual funds could be created (Feige, 1990; Lipton and Sachs, 1990b).

Furthermore, if shares were distributed equitably through means other than mutual funds, any one household would hold only a miniscule interest in any one. The distinction between the pre- and post-reform situation would be largely nominal. But how to ensure that each household receives portfolios of approximately equal value, given serious asset-valuation problems in Eastern Europe, is a conundrum yet to be addressed. Unquestionably the most serious shortcoming of this form of privatization, because of monitoring problems, is that no beneficial effects are exerted on management—normally, the principal focus of privatization. Even mutual-fund managers will not have the knowledge or incentive to assess managerial performances and promote takeovers when needed without there being a functioning capital market.

Other Forms. A form of privatization that has been explored to some degree, especially in Poland, is the distribution of user rights to social property through franchising, leasing, or management contracts. Such custodial rights could in principle be traded in functioning capital markets, but practical obstacles are likely to be so large that transaction costs would be forbidding. In fact, multiple ownership forms in combination with the gradual emergence of capital markets for the bulk of society's capital may well be the more desirable way of proceeding. Private or cooperative ownership under some conditions can internalize coordination at a smaller cost than through full-fledged capital markets. Such dilution of property rights would be based on technical economic grounds within the given environment rather than on the ideology of wealth distribution.

Another form of privatization involves the outright sale of state assets through auctions or more discretionary channels. But questions regarding how best to establish prices and how to earmark proceeds remain poignant. Apart from the fact that auction markets would have to be organized, the sale of state assets faces the obstacle of a lack of investable funds given that private savings are highly limited and it remains in doubt whether individuals would be prepared to earmark even these limited funds for the purchase of shares.

In the absence of widespread experience with auctions, careful experimentation appears to be warranted. Perhaps auction markets that are as transparent as circumstances permit, hopefully becoming so after rationalization of the state-owned enterprises so as not to encumber potential buyers, offer one important avenue toward the gradual creation of capital markets in Eastern Europe. But initially emphasis should be primarily on putting in place the foundations of a commercial banking infrastructure in Eastern Europe (Brainard, 1990).

One of the more appealing forms of selling off state assets is through debt-financed auctions, which would mitigate the lack of funds and entice individuals into adopting a share-holding culture. Such divestment would essentially be anchored to making available generous financial resources to those willing to acquire state assets and able to manage them profitably. In essence, the state as lender would become a rentier while private sectors would end up debtors and capitalists (Lipton and Sachs, 1990a).

Whereas it would in principle be possible to conduct auctions with reservation prices clearly established, the ambiance in which this would have to be carried out probably rules out the imposition of a realistic reservation price. That could be implemented much more safely through discretionary divestment. Determining a reasonable reservation price and ensuring that the discretionary sale would not infringe upon society's rights or extend favors that one was trying to rule out otherwise are no simple tasks.

Regarding the determination of a reservation price, some carefully conducted research by custodians of property under the supervision of the newly formed parliamentary organs, perhaps with the assistance of accounting firms, should yield a plausible range of asset values. For most undertakings, there should be some positive price that can be realistically established with some goodwill on the part of all actors involved. Custodians and their immediate supervisors should be denied the right to acquire property rights in order to reduce the room for conflicts of interest.

Conclusion

The prime economic task of privatization is to improve the allocation of existing capital assets, maintain the value of these assets, and ensure that new capital is formed and utilized as efficiently as possible. Recall that privatization is neither necessary nor sufficient to guarantee improved static allocation of capital resources or the efficient formation of new capital. What is required is the recognition of the usefulness of the entire range of property forms and the choice of one over another depending essentially on securing coordination of the service flows emanating from state assets at least cost.

The strategy of organizing capital markets must recognize the fact that neither private nor public ownership of the means of production by itself guarantees the most efficient use of resources. From an economic perspective, then, there is ample justification for putting in place as neutral an environment for property forms as possible (Szénási, 1989, p. 169). This is the proposition forwarded in this chapter—that user rights to capital are at stake.

By disjoining, at least conceptually, ownership from ownership rights (all property rights minus alienation of the assets), one could start thinking about the proper technical issues at stake. In that context, it is extremely important to recognize without inhibition that all property forms may coexist because there will be at least one productive endeavor for which one form (private, cooperative, corporate, public, and various mixes) will be best suited.

If that right is not available to whoever is able, and willing, to accumulate wealth or entitled to bid openly on the user rights to wealth, it is hard to envisage how the capital allocation process can be organized efficiently, regardless of who owns the assets. Whereas with exit and entry, new capital will be formed according to whatever enhances the resource allocation, subject to regulatory powers to take care of market failures, new capital cannot be anticipated for the publicly owned capital stock.

The key questions of privatization and property rights reform of existing assets, then, revolves around the allocation of capital services, that is, the usufruct of capital assets and the guarantee that those enjoying the usufruct not erode or misappropriate capital assets for "private" purposes. I contend that this applies with some minor modifications also to the use of natural resources, most of which cannot be privatized for one reason or another.

Undertaking a massive program of ill-prepared privatization in a hurry for ideological, political, or sentimental reasons may lead to casino economics. This is an unjustified way for the state to divest itself of assets that it holds in trust for the nation, however badly these resources may be utilized now. Under no circumstance could privatization be considered a panacea for raising economic efficiency. That depends critically on the creation of a competitive environment and the recognition in principle of the validity of all alternative property rights.

Even with these perspectives on privatization, the question remains of what to do with state assets in the context of the wide-ranging problem of the transition. Briefly (see Brabant, 1990a, for more on this topic), the key strategy for overcoming the multiple roadblocks to marketization and democratization of these societies implicit in this chapter is the sequencing of reforms. But the schedule of changes depends critically on the environment of the transition, so in the extreme case where a social consensus exists on assimilating an unbounded adjustment burden, all phases would be pursued nearly simultaneously.

In the first stage, all state assets have to be renationalized to establish clear property rights. Big conglomerates and monopolies have to be quickly broken up into meaningful autonomous units (see Brabant, 1990a). Other assets, especially housing, retail outlets, handicrafts, and small service centers should be privatized as quickly and as fairly as possible. Open bidding procedures would recommend themselves in most instances. This may have to be fostered through generous financing at a realistic interest rate. In any case, the entire operation should be concluded under the full supervision of a trustee appointed by parliament, to which responsibility is owed. Also a bold move forward with land reform would seem to commend itself.

Next, nearly all state-owned enterprises should be turned into joint-stock companies. Initially, ownership would remain with the state. Monitoring, however, should be entrusted to an impartial, professional body subject to parliamentary scrutiny. It should gradually prepare the firms under its supervision to be run according to managerial rules paralleling those in market economies. In time, it should also supervise the transfer of the usufruct to other bodies, such as financial institutions that, as a counterpart, assume part of the state's financial liabilities (e.g., premiums). At the same time, full property rights have to be legally protected, especially with a view to encouraging the formation of new capital from private and public savings in support of emerging competition (Kornai, 1990a; Murrell, 1990).

The next logical step is to enforce competitive behavior by creating a regulatory environment and incentive schemes that ease the principal-agent problem in state-owned enterprises. Gradually, such assets should be opened up for competitive bidding for franchises, leases, or management contracts, with the supervisory authority charged with maximizing the return on assets and seeing to it that assets are not stripped.

Simultaneously, the state has to pursue comprehensive stabilization, enact fiscal and monetary reforms, further dilute the power of monopolies and break up conglomerates, replace the material-technical supply system with genuine wholesale trading, and introduce market-type pricing. In some cases, the latter process could be helped along by first anchoring key input prices to world prices converted at a reduction exchange rate. At the same time, the job security system will need to be sharply relaxed and a social safety net put in place. Also, foreign competition through trade liberalization, including through current-account convertibility for merchandise transactions, will have to be encouraged.

Once the former state-owned enterprises begin to behave like competition firms, such as corporations in a market environment, and the most urgent structural adjustments have been completed, the process of privatizing these firms should get under way at a measured pace. This should take the form of funding the budding domestic stock market or opening the divestment process to open bids by domestic and foreign capitalists.

Notes

The author is on the staff of the Department of International Economic and Social Affairs of the United Nations Secretariat in New York. The views expressed here are his own and do not necessarily reflect those that may be held by the United Nations Secretariat.

1. See Leipold, 1983, 1988; Pejovich, 1983, 1987, 1989, 1990a,b. Their argument depends critically on the existence of freedom of entry at the pre-production stages of the competitive process (Yarrow, 1986, p. 345) and the absence of barriers to entry. Also, pure individualism and the avoidance of social conflict are key, but unrealistic assumptions (Goldberg, 1974, p. 755).

2. Of course, the institutional anchoring of markets needs to be taken care of, an issue that transcends the bounds of this paper (see Brabant, 1990a).

3. If transaction costs are zero, given Coase's theorem, alternative institutional or organizational arrangements provide no basis for choice and hence cannot be interpreted by economic theory.

4. Each contract type implies different costs of supervision, measurement, and negotiation. Also, the form of economic organization, along with the function of the visible hand, changes whenever a different contractual arrangement is chosen (Cheung, 1987, p. 56).

5. Contestable markets function well if the incumbent firm with a natural monopoly has not sunk irrecoverable entry outlays (Thompson, 1988, pp. 41–42).

6. Empirical studies of how public and private firms compare have led to ambivalent results. Although there is some support for the superiority of private enterprise, its performance depends critically on the degree of

competition prevailing in the market, the incentive structures in alternative organizational forms, and the degree of regulatory policies designed to correct market failures, rather than ownership *per se* (Yarrow, 1986, p. 333).

7. There is an organizational problem here with worker management as well, in the sense that those belonging to the former managerial group, who have the experience and know-how to supervise the firms, may be eliminated from the reconstituted firm.

8. Dabrowski (1989) argues that the rules of the labor-managed firms could be sufficiently revised to encourage greater productivity and maximization of asset value.

9. This argument is most fully developed by Jan Vanous (1989). To meet this objection, for instance, the state could guarantee loan repayment by enacting first claim to fiscal revenues from profits of the divested state-owned enterprises.

Bibliography

Alchian, A. 1987. "Property Rights." *The New Palgrave—a Dictionary of Economics*, vol. 3. London: Macmillan, pp. 1031–34.

Brabant, J. 1990a. *Remaking Eastern Europe—On the Political Economy of Transition*. Dordrecht-Boston-London: Kluwer Academic Publishers).

_____. 1990b. "Property Rights' Reform, Macroeconomic Performance, and Welfare." In H. Blommestein and M. Marrese, eds. *Selected Issues and Strategies in the Transformation of Planned Economies*. Paris: Organization for Economic Co-operation and Development, forthcoming.

_____. 1991. "Economies in Transition and Privatization—the Case of Eastern Europe." In W. Adriaansen and J. Van den Broueke, ed. *Changing Economic Order*. Dordrecht-Boston-London: Kluwer Academic Publishers, forthcoming.

Brainard, L. 1990. "Strategies for Economic Transformation in Eastern Europe—the Role of Financial Market Reform." In H. Blommestein and M. Marrese. *Selected Issues and Strategies in the Transformation of Planned Economies*. Paris: Organization for Economic Co-operation and Development, forthcoming.

Cheung, S. 1987. "Economic Organization and Transaction Costs." *The New Palgrave—a Dictionary of Economics*, vol. 2 London: Macmillan, pp. 55–57.

Comisso, E. 1989. "Property Rights in Focus." *Acta Oeconomica*, No. 4, pp. 210–16.

Dabrowski, M. 1989. "The Economic Effectiveness of the Self-Managed Enterprise—a Review of the Theoretical Literature." *Acta Oeconomica*, No. 1/2, pp. 39–54.

Dembinski, P. 1990. "Alternative Financial Approaches to Privatization." (Paper prepared for OECD conference on transition in Eastern Europe), Paris.

Demsetz, H. 1967. "Toward a Theory of Property Rights." *The American Economic Review. Papers and Proceedings*. No. 2, pp. 347–59.

Feige, E. 1990. "Perestroika and Socialist Privatization: What is to be Done and How?" Madison, WI: University of Wisconsin-Madison, mimeographed.

Furubotn, E. and S. Pejovich. 1972. "Property Rights and Economic Theory: a Survey of Recent Literature." *The Journal of Economic Literature*, No. 2, pp. 1137–62.

Goldberg, V. 1974. "Public choice—property rights," *Journal of Economic Issues*, No. 3, pp. 555–79.

Heald, D. 1988. "The United Kingdom: Privatisation and its Political Context." *West European Politics*, No. 4, pp. 31–48.

Helm, D. and G. Yarrow. 1988. "The Assessment: the Regulation of Utilities." *Oxford Review of Economic Policy*, No. 2, i–xxxi.

Hemming, R. and A. Mansoor. 1988. *Privatization and Public Enterprises*. Washington, DC: International Monetary Fund, Occasional Paper No. 56.

Hinds, M. 1990a. "Issues in the Introduction of Market Forces in Eastern European Socialist Economies." Washington, DC: The World Bank, mimeographed.

_____ 1990b. "Issues in the Introduction of Market Forces in Eastern European Socialist Economies—Annex I—Enterprise Reform Issues." Washington, DC: The World Bank, mimeographed.

Ickes, B. 1990. "Obstacles to Economic Reform of Socialism: An Institutional-Choice Approach," *Annals of the American Academy of Political and Social Sciences*, No. 1, pp. 53–64.

Kanel, D. 1974. "Property and Economic Power as Issues in Institutional Economics." *Journal of Economic Issues*, No. 4, pp. 827–40.

Kent, C. 1987. "Privatization of Public Functions: Promises and Problems." In C. Kent, ed. *Entrepreneurship and the Privatizing of Government*. New York-Westport, CO: Quorum Books, pp. 3–22.

King, T. 1990. "Foreign Direct Investment in the East European Economic Transition." Washington, DC: The World Bank, mimeographed.

Kornai, J. 1990a. The road to a Free Economy—Shifting from a Socialist System: the Example of Hungary. New York, NY: W.W. Norton.

_____ 1990b. The Affinity between Ownership and Coordination Mechanisms—the Common Experience of Reform in Socialist Countries. Helsinki: World Institute for Development Economics Research.

Lee, B. and J. Nellis. 1990. "Enterprise Reform and Privatization in Market Economies." Washington, DC: The World Bank, mimeographed.

Leipold, H. 1983. "Eigentumsrechte, Ofentlichkeitsgrad und Innovationsschwache—Lehren aus dem Systemvergleich." In A. Schuller, H. Leipold and H. Hamel, eds. *Innovationsprobleme in Ost und West*. Stuttgart: Gustav Fischer Verlag, pp. 51–64.

_____. 1988. *Wirtschafts—und Gesellschaftssysteme im Vergleich* (Stuttgart: Gustav Fischer Verlag, 1988, 5th ed).

Lipton, D. and J. Sachs. 1990a. "Creating a Market Economy in Eastern Europe: The Case of Poland." *Brookings Papers on Economic Activity*, No. l, pp. 75–133.

_____. 1990b. "Privatization in Eastern Europe: the case of Poland." Washington, DC, draft.

Moser, P. 1989. "Toward an Open World Order: A Constitutional Economics Approach." *The Cato Journal*, No. 1, pp. 133–47.

Nuti, D. 1990. "Stabilization and Sequencing in the Reform of Socialist Economies." Washington, DC: The World Bank, paper for seminar on "Managing Inflation in Socialist Economies." Laxenburg, mimeographed.

Pejovich, S. 1983. "Innovation and Alternative Property Rights." In A. Schuller, H. Leipold, and H. Hamel, eds. *Innovationsprobleme in Ost und West* Stuttgart: Gustav Fischer Verlag, pp. 41–49.

_____. 1987. "Freedom, Property Rights and Innovation in Socialism." *Kyklos*, No. 4, pp. 461–75.

_____. 1989. "Liberty, Property Rights, and Innovation in Eastern Europe," *The Cato Journal*, No. 1, pp. 57–71.

_____. 1990a. "A Property-Rights Analysis of the Yugoslav Miracle." *Annals of the American Academy of Political and Social Sciences*, No. l, pp. 123–32.

_____. 1990b. *The Economics of Property Rights: Towards a Theory of Comparative systems*. Dordrecht-Boston-London: Kluwer Academic Publishers.

Ramanadham, V. 1988. "The Concept and Rationale of Privatization." In V. ramanadham, ed. *Privatisation in the UK*. London-New York: Routledge, pp. 3–25.

Ryan, A. 1987. "Property." *The New Palgrave—a Dictionarv of Economics*, vol. 3. London: Macmillan, pp. 1029–31.

Schroeder, G. 1988. "Property Rights Issues in Economic Reforms in Socialist Countries." *Studies in Comparative Communism*, No. 2, pp. 175–88.

Swann, D. 1988. The Retreat of the State—Deregulation and Privatization in the UK and US. Ann Arbor, MI: The University of Michigan Press.

Szanási, M. 1989. "A Dispute on the Changes in Property Rights." *Acta Oeconomica*, No. 1/2, pp. 165–72.

Tardos, M. 1989. "Economic Organizations and Ownership." *Acta Oeconomica*, vol. 1/2, pp. 17–37.

Thompson, D. 1988. "Privatisation: Introducing Competition, Opportunities and Constraints." In V. Ramanadham , ed. *Privatization in the UK*. London-New York: Routledge, pp. 39–58.

Vanous, J. 1989. "Privatization in Eastern Europe: Possibilities, Problems, and the Role of Western Capital." *PlanEcon Report*, No. 38/39.

Vickers, J. and V. Wright. 1988. "The Politics of Industrial Privatization in Western Europe: an Overview," *West European Politics*, No. 4, pp. 1–30.

Vickers, J. and G. Yarrow. 1988. *Privatization: An Economic Analysis*. Cambridge, MA: The MIT Press.

Winiecki, J. 1990. "Obstacles to Economic Reform of Socialism: A Property-Rights Approach." *Annals of the American Academv of Political and Social Sciences*, No. 1, pp. 65–71.

Yarrow, G. 1986. "Privatization in Theory and Practice." *Economic Policy*, No. 2, pp. 324–77.

Zeckhauser, R. and M. Horn. 1989. "The Control and Performance of State-Owned Enterprises." In P. MacAvoy, W. Stanbury, G. Yarrow, and R. Zeckhauser, eds. *Privatization and State-Owned Enterprises—Lessons from the*

United States. Great Britain and Canada. Boston-Dordrecht-London: Kluwer Academic Publishers, pp. 7–57.

PART THREE

Dilemmas of Democratization

7

The Reconstruction of Citizenship: Reverse Incorporation in Eastern Europe

George Kolankiewicz

In Eastern Europe theoretical and ideological priorities have been cast in a language rooted as much in a rejection of "real socialism" and its ideological underpinnings as it is in an as yet dimly perceived appropriation of liberal democratic and laissez faire slogans. The kind of civil society that emerges will be as much informed by the concrete experience of countering the social atomization of real socialism as it will be by Hegelian or Gramscian exegesis.

This chapter briefly contributes to this disarray by sketching some questions raised by the new democracies in the search for a form of citizenship that takes on board those "rights," largely social and residually acceptable, while at the same time constructs a form of citizenship that accords with the systems of property rights and social and political rights fashioned in the transition to democracy.

Citizens' charters of various kinds flourish on the political landscape, and citizenship infects the discourse of parties from all ends of the remaining spectrum. In this chapter the author wishes to draw attention to an aspect of this process extant in Eastern Europe where the normal temporal sequence of post-Enlightenment citizenship gains was reversed in the transition from post-Communism. It must be taken as given that the concept is used to draw attention to some unanticipated outcomes attendant on the process whereby citizens seek to participate in societies from which they have been previously excluded by drawing on a legacy of participation, however imperfect, that differed from the Western, liberal democratic and market-led experience.

Citizenship and Civil Society

Theoretical Debate. Currently the two most powerful concepts in the political vocabulary of Eastern Europe are those of "civil society" and "citizenship."[1] These concepts are deployed in parallel, and only rarely are attempts made to reconcile these disparate analyses of the underlying processes guiding the very real activity of the new elites in Eastern Europe.[2]

The status of citizenship associated with the path-breaking work of T.H. Marshall (1973) "that basic human equality associated with the concept of full membership of a community" has connotations of human dignity, civilized society and an inclusionary ethos. All of these were destroyed in Eastern Europe through the workings of a system that reduced individuals to atomised objects, subordinated morality to political and ideological imperatives and excluded them through the perfidious nomenklatura mechanism. Even the very notion of "citizen" was devalued and emptied of meaning, but not to the same extent as "socialism" and its retinue of appendages. Thus, the symbolic acceptability of concepts of "citizenship."

"Civil society" has come to mean in popular discourse all forms of free association, unmediated and untrammelled, the antitheses to the totalising state. It reflects the heterogeneity and inherent pluralism so brutally expunged through the massification rituals and false collectivism of party rule, a collectivism hierarchically integrated and vertically segmented through the ubiquitous "leading role of the party." Authenticity is the watchword since civil society is rooted in the supposedly nonegoistic and open concerns of the group, which, springing from the grass-roots, reflect real concerns and interests. This was juxtaposed, pace Hegel, to the "dictatorship over needs" of a voracious state, which at best reflected the corrupt appetites of its leaders or at worst imposed mindless and irrational "models" with their disastrous human and material consequences.

"Civil society" is the answer found, for instance, in Poland in the horizontal collectivism of a regionally based Solidarnosc, but above all in the horizontal reform movement within the Polish Communist Party, the PZPR, in 1980–81. Responding to the bureaucratic centralism and social atomization of the party-state rule, it raised autonomous association to a prime value, often leaving concerns with individual rights and freedoms as secondary.

This civil society emerged out of or in some opinions is preceded by the "second society," rooted in the second economy, a sphere of social and economic autonomy granting some political leeway. Social initiatives and social movements are also seen as having their wellsprings in the sphere of the private, the home, club, cafe, rather than in the public sphere. That grants them further authenticity and allows them to expand into the collapsing middle ground of the artificial "civil society" created around the leading role of the party.

Whereas citizenship as it emerged in 19th century Britain was concerned with the rights (and eventually duties) of the individual, civil society seems to posit collective rights rooted in associational, communal life, which of necessity will require the limitation of individual rights for the achievement of collective ends. However, on the basis of the experience of neo-stalinism, collective rights have emerged as a guarantee of individual freedoms. Without sinking into Durkiemian "totemism" and over-glorifying the social, I would say that the search for civil society is an expression of the loss of genuine association, the latter being both the source and affirmation of societal values. The "value vacuum," which characterised real socialism and was only in part compensated for by the Church and other like institutions, is evidence of the absence of such mechanisms.

The return to Europe, an imperative so often voiced in post-Communist societies is a response to the search for an independent source of values free of the communist imprimatur. However, the reinsertion of Poland into Europe is much more than simply the rediscovery of long-obliterated values. Seen as the antidote to Sovietization, regaining Europeaness is a shorthand that involves the return of a critical reflexivity, a sense of questioning, rather than a passive acceptance fostered by the system of everything around them. A sense of responsibility, intolerance of corruption and a return of the work ethic are all included.

The inviolability of contract, a sense of trust towards bureaucracies and the state that is critical in linking the public and private sphere, was long ago undermined through the anti-state reflex that in point of fact often predated real socialism as in the case of Poland. Most importantly, real socialism destroyed trust and claimed the variety of ethoi that allowed professions and occupations, institutions and services to exercise a moral regulation over their members. Whether it was Stalinism or the more insidious world of Gomulkaist and Kadarist compromise, or even Gierek's claim to moral consensus, is a point for debate. Medicine, law, trade, police and academe were all to a greater or lesser extent stripped of their defining systems of values, norms and standards of professional conduct and codes of practice.

In the debate between the liberals and communitarians, between those accepting the sufficiency of individual rights as opposed to those tied to some idea of the common good, certain commentators such as Mouffe seek to reinject the moral into the political, to reconcile the world of private interests, wants and choices with the public world of performance and achievement through an emphasis on the nature of association. The moral community governed by rules of social intercourse would allow interest groups (universitas) to coexist in a community marked by loyalty (societas).

This "grammar" of citizens' conduct would permit an ethical community without predefining any "common good." The resulting res publica would govern the relations between groups without limiting individual freedom of association. Civil society would thus activate the citizens of Dahl's "polyarchies" as well as diffuse power to minority groups and sections of society. In the current situation the conduct of intergroup behaviour is as important as the fractured form of interpersonal relations.[3]

From Message to Medium. The spawning of myriad associations and the profusion of political platforms within the nascent and embryonic political parties jostling to take their place on the political stage in Eastern Europe is clear evidence of this hunger for freedom of association,[4] previously permitted only under the tutelage of the party (Olszewska, 1988). It is in the analysis of social movements that in their active sense represent civil society but in their more institutionalised, passive form encapsulate the achievements of citizenship that a working synthesis of these two concepts may be sought. Of course it is the ethoi mentioned above that provide the crucial link between social movements as civil society and the principles of citizenship.

It is the manner in which ethoi are shaped through the experience of social movements that then underlies the practise of citizenship. The shell of rights and artificial exercise of duties under real socialism, which saw the dual morality and superficial public behaviour, are evidence of the importance of ethoi. For instance, Solidarnosc, in seeking to sponsor something called a "citizens' movement" (ruch obywatelski), collapsed both the active and passive elements of citizenship and civil society. This is understandable given the poverty of both but was ultimately untenable once local elections, for example, got under way. At that stage, the dynamics of a unified movement rooted in the support for the new government had to give way to concrete organizations, by their very nature pluralist and diverse. The two major groupings (ROAD and the Centre Alliance) conjured up by Walesa's political maneuvering are the first evidence of this fracturing once the social movement became rooted in everyday politics.

It is precisely in this transition from a movement to a structured entity that many of the key decisions of citizenship will have to be made. It is hoped that in this task the cumulative ethos of Solidarnosc created during martial law will come to play a decisive role. Emphasizing such values as truth, dignity, work and community, the new leadership should seek to translate the message of an oppositional movement into the medium of political structures. However, the interpretation of this message, anchoring it in the rhythm of political life, is a controversial experience, as the presidential campaign in Poland indicated. The values so easily accepted in the abstract are more difficult to ground in everyday politics.

While civil rights have traditionally been seem to underpin the formation of social movements, social movements for their part have advanced citizenship.[5] However, whereas social movements in Western societies were aimed at achieving inclusion of new categories of persons into citizenship rights as well as at creating new types of rights, in real socialism social movements sought to counter the inclusionary power of Leninist regimes and to redefine citizenship rights. It was not exclusion from communist citizenship that mobilised these movements but the illegitimacy of the inclusionary regimes based upon the leading role of a single party or latterly socialist pluralism.

Critically, the achievement of citizenship is not just the positive attainment of rights but is also about the rejection of a certain type of fusion of rights characteristic of feudalism. The disentanglement of the institutional complex on which putative civil, political and social rights rested under real socialism, the nomenklatura fusion of socialist legality, the leading role of the party and the "organic labour state," was made possible by the emerging economic irrationalities of the directive-distributive state (see: Jowitt, 1975; Kolankiewicz, 1988).

Reverse Incorporation: From Social to Civil Rights

New Responsibilities. There can be little doubt that the live-wire civil society that inhabits Eastern Europe today is faced with a greater responsibility in the creation of both state and economy that any previous counterpart. As the economy shifts from Casals "property vacuum" into the many forms of legal and illegal property relations, so the control by the grass roots in the enterprises, local councils, as well as in other milieux becomes all the more important. Recent objections on the part of employee self-management representative bodies in Poland (or Yugoslavia) to rapid privatization of the economy from above—outside, as they see it, of social control—is a case in point. Charges of selling-out the national heritage for the proverbial mess of pottage emanate from most parts of the political spectrum.

The absence of an independent judiciary, still in the process of reconstruction, an unploughed legislative terrain inherited from the previous regime (as well as from the prewar period, as the abuse of 1934 economic legislation by enterprise directors has shown), requires that civil society defend the population against the predatory market forms as well as participates in shaping them. Paradoxically, even a parliament and a presidency created under the auspices of Solidarnosc can be seen as too powerful given the continued weakness of civil society. This concern was crystallised in the political crisis facing the front for National Salvation in Romania.

Likewise, as new political parties begin to take the place of movements and associations, so the possibility of new political forms emerging becomes all the more real. In Poland, in particular, the future role of local "citizens committees" (komitety obywatelskie) set up to see Solidarnosc through the June 1989 elections became contentious. Whereas some saw them as the basis of an embryonic party guaranteeing election, others, more creatively perhaps, see them as a movement for the "liquidation of the remnants of communism." It should be these committees that claim an open, grass-roots organization sponsoring democratic forms in line with the ethos of Solidarnosc.

However, the transition from an opposition movement countering totalitarianism into a political force competing with other groupings in a democratic manner is raising problems. Charges of a new hegemony, a monoparty emerging out of the doctrine claiming that Solidarnosc cannot be categorised according to traditional left-right criteria, make it clear that many are suspicious of what the Solidarnosc ethos constitutes.[6] Coupled to this is the demand that the Poles now change their attitude to the state from "Us vs Them" to "Us vs It" (it being the economic crisis), heard clearly as the January 1, 1990, economic legislation bites further into pauperised Polish society.

Is this a new inclusion? Solidarnosc must return, it is said, to civil society or run the risk of hindering the emergence of genuine political democracy. The exemplar of social movements must remove itself from the state and return to represent the nation not at the top but at the bottom of society. It may leave a presence in the form of a political party or parties or a trade union movement but it cannot be a political party encompassing civil society that seeks to "pin together various political and social currents with the single badge of Solidarnosc."

The above debate in Poland was intensified during the local government elections in mid-1990 to the 2,500 town and village councils requiring the placement of 110,000 councillors whose task was to be the reconstruction of local Polish society from below. Not only is this another arena where civil society will seek to construct organs of the self-governing republic but it is the focus of the most fundamental shift in the centre of gravity of social life. For the aim is to transfer the organization of everyday life away from the workplace to the residential milieux and thus to break with a fundamental dimension of real socialism (see Adamski, 1989).

Not only will new forms of "communal property" provide the economic base for local autonomy vis à vis central government, but it will also develop local citizenship, combining civil rights with responsibility and electoral accountability. These in turn have already created severe tensions, which will take priority over the system of industrial and social rights rooted in the workplace. These rights, rather than being liberating, were used as a means of control by the regime (e.g., between budget maximization and social justice). A case in point is the transfer of retail outlets into communal property, which frequently does violence to the desire of previous employees to manage their own workplaces.

Industrial Citizenship. Industrial rights for their part subordinated individual to collective rights, as evidenced in trade unionism, strike action, self-management and other forms of workplace cooperation, competition and conflict. However, where individual civil rights of assembly, association, and the person were themselves limited, as they were under communism, so the enabling power of industrial rights were curtailed. In fact, rather than civil rights being used to establish industrial and ultimately social rights, it was the platform of trade unionism, as in Poland, that was used to press for civil rights.

This is due to the fact that whereas under capitalism, there is a class bias towards employees in industrial rights, under real socialism the employer was the state and industrial rights, rather than being a means for collective bargaining in a market economy or for the advancement of social citizenship, were akin to and often a substitute for political rights. But here again, whereas in the Marshall sequence civil rights predated political rights (and indeed the latter were very much derivative) and secondary rights were enabled by more fundamental civil rights under the transition from real socialism, industrial and political rights such as existed (and they were intensely collective rather than intensely individualistic, to use Marshall's phrase) have been used to gain civil rights.

The freedom of speech, thought and faith have been achieved by the proposed abolition of the censor's office, the reform of the universities, and the normalization of Church-state relations. Abolishing censorship was more than just closing down an organization, since most of the press, for example, was owned by communist front organizations. The role of the Church is being redefined. It is no longer the umbrella for civil society but must now engage in a dialogue with secular authorities and with its own members within radically changed conditions. All these factors will determine the nature of citizenship in post-Communist societies. Once again the conflict over religious education in schools or the proposed abortion legislation indicates how civil rights may not easily evolve out of an emancipatory social movement.

The liberty of the person (where law and order has to be imposed on the basis of legality), the development of property rights and contracts are all in the process of reestablishment. Equally, new rights will be on the agenda that reflect the appalling problems inherited from the communist rulers. Ecological degradation, human morbidity and mortality rates will raise the profile of the right to life, leisure and landscape. Can there be any doubt that the reconstruction of citizenship on the basis of devastation will not be rooted in such concerns?

Most critically, the right to justice—a key item in the "round-table" negotiations—an independent judiciary and equality before the law are high on the new governments' agendas. The emergence of the "legal state" as a term within the constitution as much as the subordination of the procuracy to the ministry of justice is evidence of this. In the anti-ideological atmosphere of transition, the rule of law and of the constitution takes priority over the formation of nascent political platforms. The freedom of association and assembly are in principle accepted except that their legal codification contained some points of controversy in what was still, after all, an uneasy coalition government.

The continued presence of the dual functioning Solidarnosc, both union and government, is an indication that industrial rights are still seen as guaranteeing the emerging civil and political rights. The recent controversy over the use by the Citizens' Committees of the Solidarity label in the forthcoming local government elections was a case in point. Denied the right to do so by Walesa, the Committees were the only bodies that could deliver a victory at the polls to compare to the June 1989 success at the national level. This was doubly the case because of the admitted weakness of NSZZ Solidarnosc in the workplace. Forthcoming general elections will, however, see industrial rights removed from the political arena.

The question that needs to be asked is as follows. What will be the impact on the nature of the civil and political citizenship as it emerges, given its roots in industrial and social citizenship? One can well speculate that the increased interest, for example, in "worker-share" ownership (e.g., ESOP and various voucher systems) as the most popular form of extension of property rights rests in part in the legacy of employee self-management both pre- and post-1980 but also in objective financial limits to other forms of destatization. Outright privatization of state industry is not acceptable to key sections of the working class and intelligentsia, although in the area of services broad-ranging private sector activity is supported. Sentiments of the kind "this factory is ours since we worked for it" are not often met in other work forces facing privatization within largely capitalist economies, for example.[7]

If economic reform requires the depoliticization of the workplace, with the removal of all party organs, it also more controversially implies the elimination of the social role of the enterprise. Paradoxically, the elements of social citizenship that Marshall defined as "a modicum of economic welfare and security . . . the right to share to the full in the social heritage and to live the life of a civilized being according to standards prevailing in the society" are those apparently most threatened. As enterprises come to shed their medical and welfare appendages, which have been highly subsidized, they will require a counterbalance at the local level in provision.

However, social citizenship was also largely compromised through its attachment to the mode of collective consumption under real socialism, and there social rights may well be sacrificed in the short term because of their association with the previous regimes. If social citizenship modified distributional inequality, although not the distribution of wealth as such in emerging capitalism, then the growth of civil rights—in particular the right to private property—in Eastern Europe will be associated with increasing pauperization and felt insecurity. Thus, civil rights will come into conflict with established rights of social citizenship and this will of necessity affect the nature of both. It is clear that the distributional subsidies enacted by the state and affecting all strata and segments of society are interpreted as social rights that are endangered by privatization.

This is, however, to an extent, a misleading perception. As Barbalet points out, after Marshall, social rights are claims against the state, they are benefits in effect and therefore potentially exclusionary since they are of necessity targeted and not universal. Furthermore, according to the "state redistributive thesis," social rights in the form of subsidies to health, housing, education and food, rather than diminishing inequality, under real socialism concealed a form of cumulative inequality in favour of the party-state apparatus. Collective consumption, the supply of goods and services in kind rather than through transfer payments, increased inequality. However, as under capitalism, these payments may have served to ease tension, if not between the inegalitarian effects of the market and the equality of status presumed in civil citizenship, then between the inegalitarian effects of the plan and the equality postulated in Marxist-Leninist ideology.

More importantly, in the absence of well-grounded civil rights, social rights were used to discipline employees and citizens. This was legitimated by the regimes through stressing the symmetry of rights and duties, the one conditional on the other, as well as by the absence, more pragmatically, of other disciplinary tools such as unemployment.

It is often observed that the state exacted a whole range of duties and obligations largely of an economic and occupational nature from its citizens and in this way crowded out the space for individual autonomy and the exercise of rights. Furthermore, this emphasis upon duties—to vote, to work, to join state organizations, to obey laws and their associated enabling regulations—produced a tyranny of obligations whereby anything that did not accord with these stated obligations was viewed with suspicion (Marshall, 1973, p. 88).

The New Citizenship

However, it would be naive to assume that the emergence of key citizenship rights within the existing structure bequeathed by real socialism will not effect the constitution of these rights. The tyranny of obligations coexisted with the promise of full employment regardless of the consequences of this policy. Local fiefdoms may not have fostered local self-government, but local politics still managed to bring forth a sense of localism absent in more democratic systems and a modicum of order. The remainder of this chapter will examine in brief the possible scenario for the development of civil, political and social rights respectively, each in one area, namely property rights, local self-government and welfare provision. Hopefully some useful indicators of the possible syncretism between existing rights and postulated rights may emerge.

Substantive rights to property. "A property right is not a right to possess property, but a right to acquire it if you can and to protect it if you can get it," argues Schroeder (1988). Given the history of ownership of both personal property and property as capital in Eastern Europe and under real socialism, the codification of property rights thus defined would be a significant advance. However, in the case of Poland, Hungary, and Czechoslovakia, which appear to be the most advanced in the process of reprivatization, certain factors may intervene to translate this formal right into a substantive one.

The argument for private property rights as the bulwark of any political reform is now well rehearsed. However, the argument from private property rights as a sine qua non for market reforms and therefore increasing efficiency is also familiar. Because market reforms bring to bear on the owner all the consequences of ownership (economic, social, ecological and political), they appear as the antithesis of the property vacuum. Paraphrasing Plato, what belongs to everybody will be thought of as belonging to nobody and thus no one will care for it. This admirably sums up the fate of state property in terms of both industrial property and the public good under real socialism. Further, such privatization is also seen as a major instrument of the depoliticization of the workplace, a source of budget revenue, an incentive to foreign capital, and a panacea for a whole range of other problems.

In Eastern Europe, however, a host of obstacles to privatizing the socialised sector, which produces 90 percent of industrial production, has raised interesting prospects. Crucially, the government's economic programme perceives an evolutionary path to structural transformation, with preference shown to employee or citizen shareholding. It is equally obvious that the manner, therefore, of privatization will be a major political issue shaping the political platforms of the nascent parties for the foreseeable future. Already the stabilization plans are taken by the ex-communist opposition as a new short cut to primitive accumulation, using the transfer of state property into private hands for takeoff.

This has been further highlighted by the variety of legal and illegal "buy-outs" of state capital by managers and related persons as well as by fictitious companies used solely for the purpose of raising prices without incurring government taxation.[8] The whole question of pricing state property, the extent to which the population could possibly partic-ipate in such a privatization exercise given the increasingly impover-ished state of whole sectors of society, leaving the field to the affluent minority or to foreign capital, is a major problem. As a consequence, it is not surprising that opposition to outright privatization as opposed to worker shares has grown amongst employees.

Self-Management. The usual response to this concern over the sell-off of state property was to underline the control function of employee councils in the enterprise (Fedorowicz, 1990). However, more recently after a review of these so-called nomenklatura companies, the industry minister has raised doubts as to the control function of self-management bodies as well as to the future role of these organs in a market economy. Self-management activists for their part have come to the defense of "social property" both as an important form of ownership in its own right as well as a possible interim type of property in the transition to privatization. Symbolically, the recent resurrection of the 1980–81 "Siec," or self-management network structure within the trade union Solidarnosc proclaiming employee share ownership as its policy, provides evidence of the link between the self-management ethos and share ownership in Poland.

It is clear that other than purely capital market considerations have to be taken into account, not least the distorted form of the housing and labour markets in Eastern Europe, as well as the importance of other relations created under real socialism that will be a long time in dispersal. Privatization will be taking place within a complex of social conditions, social relations and dependencies not present in the West (see Rychard, 1989, p. 319).

However, it is as well to remember that behind the flag of self-management can be concealed both conservative as well as managerialist groups, not simply those committed to the interests of the direct producer. The recently formed Union of Employee Ownership brings together some of the largest enterprises, such as FSO, Ursus, and some steelworks, all pressing for a greater employee share-ownership than the 20 percent guaranteed by the Ministry of Finance. The suspicion is that they wish to use the form of employee share ownership in order to retain their dominant positions in the market.

The government for its part is committed to increasing competition and thus moving from formalised state property to share sales on the open market. This, for example, appears to be the likely fate of the Gdansk Shipyard. In such a situation, according employees more than 20 percent of shares at preferential rates would be economically irrational. Despite the avowed rebuttal of the government that it will not seek any "third path" but will keep to tried and tested solutions from the West, there are obvious signs of political mobilization in favour of just such a middle of the road formula.

Self-managed social property has well-known limitations when compared to capitalist markets, but it is clear that collective property rights may play an important role in alleviating the pangs of transition associated with the withdrawal of social welfare functions from the enterprise—the growth of unemployment, impoverishment and greater economic inequality. In this sense the nature of a key civil right will alleviate the reshaping of social rights, truly a case of reverse incorporation.

The ethos of self-management is being mobilized in professions and occupations long ago reduced to the status of functionary. Medical councils will not only represent the medical profession but will also speak out on national health policy and ethical matters, control promotion and generally intervene in the disposal of medical resources. Similar changes in the legal professions will hopefully establish the ethos critical to the exercise of new rights of citizenship but will again be rooted in an experience of the pathologies of "socialist legality" and bureaucratized health.

The urge to self-organization, internal control and democracy will be a powerful force in overcoming the learned inertia and passivity that came with state-socialism. As such self-organizationwill stand next to the right of assembly and association and thus will blur the distinction between the paramount nature of individual rights and duties and those of such collectivities, since here corporations with property rights will also have clearly defined responsibilities and duties.

State and Citizenship

Socialization of the State. Although it is now recognised that Marshall rather sanguinely accepted the role of the state in the promotion and guardianship of citizenship rights, this cannot be the case in Eastern Europe. Given the roots of the reform movements in civil society and their search for the pays réel, there is a paradox in the fact that these movements seek to emasculate the state, but sufficient power must reside with the state to initiate the reforms, both economic and political.

It is to local and territorial self-government that the task of limiting central state power in the future is to be accorded. Perhaps the most distinctive nature of citizenship rights in post-Communist societies will be that these rights will be guaranteed at the level of community and that citizen as subject rather than object will be devolved to the lowest level possible, reducing the sphere of state intervention to a minimum.

Given access by local self-government to its sources of raising revenue, a key part of the process would be the resolution and identification of the confused state of property at the local level. The distinction between this body, the gmina and state administration would be paramount, with accountability of local governors and mayors clearly resting with their electorate and councils. The gmina would be a size known to the citizen through daily observation (thus providing a critical unmediated control and supervisory function). How this will work in the cities is not made clear in the rather long and dense proposals submitted by the Polish Senate.

Obviously certain services and provision would have extraterritorial implications, e.g., roads, universities. However, such services as health, education, policing and the like would be the object of considerable debate. At present the self-government lobby would seek to appropriate all the assets and powers necessary to ensure its independence of the centre whilst not taking on burdens that would entail excessive obligations. Deficit, highly polluting and other types of enterprises are a case in point.

At present the nascent local councils elected in May 1990 will have to work with the existing bureaucratic apparatus, which is in fact being compelled by law to stay in post until the end of the year. The shortage of personnel competent to administer local government is the first sign of the kind of problems facing this peaceful revolution. Concrete solutions apart from the position of the local self-government organs would be between the private individual and their associations and the state administration. Its transparency would contrast with the distant and opaque nature of relations with the state.

It is likely that political activity will be concentrated at the local level for some time to come, as parties take shape and the rather amorphous nature of state power in the transition deflects organised antistate actions. In many ways local government will be the vehicle for civil society, and the possibility for associations of such bodies (sejmiki) designed to deal with specific economic and social tasks is in the best tradition of anticentralist horizontalism. Obviously, on such matters as who subsidizes the weaker regions, those with fewer sources of income such as property tax, rents and the like, controversy cannot be avoided (Barbalet, 1988, pp. 21–22).

In all likelihood, the factor that may be most conducive to rebuilding the social bonds at the local level—where problems become real and individualised—will not be elections or economic reforms but the need to deal with the effects of pauperization attendant on this reform, self-help in the most basic meaning of that term. For social rights are likewise to be decentralized, loosened from the grip of the state umbrella and put into the hands of the community. In this way perhaps the greatest asset to citizenship, other-directedness, civilized community, civic honesty, and integrity will be reconstructed from the grass roots. For, if nothing else, associations, groups and movements are above all moral communities, and unless the locality can deal with this problem, the foundations of res publica will be precarious.

How the societies of Eastern Europe throw off their "dependency cultures," rooted in demoralizing overemployment and the state provision of "barracks socialism," is an open question. Whereas an enterprise culture is clearly in the making, the "active citizen" giving of time and money to the community is less obvious. However, this is not to pre-judge the emergence of just such "citizenship" based on the syncretism of imposed self-help, disaffection with the central state and values borrowed from church and traditional socialism.

Work vs Employment. Whereas civil rights are largely defensive against the state, social rights are by definition invasive, requiring the state to guarantee the provision of certain benefits. Not only do they generate an administrative apparatus, but they also place considerable budgetary constraints on the state. During hardship, as Barbalet nicely points out, "a pressure against social rights may take the form of the reassertion of civil rights" not just in property but as an individual unit in economic competition (Marshall, 1973, p. 97). Since social rights create "a universal right to real income which is not proportionate to the market value of the claimant," the incentives are very different; one is for personal gain, the other is that of public duty.

Under real socialism both were distorted, incentive to personal gain being in large measure corrupted or prohibited whereas the notion of public duty was rooted in an illegitimate regime and therefore trans-formed into an onerous obligation. Although social rights under social-ism may have reduced risk and insecurity, they did little to enrich civilised life, being low level and eventually of the last resort. Thus, the collective as well as individual aspects of social rights, the provision for society as a whole and for individual instances, was severely criticised.

The thesis of the "over-protective state," which was coined in the run up to market reform, brought forth the retinue of data concerning exces-sive morbidity and mortality rates, unequal educational opportunity, pension-based poverty, squalid and overcrowded housing conditions, and many other indicators of declining quality of life. What is incontro-vertible is that alongside this decline in living standards, Polish society became incapacitated, unable and unwilling to act for itself.

The key social right fundamentally affecting the notion of socialist citizenship was the much lauded "right to work." It was the common qualitative experience of job-security, political security at the top, security in the face of absenteeism, alcoholism and petty corruption at the bottom, which fostered the demoralization and disintegration of the work ethic. When 53 percent of workers see drinking at work as normal, 58 percent condone theft at work, and 71 percent accept working on the side during official working hours, then it is difficult to deny the claims of those who see the fault in the noncommodification of labour. The degradation of labour itself was clearest when labour costs dropped from 20 percent to as low as 5 percent of production costs.

It is difficult to foresee the effects of the fundamental transformation wrought by the introduction of legislation on unemployment and the termination of the work contract. Unemployment is a last resort and no one doubts the commitment of the Polish and Hungarian governments to the reestablishment of the balance between incentive and duty. At present there is a general disbelief as to the possibility of bankruptcy, and many enterprises believe in the myth of privatization, that turning themselves into private companies will deflect the laws of the market-place.

Conclusion

There are many issues affecting the emergence of citizenship that this chapter has not addressed. The role of the peasantry, class inequality, nationalism and the legacy of Soviet hegemony, the collapse of Marxism-Leninism as well as the devaluation of the socialist project are just some of them. Marshall rightly asked the questions as to whether there was a limit beyond which the modern drive to social equality could not pass. We could well ask the obverse, whether the reforms in Eastern Europe will have a level of inequality beyond which post-Communist societies will not go. What are the factors creating these limits, if any?

Social rights might once again become embedded in local communities and functional associations under the banner of self-management. Or they could stand in defence of the old against the civil rights siding with the new. Social citizenship may place a limit on the emergence of new political and civil rights simply because neither is possible without an educated, healthy, and civilized populace. At the same time, class will emerge alongside citizenship rights and not antedate it as in western societies, and this in turn will modify the resulting class structure.

If civil rights were indispensable to the development of a market economy, and as status moved to contract, civil rights were intensely individual rights, as was mentioned above. It is doubtful if the collectivist heritage of the last forty years can be as easily shed as other vestiges of real socialism. Although research points to various attitudes that are pro-privatization, pro-unemployment and inegalitarian, these were as much due to a rejection of the previous regime as based on a concrete calculation of personal interests. Finally, the establishment of full civil and political rights may relegitimate many of the social rights previously associated with real socialism and may once again temper class inequalities fostered by the former.

Notes

1. Another concept has entered into the ranks of the "essentially contested concepts" where the definition of the term is part of the problem. Alongside "civil society" and more recently the "private-public" distinction, the concept of citizenship has made a career for itself both in Eastern and Western Europe. Drawing on the work of T.H. Marshall, it identifies the civil, political and social rights which emerged in England since the 19th century as a condition for participation in society. Obviously, some of these rights were primary and others secondary or enabling. Some were more formal, others substantive in nature.

These rights deemed to be an inheritance of the Enlightenment have been formally inscribed in constitutions and declarations have been observed more in the breach than in the adherence of states. They have been the object of struggles by social movements seeking to widen the compass of these citizenship rights to include ever greater excluded sections or categories of society. Citizenship is therefore less a static status or condition, more a process of definition and redefinition of what constitute the conditions for meaningful participation in society's institutions.

However, as to the explanatory power of the concept of citizenship, there must remain some doubt. Is it more a symptom of societies' subjects searching for greater control over their lives vis-a-vis a totalising state? Is it a moral discussion about participation, or a concept which points to the conditions for such participation? Is citizenship the outcome of a democratizing process or is it the language of this process? The normative and descriptive, the evaluative and cognitive as ever bind the expectations, practices and precepts tied to this concept into a Gordian knot.

2. As an example see the papers to the "State and Civil Society" conference in Budapest 1987. See: Gathy, 1989.

3. Using the ideas of Michael Oakshott, Mouffe (1989) strives to reflect the imperative which would give greater primacy to association without endangering individual rights. Also see: Arato, 1988.

4. Prior to the emergence of the new law on associations which immediately required amendation, there was a veritable flood of new associations seeking registration. As for the "political panorama" as it is called, revivified prewar parties as well as new outgrowths of existing parties make a confusing picture see "Polityczna panorama" *Rzeczpospolita* 18–19/11/89. Also "Demokracja kwitnie" *PWA* 1/12/89.

5. Barbalet (1988, pp. 97–99) *Citizenship*, OUP. This excellent account of the Marshall thesis as applied to Britain is invaluable to an examination of the relationship between rights and class.

6. See: M. Drozdek (1989). For a sample of the discussion on the future of Solidarnosc, see also L. Bedkowski (1989). For a discussion of "ethoi," see M. Ilowiecki (1989).

7. See R. Kubiak (1989) as an example of the debate over how to deal with the anticipated and extant pauperization. Also Zielinska (1989).

8. The Procurator General discovered 1593, or 10 percent of all companies registered were so-called Nomenklatura buy-outs. They involved 700 enterprise directors, 680 chairmen of cooperatives, 9 wojewod or regional governors, and 80 high ranking political and professional persons. Many were found to be parasitical on state property, paying no rent, service charges, etc.

Bibliography

Adamski, W. 1989. "Obszary i granice spolecznie oaprobowanej prywatyzacji gospodarki w Polsce." In *Polacy '88*. Warsaw.

Arato, A. 1988. "Social theory, civil society and the transformation of authoritarian socialism."

Barbalet, J. 1988. *Citizenship*. OUP.

Bedowski, L. 1989. "Zamki na etosie." *Przeglad Tygodniowy*, vol. 12, pp. 24–31.

Drozdek, M. 1989. "Michnika projekt monopartii," Lad 10/29.

Federowicz, M. Jan. 1990. "Inicjatywa gospodarcza spoleczenstwa." *Samorzad i Zycie*.

Gathy, V., ed. 1989. *State and Civil Society: Relationships in Flux*. Budapest.

Ilowiecki, M. 1989. "Powrot." *Gazeta Swiateczna*, vol. 12, pp. 16–17.

Jowitt, K. 1975. "Inclusion and Mobilization in European Leninist Regimes." *World Politics*, vol. 28, No.1.

Kolankiewicz, G. 1988. "Poland and the Politics of Permissible Pluralism." *Eastern European Politics and Societies*, vol. 2, no. 1.

Kubiak, R. 1989. "Z czym do nedzy." *Tygodnik Kulturalny*, vol. 5, no. 11.

Marshall, T. 1973. Westport, Conn.

Mouffe, C. 1989. "Democratic Community and the Political Community." Paper presented to the Conference on "Citizenship in Europe" Budapest, May 26–28.

Olszewska, B. 1988. "Rejestracje i odmowy." *Polityka*, vol. 15, no. 10.

Rychard, A. 1989. "Lad polityczny: Centralizm i Pluralizm w Opinii Polakow." in *Polacy 88*, op. cit., p. 319.

Schroeder, G. Summer 1988. "Property Rights Issues in Economic Reforms in Socialist Countries. "*Studies in Comparative Communism*, Vol. XXI, no.2.

Zielinska, H. 1989. "Strefy nieswiadomosci." *Przeglad Tygodniowy*, vol. 10, no. 15.

8

From Social Idea to Real World: Clash Between New Possibilities and Old Habits

Mira Marody

For all the differences in goals and social support, the transformation of the social system now being attempted in Eastern Europe has at least one feature in common with that initiated by the Communists forty-five years ago. In both cases, there has been an endeavor to introduce, from the top downward, new institutions of public life to societies accustomed to entirely different institutional frameworks. Thus, in both cases, the basic problem with transformation is that everyday actions of individuals within new institutions have been molded by expectations and dispositions developed mostly in old ones.

There is also, fortunately, an essential difference between the two historical movements. It pertains to the mechanisms adjusting the actions of individuals to the new institutional sphere, mechanisms preferred by the authorities. For the Communist system, political coercion (often by the police) was to be the basic modifier of human behavior. Today that role is assigned to economic coercion, on the assumption that without interference by the government and its agencies, people will increase productivity, enterprises will begin economizing, and various interest groups will emerge, availing themselves of democratic principles.

Basic Conflict of Rationalities

Societas Perfecta. The one factor that was most essential in forming postwar social practice and its related attitudes was that at the beginning of that period, Eastern European societies were furnished with a system of institutions and principles of functioning that were not the result of spontaneous social processes. Rather, they were designed according to a doctrinaire vision of the ultimate goal: mankind liberated from the vices and imperfections that had plagued it from the very beginning. In other words, the system was founded on a particular vision of *societas perfecta* (Flis 1988).

Communist society was to be the embodiment of all the fundamental ideals of humanity—equality, justice, freedom, abolishment of exploitation, respect for human dignity, and total fulfillment of social needs. The blueprint for such a *societas perfecta* was the ultimate goal, and the Communist party, holding all power in its hands, became the main executor and guardian of that Design. This Design was responsible not only for setting the direction of social development but was also seen as a tool for mobilization of the social forces behind the predetermined collective aims.

T.H. Rigby (1982) rightly shows that in Communist systems the basic justification for society's submission is the constant reference by the authorities to a rational relationship between the ultimate aim—the establishment of communism—and the specific tasks subscribed to different social groups or individuals. The rationality that was built into the social system was, to use Weber's (1956) typology, a value-oriented rationality (Wertrational actions) as opposed to a goal-oriented—or, as we would say today—instrumental rationality (Zweckrational actions).

The purest form of rationality was to be, in Weber's opinion, goal-oriented rational actions distinguished by the conscious choice of the most efficient means for achieving clearly specified aims. In such actions, individuals assess not only the costs of achieving a particular aim in a particular manner but also the value of the aim itself, because it is often perceived as a means for achieving other purposes.

In contrast, Wertrational actions, as claimed by Weber, are oriented toward aims that are of an ultimate character and cannot be used as a means for achieving more general goals. It is true that here also the individual might consider the choice of the most efficient means. However, due to lack of external criteria, which in the case of goal-oriented actions are the assumed costs, assessment of its efficiency is hindered and often taken as given in itself.

This differentiation seems particularly convenient for analyzing political functions in postwar Eastern Europe. For, it might be said that the existence of the Design provided a substitute for politics; it was intended to somehow realize the fundamental political functions of the system from above society. For the Design to be able to play such a role, however, at least two conditions had to be fulfilled: first, society would have to accept the aims of the Design, or its definition of directions of social development; and, second, it would have to accept on the level of individual actions the same rationality that was in force on the system level.

One can say concerning the first condition that the system of basic social values accepted by the majority of Eastern European societies is to a large degree in accordance with the social ideals of the projected *societas perfecta*. These ideals include, in particular, equality of opportunity, freedom of expression, democracy understood as the influence of citizens on the authorities, justice, truth, respect for human dignity, and general affluence (or economic efficiency as a prerequisite of this affluence).

The above set of values has been researched many times and found to exhibit considerable stability.[1] The marked similarity in the system of society and slogans derived from the Design should not come as a surprise, as in both cases, they expressed the social ideals that for centuries have been animating humanity's imagination. Proof that Eastern European societies directly identified these values with the content of the Communist Design is that the reason most often given for lack of obedience to the state powers was the complaint of "unfulfilled promises." This was clearly a far more important cause of social disorders than, say, frustration with the incompetence and corruption of the administration, its repressiveness, or its enforced character.[2]

The situation is different when it comes to the second condition, the acceptance of the system's rationality on the level of individual actions. Even the creators of the Design must have had serious doubts in this respect since they needed to have the party as its guardian. Their successors went even further when, with the passage of time, they began to limit the requirements imposed upon society to one only: that it should not disturb the work of building the *societas perfecta*. From the time the Communist system was first introduced, this requirement was strengthened with considerably painful social training.

The sphere of politics was always most diligently guarded and controlled by the authorities and any deviation from the Design assumptions was most expeditiously and severely punished. This training resulted in Eastern European societies perceiving politics in a way that made it into an area of a peculiar sacrum. It was, so to speak, a negative sacrum, whose influence radiated upon all, but the borders of which were crossed rarely, reluctantly, and only in situations of extreme necessity.

Political Conflict. Consequently, a peculiar political contract binding the authorities and society was formed. It assumed division of roles according to which society was meant to profit from the goodness of the

created system while leaving all the executive decisions to the preroga-
tives of the authorities. This division of roles only sealed the earlier
existing differentiation of rationalities built into the social system and
dominating on the individual level. For, while the system was based on
actions of the Wertrational type, the everyday actions of individuals
were of a Zweck-rational character.

The different rationalities used by the authorities and by society were
connected with the difference in aims on which both political subjects
were focusing their actions. Despite the identity of society's values with
those of the *societas perfecta*, the strategies of action of the authorities and
society were marked by two different aims. The authorities were playing for the realization of the Design, while the people were playing for
"setting themselves up" in the existing social system (see more, A.
Rychard, 1985). Both sides generally tolerated their differences and
often even declared that the game they were playing and their main
interest was in essence the same, treating these declarations as effective
means for achieving their own purposes.

The authorities' increased interest in fulfilling society's needs served
as much to pacify the social mood as the increase in ideological fervor
served to accelerate individual careers. Because of the different rationalities used by both "partners" to the political contract, the mobilizing
functions of the Design were therefore replaced by the mutual inter-
twining of their interests. For one side to realize its interests, it was
necessary to consider the peculiar reasoning of the other (Marody, 1986,
1987). However, such peaceful coexistence had its limits, and it began to
break down when the rationality of the system came into sharp conflict
with the rationality of society, with the main source of conflict being
usually the economy.

Economy as a Substitute for Politics

Because the system of real socialism inhibited any political processes
from taking place, it was the economy that became the main arena for
articulating and negotiating social interests. The frequent overlapping of
political and economic crises demonstrates the importance the economy
had in establishing the system's credibility.[3] Moreover, an inversion had
occurred in the classic relationship binding these two areas of social life:
the economy became the guardian of political interests, while politics
became the overseer of economic interests.

Return to Politics. These characteristics of the Communist system—
the abolition of politics as an autonomic area of social life, as well as the
politicization of the economy, obliterating economic principles and

social interests from the economy—made it essentially impossible to articulate political interests (Rychard, 1983). Nevertheless, even within such a structure, one might talk about political interests in their most rudimentary form, namely, societal acceptance of the continuation of the political status quo, or else an attempt to destroy it, and for the authorities, its preservation.[4] Again, this was the case despite the identity of values shared by the authorities and society.

The construction of *societas perfecta*—desired by the authorities—and "setting oneself up"—driving individuals—could have appeared complementary and in fact were presented in this manner by the authorities to society. Their conflicting character came to the fore only when the anachronistic, wasteful economic system collapsed and the authorities were forced to choose between allowing systemic reforms and permitting a drastic lowering of living standards. Only then did the differences between the two types of rationalities—that built into the social system and that dominating on the individual level—emerge, bringing with them the beginning of a conflict of political interests.[5]

In this context, the statement that in the postwar Communist system, the economy safeguarded political interests has a double meaning. The way the economy functioned determined not only the authorities' chances for preserving the political status quo but it also determined society's chances of articulating and presenting its interests in political terms by connecting the possibilities of personal "setting oneself up" with the structure of the social system. The basis for social demands was that component of the Design that described the effects the system meant to bring about to the people living in it.

It is important to note that the economic and political crises were accompanied by a total change of the rationalizations used by both sides in their political rhetoric. At that juncture, the authorities were trying to justify the necessity of making unpopular decisions by referring to pragmatic arguments. Individuals, for their part, were defending their interests by recalling the social ideals underlying the social system (Marody et al., 1981; Linderberg and Nowak, 1987). Because of the content of the political contract binding both sides, the complaint of unfulfilled promises helped society to legitimize its trespassing into the area of politics reserved for the authorities. This was especially the case when the extent of social protest was sufficiently wide.[6]

However, this return of society into politics through economics differs in its effects from a situation in which the political interests of the population are shaped by economic interests, which in turn are determined by the social position of the individuals. In this kind of return, the political interests of society were identified with the interests of the community of consumers and not of producers. This was not only because the sphere of production constitutes the systemic part of the Design and therefore belongs to the domain of the authorities but because the politicization of the economy and the abolition of politics as an autonomic area of public life obliterated the possibility of social integration on the basis of economic interests.

The abstract values describing the shape of a just, free, and affluent society in which every person can without limits, and on an equal level, fulfill his/her needs remained the only bridge connecting the concrete concerns of individuals and the general interests of society as a whole. By this token, these values were becoming the main realm of integration at a time when individuals were confronting the decisions of the state powers striking at their interests.

Of course, general acceptance of the acknowledged abstract values doesn't negate the differentiation of social interests. Consequently, the integrative power of these values was limited to situations in some sense extreme when society attempted to change the decisions of the authorities or the authorities themselves. The return to politics was in this case a short excursion[7] that basically disturbed the essential division of roles, but politics remained in the hands of the authorities and the average citizen became a suspicious observer ready to show disobedience.

Threat of Politics. Clearly, during all this time, politics as a tool of managing society was above all a source of threat to the average person. It was a direct threat that struck at those who, purposefully or unknowingly, crossed its borders and an indirect threat in that political decisions regulating all manifestations of social life were subordinated to a rationality different from that of the average person. As such, politics introduced an element of unpredictability and uncertainty into a social reality to which people had somehow grown accustomed.

However, politics during this entire period was also a source of hope. Hope for a better life, which would be delivered by the authorities to society. This was a hope that diminished under the experience of everyday life but re-emerged with amplified strength every time there was a change of governing personalities. This hope not only turned politics into the fundamental tool for the distribution of all social goods but was also the fundamental source. In this way, politics can take the place of economics in the social consciousness as the basis of social affluence.

If in the Communist system politics was the area of sacrum, then society's attitudes toward this sacrum most closely resembled the disposition of the disciples of the cargo cult.[8] In both cases, we are dealing with expectations for gifts from outside that are controlled by the powers' capricious and fear-instilling behavior. In both cases, there is an emphasis on just distribution and also an identical lack of interest in the processes necessary for the creation of the required goods or states or reality.

Naturally, we might say that both the feeling of being threatened and that of hope were shaped in society through the concerted efforts of Communist authorities using specific political rhetoric that evidently served their interests well. Yet the existence of these attitudes will for a long time significantly influence the expectations and actions of society in the sphere of politics, irrespective of who holds power.

Tossed about in turn by fear and hope, people are likely to look for solutions to the problems besetting them above all in changes of the authorities. For passing on responsibility to the ones who govern doesn't mean total surrender to their decisions. It leads, though, to a situation in which the fundamental dimension defining political life is that of "confidence versus lack of confidence" and the essential category explaining political options becomes the category of faith.

Both faith and confidence in political leaders are built on abstract values describing the shape of an ideal society and usually have a somewhat distant relationship with the condition of the society empirically existing. Therefore, as Weber wrote (1987: 36) many years ago: "After the emotional revolution usually comes traditional everyday reality. The hero of the faith, and above all the faith itself, disappears or (which brings even more visible effects) becomes the object of the conventional, empty talk of political philistines and technicians." The faith disappears, but the unsolved problems remain. Their pressure pushes people toward finding new, better, more caring leaders. And so da capo al fine.

Rejection of the Design

Examination of studies on the sources of inefficiencies of the social system indirectly shows that the development of political consciousness of Eastern European societies was a laborious process strongly connected to the recurring economic difficulties (Marody et al. 1981; Lindenberg 1986; Kosela 1989; Banaszak 1989). In Poland as late as 1978 people overwhelmingly blamed the bad state of affairs on "laziness," "drunkenness," and "wastefulness," that is, on the failures of human nature rather than on the social order. Only after 1980 did the blame start shifting toward systemic factors such as "abuse of power," "suppression of criticism," or "lack of competency on the part of persons at leading positions" (Banaszak 1989). At this point, however, the socialist system continued to be seen as having certain advantages over the capitalist, particularly in social relations, including job security (Adamski et al. 1986).

The radical rejection of socialism as an ideology determining the shape of the social system came only after 1985. First, there was an almost total rejection of the state monopoly of the economy, seen most clearly in foreign trade and heavy industry. Other meaningful shifts took place in the description of good social order. Specifically, there was a movement toward views accentuating nonegalitarian division of goods, pluralism of worldviews, and a polycentric model of political power (Banaszak 1989; Kolarska-Bobinska 1989). The change that came after 1985 lay above all in an awareness of much of Polish society that the system was no longer able to perform social security functions for its citizens, thus the last argument for its existence was gone.

The standard explanations of the rejection of the socialist system were pointing at the growing disproportions between human aspirations and the possibilities for their fulfillment within the framework of the existing institutional order. While this factor certainly played a substantial role in the delegitimization of the socialist system (Tarkowski 1988), it is nonetheless unsatisfactory because objectively these disproportions were occurring in just as high if not higher degrees in the first part of the decade, during which a relatively high percentage of persons were accepting socialist principles of the organization of social life. The factors responsible for this change should be looked for in another sphere, in those processes influencing not only the economic but also the normative order of the social system.

After a "decade of success" in the seventies the steep fall in consumption during 1980–82 was for Polish society a traumatic experience, in particular when the rapidity and depth of changes in life style that followed contained an element of surprise. It is true that the stagnation in consumption started earlier, but the ruthless regress of material conditions was concentrated in the space of less than two years and its most visible manifestations appeared within a few months and affected everyone. The shops became emptier from one day to the next and growing queues for the most essential products were forcing consumption restrictions on even relatively well-off people.

Particularly important is that the fall of consumption was accompanied by the breakdown of the social order both on its institutional and normative levels. All this caused the introduction of martial law in 1981, which, although generally condemned, was accepted by many people with a kind of relief, as something that brought back order and stability to social life (Adamski et al. 1986; Wnuk-Lipinski et al. 1987). Such an order and stability would let individuals try again at "setting oneself up."

After the imposition of martial law, Polish society was marked by individual actions aimed at protecting the previously achieved levels of consumption and at "biding one's time" through the economic crisis. Common to most of these activities were attempts to go outside the system, to take advantage of all the social devices that would replace or complete ineffectively functioning state institutions. However, with the passage of time, it slowly became obvious to an ever larger number of people that waiting through the crisis was an unattainable goal.

Escape outside the system more and more often ended with the discovery that the system, to coin an expression, "runs together with me." Money made was eaten up by inflation, shortages of goods on the market entangled people in activities taking all their time, disorganization of systemic institutions disorganized family life. The feeling of disproportion between the struggle toward protecting previously attained standards of living and its resulting effects, the feeling of moving backward in spite of doubling efforts, became the dominating experience.

These subjective experiences had their objective causes. The "second society" that had been built during the individual and group processes of adaptation was not creating its own institutions independent of the system. Rationality of individuals was a rationality of a micro scale, directed above all at changing the individual's situation in the social system, not at changing the system itself. Improvement in individual well being was taking place not by implementation of new norms of social life but rather through dismantling, breaking down, or at least bypassing the norms and rules operating until then.

This process, whose roots lay in much earlier periods but which in the eighties underwent an exceptional acceleration, was accompanied by two phenomena that with the passage of time started to affect the effectiveness of individual adaptive activities. The first of them can be called in short "the cooling down of institutional order," manifested by the growing institutional chaos, disorganization of public life, and the falling apart of the material infrastructure of society. The second was described by Lamentowicz (1988) as "an expansion of factuality" as a main regulator of human activity that instead of following general rules and norms was becoming ever more often and in an ever more widening scope conditioned by situational factors.

Both these phenomena were the expression of one and the same characteristic of social reality—the social system's loss of ability to coordinate individual activities on the global level. The full analysis of the mechanisms that resulted in the development of this characteristic goes beyond the scope of this text, but it has to be emphasized that the different rationalities used by the authorities and the society was significant.

Most generally it can be said that the rationality from macro level resulting in economic and political decisions was diametrically opposite to the micro-level rationality that directed the individual adaptation activities to these decisions. It diffused the norms defining the ways of functioning of the whole system and in consequence also the rules determining people's actions in the social space. Social reality was becoming *normatively indeterminant,* which is equal to the statement that it stopped to be the reality of shared meanings and rules of action.

Instead of norms and principles holding at all points of the social space, there started to appear local "ethics" valid at the moment for only a given group of people engaged in a concrete interaction. Although in the short run, they were raising the chances of achieving individual or group aims locally, in the longer time span and in society as a whole, they were making the reproduction of the whole social order impossible, thus leading to social disorganization on all levels.

While the decomposition of the social system seemed to be stopped with the introduction of martial law, it was not. This process in the following years, although less visible, constituted a permanent element of social life. Its objective consequences were a lasting lowering of material benefits, but much more essential was the impact on social consciousness. First, the advancing impoverishment of society, which was due to the inadequate fulfillment of social needs, was turning into a feeling of civilizational degradation (Marody 1988b) that could not be justified by any general norms that would give the reason for the necessity of sacrifice.

This was so because social order, or rather the *lack* of it, took away from the majority of such norms the power to regulate social behavior. Moreover, there was an increasing visibility of affluent groups of people who thus provided examples of spectacular financial careers based on rules difficult to comprehend but nonetheless unmistakably from an origin outside the system. By their very being they advocated the acceptance of paradigms of rationality different from those provided by the system.

Transition from the conditional acceptance to radical rejection of socialism as an ideology defining the shape of the social system was a process extended in time, one whose development was influenced by the growing normative indeterminance of the social reality being the result of the adaptation processes and at the same time limiting to a significant degree their effectiveness.

On the systemic level this led to the breakdown of a socially indispensable minimum of conformism and integration. On the individual level it took from people the minimum knowledge of the rules by which others were playing, thus preventing the rationalization of individual activities. In both cases, it created a singular vacuum that could be filled with norms and rules diametrically opposed to those existing before.

New Possibilities, Old Habits

The change in institutional order, or rather the series of changes undertaken by the non-Communist cabinets, has in view, generally, the introduction of the market economy and a democratic political system. Those changes are accompanied by what appears to be a high level of support for the governmental policy, a very high level of confidence in the leading figures in political life, and an acceptance of the necessity of even considerable, though relatively brief, material deprivation. That support, in fact, is rather shallow since the new institutional possibilities have only slightly influenced the sphere of habitus, modifying the dominant patterns of action.

Social attitudes operate at different levels of consciousness, the deepest being a habitual level. This category, called "habits," comes closest to Bordieu's concept of *habitus*, which is a system of unconscious schemata of thought and perception or dispositions that act as mediation between the system of public institutions and the system of individual behavior. At the collective level, it is responsible for the continuities and regularities empirically observable in the social world. At the individual level, it is both a socially constituted structure of cognition and a motivating structure.

Because of the fit between individual ways of being and empirically observable objective structures, habits are perceived as self-evident and natural, and hence they go unquestioned. A change in those objective structures alters all the goals of human actions without infringing, in the initial period at least, the habitus that by being part of what society takes for granted, escapes critical reflection and continues inertially to shape human actions.

The new possibilities of action were first created in the political sphere, as in Hungary or Poland, where by mid-1989 most institutional limitations were practically removed. It could have been expected that the related differentiation of social interests would manifest itself in the emergence of new parties and political groups, and then in a new division of the electorate.

The first of the two expectations has been confirmed. Many new groups emerged, even though most of them remain numerically very weak. But when it comes to the second expectation, the picture is that of a highly asymmetrical configuration of political forces in which one dominant political bloc—Civic Forum in Czechoslovakia or Solidarity in Poland—finds no counterbalance in any other group or even in their theoretical coalition.

These blocs are perceived by the electorate as an element of the one-party model (the governing party—the satellite parties—the extra-systemic opposition) rather than a parliamentary model (the governing party—the undecided center—the opposition parties). As in the past, there are in the collective consciousness two principal actors: the governing, non-Communist party (or social movement), which is the leading force, symbol, and guarantor of social change, and society, which benevolently (for the time being, at least) watches the governing party's doings without engaging itself in them.

The new institutional solutions in the economic sphere have a much shorter history. Only now are the first important changes being introduced, though those in the property system proceed very slowly. Nevertheless, it might be said that at least in Poland, people have for some time been intensively preparing for the approaching economic reforms. Thus, after the first month of real reforms, one should notice some changes in the organization of work and the underlying social consciousness.

Nothing of that kind has taken place, even in Poland, where shock treatment has been applied. The financial deterioration of enterprises remains the primary practical and directly experienced effect of the reform. People are not much more willing to work, the organization of work has not improved, nor are the time and qualifications of the employees better utilized. Even though many people take into account the possibility of losing their jobs, few view it as an important problem.

The impact of economic coercion in the sphere of political attitudes seems weak as well. The growing sense of financial handicap and the fear of deteriorating living conditions are not a foundation for the emergence of a sense of identity that is conscious of distinctive features of the social situation. Neither the present nor the expected financial differentiation has led to political differentiation. Even Polish farmers, with their clearly articulated interests, still have a weak connection with group interests in their political choices, their attitudes toward economic liberalization: they manifest moral rather than political support.

That economic coercion does not dramatically influence human behavior in the appropriate, predicted direction does not mean that it has no influence whatever. It activates primarily the traditional adaptive strategies learned in past economic practice. People mainly resort to moonlighting rather than to seeking jobs and ways whereby one can earn more and to limiting their expenses in the situation, even when those expenses threaten biological survival. The most frequent reaction in enterprises is stopping or drastically cutting down production, forcing employees to take leaves, and taking credits to pay salaries and wages. These are both actions that not only do not undermine but outright consolidate the sphere of habitus as it has been to date.

A similar tendency is observed in political attitudes in Poland. The potential electoral support of Solidarity has fallen lately, while support for all the remaining parties and groups has been the same and relatively low. Those who withdrew their support from Solidarity have joined those who are dissatisfied with the policy of the present governing team but find no alternative to it in the programs of other parties. When translated into potential action, this means that practically the only potential form of political reaction (we are not interested here in psychological reactions taking the form of apathy or withdrawal) to unacceptable decisions of the authorities still consists in society's declaring its disobedience to those authorities.

The belief in the effectiveness of economic coercion is based on observation of Western societies. However, when drawing conclusions from the functioning of Western societies, we have to keep in mind that economic coercion is effective there, among other things, because it is perceived at least by a significant majority as a natural element of social reality. In fact, it ceases to be coercion because it is included in the habitus, hidden in learned cognitive schemata and dispositions, reinforced by interactions with other persons and by contacts with public institutions. It ceases to be an external force and becomes internalized and hence a way of life for individuals.

Confidence in, and support for, the reformist actions of the present non-Communist governing team are based mainly on confidence in the persons who form it. Willingness to accept the consequences of the market mechanisms introduced into the national economy by the government is thus a moral choice, unlike the acceptance of necessities that would have to be taken for granted. It is a form of "escape into the collective lot," a reaction to the danger perceived (consciously or not) as external, and the search for psychological support in the spirit of community and the sense of social solidarity. It is a result of that confidence that delegates to the authorities the full responsibility for reforms and at the same time absolves every person from the necessity of making individual decisions about his or her future.

What further dilutes individual interests in the rather abstract public interest is the poor sense of choices offered by governmental policies. For instance, the common statement that everyone must carry the costs of overcoming the crisis and that everyone is to profit from this sacrifice does consolidate social solidarity. But at the same time, is left every person without information about where to invest his/her efforts and energy and how to guide his/her actions. It renders difficult the formulation of individual interest in social terms, that is, by reference to clearly defined criteria of social differentiation, and thus delays the emergence of such social groups, which in supporting the policy of the government would see their own and not only the all-national interest.

It is that collectivist thinking that poses the basic threat to the transformation of Eastern European economies. The institutional changes form only a framework that, if it is to work, requires that society adopt an individualistic attitude. This framework requires that people look at dangers and profits as something that is societally differentiated and is inherent in, rather than outside, the social system. Such an attitude is the foundation of the functioning for the market economy and a democratic system, and without individuation, only a dummy market and dummy democracy are possible.

Of course, the crystallization of new ways of perceiving social reality and of new attitudes toward it require much time. But this does not imply that the time available to Eastern European societies to transform themselves is unlimited. It must be borne in mind that the attitude of escaping into the collective lot, as is now dominant in Polish society, for example, carries a risk that should be taken into account. This attitude might any day, without warning, change into "escape from the lot."

All these habits, attitudes, and expectations created in a collision between the systemic rules and human aspirations and needs were the basis for two fundamental forms of socialization of individual activities between which Polish society is spanned. The first of them, arising from adaptation processes, copied the family matrix as the standard for cooperation of individuals at all levels of social reality. In this form of socialization, small groups connected by common interests, views and/or customs became the fundamental settings of social identification, whereas the division into "we" and "they" was the basic social division. This division involved "ethical dualism" (Dobrowolski 1967; Tarkowska 1987): standards and norms observed in "our" groups were invalid with respect to "them." The claims of "their" groups were treated as illegitimate and a threat to "our" group.

The other form of socialization, coming out of social protests, generated in response to a threat perceived as external the feeling of unity and solidarity based on the social interest as opposed to the "selfish" interests of the authorities. In view of the normative indeterminism of social reality, collective activities were to be regulated in it by reference to the fundamental moral values of dignity, autonomy, responsibility,and altruism. At the same time, because of the lack of crystallized political interests, the goals of collective activities were set by reference to the ideal vision of "normal life," the shape of which was defined by fundamental social values such as freedom, justice, equality, and the general affluence.

The first form transformed the society into an aggregate of primary groups, whereas the other form generated a mythologized feeling of unity that disintegrated in a collision with the reality of everyday life. Both struck at the existence of a state as an entity subordinating the activities of individuals to generally observed principles and rules. The first did so by attempts at "privatization" of them, the other by trying to replace them by moral norms. Both also eliminated the need for politics as a tool for reaching an agreement on the goals of social development, of shaping the collective will and mobilizing the social forces. The first did so by directing people's attention to the possibility of individual "setting oneself up" in the system, the other—by subordinating social activities to the search for leaders promising the implementation of the ideal vision of "normal life."

The change of system is above all the change of human action. In turn, the actions are determined not only by the *current* institutional possibilities but also, or perhaps even first of all, by social habits rooted in the structural characteristics of the society, which result from the *past* systemic regulations. The institutional changes introduced so far in Poland have created a certain set of instruments. For them to work, the majority of society must assume attitudes and habits completely different from those formed in the adaptation processes. After all, the myth of social solidarity will not supersede the processes of crystallization of social interests reflecting the social differentiation of modern societies. The myth of civil society is a poor basis for solving social conflicts in a disintegrated society intent on looking for direct gratification. Finally, the myth of normal life will not bring a solution to social problems augmented over the years immediately after the market economy and a democratic political system have been introduced.

Conclusion

The attempt by which Communist power in postwar Eastern Europe shifted political functions beyond politics resulted in the creation of a system that had a built-in collective aim but no mechanism to ensure the necessary mobilization of social forces for its implementation. The Design's social ideals for the establishment of the *societas perfecta* could have determined the general direction of social development. However, a division into separate systemic and individual rationalities, forced by practical reasons (as the empirically existing *societas perfecta* was unfortunately imperfect) made impossible their transformation into concrete aims capable of animating social activity.

The role that the authorities determined for the citizens, one of consumers of all the benefits bestowed on them by the state—from guaranteed work and health care through social advancement and education all the way to retirement, and the most important benefit, the possibility of setting oneself up in the system—did, in fact, mobilize some social energy. However, it was an energy that could not find expression in common aims, because consumption par excellence is an individual activity even if statistical reports define it as a "collective" one.

The supporting basis of the system—and, at the same time, its main threat—was the economy. It bound the activities of individuals in their double role of producers and consumers, and in the further perspective brought about the possibility of connecting the chances for "setting oneself up" and the failures of the social system. Recognition of the sources of the social system's inefficiency and development of a political consciousness in society was a laborious process closely connected to the recurring economic crises.[9] Only in recent years have popular perceptions changed so that Poland's bad state of affairs is seen as caused by "laziness," "drunkenness" and "wastefulness," that is, by the vices of human nature rather than by the social order.

It is characteristic that the massive questioning of the system's solutions is not accompanied by changes in the values describing a "good society." It might therefore be said that the process that in 1989 brought about the radical rejection in Eastern Europe of the system founded on the establishment of *societas perfecta* basically embraced the means, though not the aims, of the system. What may be even more important is that in the recent alternative systemic solutions, little concern has been generated among the public by issues relating to widening citizens' influence on the functioning of the state.

One might, of course, imagine many ways of breaking the vicious circle of politics. Each one of them would, however, have to meet the same fundamental condition: it would have to lead to a unification of the rationalities operating in public life and in individual private activities. Only under this condition can individuals become the rightful "producers" of the social system rather than mere passive "consumers" whose destiny and success depend each time on the good will and moral qualifications of those people holding power over them.

Notes

1. For more, see: S. Nowak, 1965, 1975; Marody et al., 1981; Lindenberg, 1986; Banaszek, 1989a.

2. As, for instance, in: Marody et al. 1981, Rychard, Szymanderski, 1986.

3. See, for instance, Staniszkis, 1976; Feher, 1982; Pankow, 1983, Rychard, 1983; and Tarkowski, 1988.

4. On the assumption that the stability of the given system is not based only upon the application of physical violence, which seems well founded in the case analyzed here.

5. This thesis is well illustrated by an analysis of data from research undertaken by L. Kolarska and A. Rychard (1983) showing that political interests (defined by the authors as acceptance of changes in the manner of ruling, which could be considered here as systemic changes) were connected primarily with the organizational structure, while economic interests were connected with the social structure.

6. Compare here an interesting analysis by A. Flis (1988) on the symbolic means employed by the state in a situation of crisis and having as its aim the reestablishment of the character of sacrum to politics.

7. With one exception when the "excursion" lasted more than a year. Of course, I have in mind the period 1980–81.

8. This comparison is used by P.L. Berger (1986) in relation to the role that the modernization ideology played and is still playing in the countries of the third world.

9. E.g., Marody et al, 1981; Lindenberg, 1986, Kosela, 1989; Banaszek, 1989a.

Bibliography

Banaszak, H. 1989a. Postawy polityczne studentow Warszawy 1958–1988. W druku.

_____. 1989b. Postawy polityczne mlodego pokolenia Polakow w okresie przejscia modernizacyjnego. W druku.

Berger, P. 1986. "Trzeci Swiat jako idea religijna." *Pismo Literacko-Artystyczne*, no. 6–7, pp. 79–90.

Dobrowolski, K. 1967. *Studia z programma historii v socjologii.* Wroclaw.
Feher, F. 1982. "Paternalism as a Mode of Legitimation in Soviet-Type Societies." In T. Rigby and F. Feher, eds. *Political Legitimation in Communist States,* pp. 64–81. New York.
Flis, A. May–August 1988. "Crisis and Political Ritual in Postwar Poland." *Problems of Communism,* pp. 43–54.
Kolarska, D. and A. Rychard. 1983. "Interesy polityczne i ekonomiczne." In W. Morawski, ed. *Demokracja i gospodarka,* pp. 427–60. IS, UW, Warsaw.
Kolarska-Bobinska, L. 1989. "Poczucie niesprawiedliwosci, konfliktu i preferowany lad w gospodarce." In *Polacy '88: Dynamika konfliktu a szanse reform.* Warsaw.
Koseka, K. "Opinie na temat zrodel spolecznego zla." In S. Nowak, ed. *Ciaglosc i zmiana tradycji kulturowej,* pp. 177–203. Warsaw.
Lindenberg, G. 1986. *Zmiana spoleczna a swiadomosc polityczna: Dynamika postaw politycznych studentow Warszawy 1979–1983.* IS UW Warsaw.
_____ and K. Nowak. 1987. *Swiadomosc spoleczna wobec kryzysu i konfliktu spolecznego: Robotnicy i studenci Warszaway 1983–1984.* IS UW Warsaw.
Marody, M. 1986. *Warunki trwania i zmiany ladu spolecznego w relacji do stanu swiadomosci spolecznej.* IS, UW Warsaw.
_____. 1987. "Social Stability and the Concept of Collective Sense." In Kowalewicz, I. Bialecki, M. Watson, eds. *Crisis and Transition,* pp. 130–58. Berg Publishers.
_____. 1988. "Antinomies of collective subconsciousness." *Social Research* 55, nos. 1–2: 97–110.
_____. 1989. "Sens zbiorowy a stabilnosc i zmiana ladu spolecznego." *Kultura i Spoleczenstwo,* no. 1, pp. 51–70.
_____. 1990. "Perception of Politics and Political Participation." *Social Research,* in press.
_____, J. Kolbowski, C. Labanowska, K. Nowak, and A. Tyszkiewicz A. *Polacy 80.* IS, UW Warsaw.
Narojek, W. 1986. "Perspektywy pluralizmu w upanstwowionym spoleczenstwie." Unpublished paper. Warsaw.
Nowak, S., ed. 1965. Studenci Warszawy, maszynopis.
_____. 1987. Spoleczenstwo polskie w drugiej polowie lat osiemdziesiatych, ekspertyza ZG PTS.
Pankow, W. 1983. "Gospodarka i system spoleczno-polityczny PRL: trzy modele rozwiazan." In W. Morawski, ed. *Demokracja i gospodarka,* pp. 63–116.
Rigby, T. 1982. "Introduction: Political Legitimacy, Weber and Communist Mono-Organizational Systems." In T. Rigby, F. Feher, eds. *Legitimation in Communist States,* pp. 1–26. New York.
Rychard, A. 1983. "Wladza i gospodarka: trzy perspektywy teoretyczne." In W. Morawski, ed. *Demokracja i gospodarka,* pp. 23–62. IS, UW Warszawa.
_____. 1985. *Ludzie i system: mechanizmy destosowawcze.* maszynopis.
_____ and J. Szymanderski. 1986. "Kryzys w perspektywie legitymizacji." In

W. Adamski, K. Jasiewicz, A. Rychard, eds. *Polacy 84: Dynamika konfliktu i konsensusu*. IFiS PAN, Warsaw.

Staniszkis, J. 1976. "Struktura jako rezultat procesow adaptacyjnych w organizacji." In W. Morawski, ed. *Organizacje. Socjologia struktur, procesow*. Warsaw.

Tarkowska, E. 1985. "Zroznicowanie stylow zycia w Polsce: Pokolenie i plec." *Kultura i Spoleczenstwo*, no. 2, p.71.

Tarkowski, J. 1988. "Sprawnosc gospodarcza jako substytut legitymacji w Polsce powojennej." In A. Rychard, A. Sulek, eds. PTS, pp. 239–68, UW, Warsaw.

Weber, M. 1956. *Wirtschaft und Gesellschaft*. Tubingen.

_____. 1987. *Polityka jako zawod i powolanie*. Niezalezna Oficyna Wydawnicza, Warsaw.

9

Main Paradoxes of the Democratic Change in Eastern Europe

Jadwiga Staniszkis

The concept of "democracy" belongs to the vocabulary of ideology, but it also has an analytical content. Contemporary Western visions of democracy are linked to the complex institutional and legal framework through which those who rule are checked by the ruled and conflicts that occur among the latter are mediated. The alternative concept of mass democracy executing a mythic "general will" is rejected and treated as remote and dangerous. However, it is worth remembering that these two models of democracy are also linked to the different patterns through which community/society constituted itself (or defined itself) as a political entity. This chapter discusses a few such patterns that have appeared during the recent transformation in Eastern Europe and analyzes how these patterns could prevent the development of representative democracy based on the rule of law. I also discuss the type of state that is now replacing the old party-state by referring to the category of Standesstaat,[1] as well as the concept of "exclusionary corporatism."

Dilemma of Political Transition

One pattern of democratic change in Eastern Europe is related to society forming itself into a peculiar type of political entity during the first stage of transformation. And now, in the second state of transition, the dilemma for democracy is that the very same form of political articulation has to be demobilized from above by a new elite composed of some ex-opposition leaders. The dramatic paradox of this stage of breakthrough in real socialism is that a popular, massive, political mobilization is possible only in a nationalistic or fundamentalist way when an economic base for a genuine civil society does not exist. The term "civil society" is used here in a Hegelian sense,[2] as synonymous with the peculiar pattern of socialization through which both inner differences in society and the necessity for the state's mediation are recognized and legitimized. Only such a society can put into practice the representative, not the mass, pattern of democracy. The fundamentalist or nationalist articulation is unavoidable at this stage but highly dysfunctional for both gradual change and emerging politics.

Another feature of political change in Eastern Europe is rooted in the character of the transformation itself and may be traced to the days long before the whole process started. The ontology of real socialist societies is such that all change—not just political—has to be conducted from above in the name of "theoretical interests." This dilemma is particularly visible in the privatization process that is essential for the whole transformation. Groups that would have "real" (own material motives), not only "theoretical" (based on knowledge of what is economically rational), interests in such change are lacking and must be created by the state. The crucial point of the breakthrough is exactly the change in the web of interests, with an increase in the number of subjects interested in privatization as it continues.

In other words, during the first stage of transformation the new political elite—composed largely of reform-oriented ex-party leaders—are projecting on society their vision rather than representing the interests of concrete social groups. In such a situation the idea of general interest cannot be reduced (as liberals would wish) to the interest in reaching an agreement. Some alternatives have to be defined by the state itself as being clearly in no one's particular interests. The state has also to create actors who would treat those alternatives as being in their own best interests or somehow imitate such actors as the party to a contract. The legitimizing argument here is the interest of society in abandoning real socialism and not in the expansion of interests of a particular, well-defined constituency.

Most of the leading perspectives on social change assumed that the origins of social transformation are to be found in processes internal to society. Change is presumed to occur via mechanisms "built into the very structure of a given society."[3] However, revolutions from above in Eastern Europe ask clearly for a more elaborated paradigm that would take into account not only systemic contradictions and social forces mobilized by them but also the active role of the state, as well as the effect of chance phenomena. In fact, even in advanced capitalist societies, the idea of the public interest cannot be fully rejected and politics cannot be reduced to legislative activity only (or to defending a free competition structure against special interest groups). Some interests, such as environmental problems, have to be defined from above as "quasi-objective goods" without waiting for the spontaneous contracts decided on in the marketplace.

The issue of privatization is especially instructive here. It is the key issue of transformation, and strong arguments are formulated to depoliticize it as much as possible (with the "minimal state" claim as an "anti-politics" attitude). But even where privatization would be eventually conducted through commercial agencies selling stocks, the role of the state would be crucial; it would not be substantially reduced. It must be remembered that it is the state that is shaping economic conditions during the privatization procedure.

The state defines not only which capital is legitimized but which is not; the recent attacks on capital accumulated by ex-party functionaries, the nomenklaturists, have been through a "political capitalism" mode. The state also makes decisions about the future distribution of property rights (as in Poland where distribution is decided through administrative limits on stock sold to employees, which is kept at 20 percent of the privatized enterprise's fixed capital). The state also creates the legal and institutional framework—for instance, credit facilities—that is decisive to the speed and mode of privatization.

These actions by the state, unavoidable as they are, create a danger of making newly elected democratic institutions a sort of façade, for they can be manipulated by the new vanguard, often in the name of pure politics and power struggles. The lack of well-articulated interests in a society that is in transition gives the new elite the illusion of a free hand. The possible consequence is not only an eventual fallacy of representation but also the danger of abuse by the state of its power of defining public interest during the period of transition.

The strong impact of the new elite on the evolutionary character of change,[4] followed by the very good adjustment of the old party nomenklatura, created a peculiar type of cynicism (both among the well-informed public and the new elite itself). It also increased the passivity of society, leading to all the paradoxes of representative democracy in an apathetic society. This is especially true where the majority is not absolute but relative. This was sometimes the case during the June 1990 election in Poland and, as a result of growing passivity, is now the rule. With growing social apathy it is appropriate to question with what right the will of the greatest number is substituted for the will of the majority. This is especially valid when choices are made not between well-elaborated alternatives but between symbol, loyalty, and ethos, and it is these latter choices that are often the choices in Eastern Europe.

It is worth adding here that the aura of cynicism, delicate as it is, corresponds well to the peculiar cynicism of Western politicians and professionals dealing with Eastern Europe. Those who know the rule of cynicism are impatient with those who deny it, as Lithuania did.[5] Those who are responsible for the monitoring of Eastern European transformations are tired of its unpredictability. The cumulation of nearly unsolvable economic problems decreases the credit-worthiness of Eastern Europe. All such attitudes existing in the West have the effect of a self-fulfilling prophecy. The lack of Western capital involvement that follows this perception by Western politicians would stop the transformation midway, especially when no capital is available for privatization. This could only increase the dilemmas for democracy and would lead to a peculiar "argentinization" of that region and to the electoral fallacy (i.e., the illusion that the new electoral rules are enough to guarantee democracy).[6]

Politicians debate on how to control and check the unavoidable strengthening of the state during transition. A frequent proposal is (like that from neo-conservative groups) to create such a system of checking standards on the basis of prefigurative communities, like, for instance, those discussed in the social teaching of the Catholic church. This proposal reflects the belief that "neo-traditionalization" is the only possible way to get safely out of real socialism when a civil society does not yet exist.

The response to neo-traditionalization has to be positive given the experience with transition. The dilemmas described above are rooted in a specific attitude that reflects to some extent post-modernist culture. In the case of the elite, which is proceeding, say, towards privatization from above, neo-traditionalization is a peculiar politics of pastiche with its half-mocking and self-doubting imitation of some forms of nineteenth-century capitalism, i.e., a "pure" market and personalized ownership. Such an imitation of capitalist prehistory is seen as the necessary step to enter the modern capitalist world, reflecting the assumption by Fukuyama[7] that stylistic innovations are no longer possible.

On the popular consciousness level such a post-modernist attitude can be observed in society's efforts to overcome its own atomization and to form itself into a political entity. This is done with the help of action on the one hand (rebellion as the politics of identity) and, on the other hand, with a peculiar neo-traditionalization. Paradoxically enough, such post-modernist attitudes by the elite and by society are treated as instruments to enter the modern world, i.e., to make two steps forward to actually make one step. Is such post-modernist culture rational given the Eastern European current problems, or is this a refusal to engage the present and to think historically?

Society's Self-Organization into a Political Entity

Politics of Identity. The first stage of the transformation in Eastern Europe should be labeled as the "politics of identity" and is connected with the shift from a "desocialized" society to society as an agent of change. In other words, from a society that is atomized and system-atized by the state—even in the actions of previous rebels that were to some extent mere rituals of change,[8] directed from above[9]—to a society acting on its own as a political entity. The functional imperative that would make such change possible is a shift in the collective imagination of society and its new perception of itself. This shift is connected with the search for the concepts that would define the terms of society's inde-pendence from the state, as well as for values that would justify such independence. The new existential experience (solidarity, "unegoistic" strikes of 1980) activated latent values and promoted them to the role of cognitive categories.[10]

These cognitive categories made possible the "politics of identity" when the axis of society's conflict with the state was defined and the value base for society's independent status as well as the limits for the penetration by the state were articulated. Values inherent in political fundamentalism and in rapidly accelerating nationalism can play such roles. They are alternative patterns of the initial mass mobilization that becomes a generalized threat, one of the main reasons for the ensuing revolution from above. But both patterns of mass articulation have to be demobilized when such revolutions from above take place.

What is more, such demobilization has to be administered from above when an ontological base for a genuine civil society is not yet created and the eventual reform of property rights is still being dis-cussed. This adds, as in Poland today, to a peculiar social vacuum and passivity when fundamentalist political articulation is gone and the new political entity has not yet emerged. The other reaction is that observed in Romania or in the Soviet Union, which has taken the form of violent clashes between society's vision of how to achieve the newly created space for autonomous activity (as reflected in the nationalistic fights with minorities) and the vision of politics formulated from above.

In all Eastern European societies the base for the pattern of socializa-tion typical of civil society will emerge only after the dissolution of state ownership. The presence of political space is clearly not enough, since the state-controlled economy, even when it is deregulated and decentralized, continuously leads to the atomization and segmentation of society. In such an economy, the universalized market rules as well as concepts are lacking that would make possible a perception of economic activity as a process. The étatism is also one of the causes of the "natural" anarchism so characteristic of Eastern Europe, where the state is treated as a particularistic body acting in the name of its own interests. The popular answer concerning the prerogative philosophy of power (treating law as the mere instrument of politics) entails a substantive, not a formal, vision of justice.

Bases for Socialization. The legitimacy of the new elite, built on trust, has reduced that attitude of substantive justice but has not created a new pattern of socialization that could eventually substitute private property rights as the base for a socialization leading to a civil society. Such an alternative base is not possible at all, and its absence now is responsible for the initial form of society's self-articulation as a political entity separate from the state, being either fundamentalist, as in Poland in 1980, or nationalistic. Nationalism can be the variant of or the claim for a select sovereignty (as in the Baltic republics) or, as in the southern republics, it can take the form of aggression against both Russians and local minorities rising out of unsolvable territorial claims.[11]

The other forms of political articulation now observed in Eastern Europe and the Soviet Union and, to repeat, emerging only when society is relatively passive and only the elite is mobilized, include what one could call a soft national orientation. Moreover, some claims of sovereignty, including strong nationalistic actions directed against minorities or without claims of immediate independence, are combined with a decisive movement toward institutional reform.

Such articulation appeared recently in some former Soviet republics, for instance, in the Ruch formula in the Ukraine, as well as in Czechoslovakia and Hungary. However, this can very easily shift towards nationalism. A related form of articulation is the drive toward technocratic autonomy, which through decentralization would make it possible to solve at least some local problems (e.g., such orientation is often represented by the Russian elite in the Soviet Far East[12]).

Another form can be found in East Germany, where party politics awakened the old political façade and were reinforced by the East German party machines and the challenge of reunification. The surprisingly good electoral results of the reformed Communist party[13] can be explained only by the voters' rejection of the fundamentalist attitude, which would eliminate the Communist party on moral grounds as during the June 1989 Polish election when both party reformers and hardliners were crossed out.

With voting based on merit, the Communist party in East Germany gained some strength due to a position on unification that was shared by some East Germans. Such party politics took place in the initial articulation—the Popular Front—that combined elements of political fundamentalism with a strong revisionist orientation (reminding one of the politics of the Polish revisionists inside the Communist party [PUWP] in October 1956).

Finally, the corporatist orientations that have developed in the late seventies were not a viable option during the recent transition. They have gained some currency only by a professional elite that formulated a theoretical proposal for reforms based on professional standards and knowledge, not on the interests of its own social group. In the eighties such forms of separate articulation of society were rejected consciously by many as leading only to local concessions and as isolating the intelligentsia from the rest of society. However, further rejection of corporatist bodies as political channels has only reinforced the tendency to operate in the paradigm of the "general will" and mass democracy.

Demobilization from Above. Nationalism and fundamentalism, in their religious as well as secularized forms, have now to be demobilized from above, that is, by the state. The techniques of such demobilization oscillate between the two extremes, exclusionary corporatism on the one end and the threat, or even implementation, of state violence (as in Lithuania or the southern republics), on the other end. The technique of exclusionary corporatism is connected with the elaborated web of selective mobilization of electoral support, in the form of a supra-party bloc that is based on trust and loyalty rather than on a defined political program and the demobilization of articulation of social conflicts.

This is assuming that political parties that emerge from below are too weak (and without access to the mass media)[14] to compete effectively with the supra-party bloc that captures symbols of anti-Communist opposition (e.g., Democratic Forum, or Solidarity). The lack of an economic base for a genuine civil society increases the remote and abstract character of the party-type articulation, as these supra-party blocs do not even know who forms their constituency.

The remaining forms of articulation can be to some extent combined with the representative democracy model. These forms are possible only through the relative passivity of society and its lack of mobilization. The resultant democracy is without the broad will to participate, and only the elite is active. In other words, when the revolution is from above from its first step, not from below, the atomization of society does not cease to exist and its new identity vis-à-vis the state is not created.

The mutiny of society is, however, now due not to the lack of legal possibilities to organize or to the threat of repression but is rather rooted in the new elite in an effort to demobilize fundamentalist or any radical articulation and to reinforce with the elite's whole authority structures of articulation that are largely irrelevant to the real axis of conflicts and the matrix of social interests.[15]

The phenomenon of "local revolutions" that took place recently in Poland[16] is a good illustration of conflict between not fully demobilized fundamentalist articulation and the orientation of the new establishment, but the potential for such clashes is everywhere. The clashes appear on two levels, including, first, a clash between two perceptions of revolution. On the one hand, the elite presents revolution, mostly for tactical reasons, as an evolution, but in spite of this introduces basic structural changes. This elite vision is labeled a "legal revolution" and rejects both a substantive concept of justice and a rapid change of the old executive apparatus of power.

On the other hand, there is a popular vision of the revolution as the rebellion of those without power, with strong elements of status politics, the destruction of the old hierarchies, and a dramatic change of the relationship between state and society. The elements of "cultural revolution" are seen as more essential than slow legal reforms that are not only difficult to grasp on the level of common consciousness but do not give the immediate taste of victory due to the adaptation of the late nomenklatura.

Second, at a different level there is a conflict between two types of economic rationality: technical (or macro) and moral (or micro). Based on elegant macro logic, the government's stabilization plan (reinforced by the International Monetary Fund) has attempted to fight inflation with the help of correctional inflation and demand reduction. This program is not well understood by the population, particularly because the popular vision of how to fight inflation involves a more entrepreneurial approach.

The now introduced tight credits, high taxes, and so forth not only make the setting up of new businesses more difficult[17] but lead to a pattern of bankruptcy that is seen by average persons as irrational.[18] And the concept of the demand barrier as a cure to inflation is seen as immoral when basic needs are not met and because by January of 1990, real incomes fell 25 percent. A rational adjustment by reducing costs seems nearly impossible both to individual workers and to enterprise collectives.

Such clashes create a threat to the government's legitimacy and thus reinforce the new elite's opinion that society has to be somehow demobilized. This, together with the new regime's being tempted to consolidate its power, poses a serious threat to democratic rule. The dramatic paradox at this stage of transformation is rooted in both fundamentalism and in the methods of demobilizing fundamentalism, which are for different reasons dangerous to the development of a genuine democracy. This is especially so when the argument of "fundamentalism as a danger to reforms" is used as a justification by the state for the exclusion of opponents in the political arena.

The Awakening of Nationalistic Feelings

Multifunctional Nationalism. Nationalism, in its soft or hard form, can be treated as a functional equivalent of the fundamentalist articulation in its role of overcoming the initial atomization and indifference of society. The relative independence of the Catholic church and the high authority of the pope were the main reasons for the origin of the political fundamentalism that activated ethics as a political tool in Poland. In the Soviet Union, however, the situation of the Orthodox church is different, and nationalism rather than fundamentalism serves as the initial pattern of popular mobilization.

As Albert Hourani wrote, "Other people's nationalism is as incomprehensible, and even as absurd as other people's love."[19] Such relativism of nationalism leads unavoidably to dual standards (different standards when dealing with one's own as opposed to others' nationalistic feelings) and together with its "moral neutrality" (also rooted in dual standards), such relativism is one of the main causes of the danger inherent in each form of nationalism. The role of nationalism in the present transition in Eastern Europe is difficult to understand not only for the reasons mentioned above but also because it pursues aims not linked directly to national sovereignty.

The multifunctional role of nationalism can be seen at both elite and mass-consciousness levels. For the local political elite in the former Soviet republics, reinforcement of nationalistic feelings of their own people is often the only way to survive. A good example is the split of local Communist parties from Moscow with the new rhetoric as a practice as well, adding to their legitimacy. This has been clearly going against Gorbachev's policy, beginning in 1986, aimed at reinforcing populistic feelings that would then cut the local elite off from the people and prevent nationalistic articulation from endangering the interests of the Soviet empire.

Sometimes nationalism is also an instrument in the hands of the local elite in its competition with the Russian elite that dominates in other spheres—the army, important segments of the economy, and often the KGB. The fight for official status of the local language makes it easier to get rid of "strangers" and to take their positions. Nationalism is also often an argument reinforcing the local elite's fight for genuine economic decentralization, which in the better developed republics translates into more control over local resources and capital.

The awakening of nationalistic feelings in popular consciousness, like the Poles' fundamentalism in 1980, represents the fastest way of reconstructing limits to penetration or autonomy by the state. Such feelings help, as well, to overcome indifference on an individual level, which is rooted both in the totalitarian distortion of ethical reasoning (in relation to ends and means) and in the cynicism of the repressive tolerance of the 1970s that even coopted some rebels. In theory, nationalism can be treated (as fundamentalism was in Poland in 1980) as a basis for suspended logic in political life.

The reaffirmation of traditional ties can be seen as a barrier to the imposition of ideological projects that treat society as a plastic body composed of malleable individuals. But crystallization of the public sphere through nationalism is not neutral and has its own dynamics. It is extremely difficult to keep it on the level of skeptical and tolerant feelings combined with the secularized fervor of Christianity, a fervor the new, enlightened, opposition elite in Eastern Europe would dread.

To exploit nationalism as a tool in the fight for the limitation of totalitarian power, as a source of resistance, and in the fight for autonomy is very risky indeed. First, it has to be remembered that nationalism is to some extent a substitute for the institutional (democratic) limit to the arbitrary state: nationalism is usually a base for plebiscitarian mass democracy. Second, when a mixture of exaltation and brutality characteristic of nationalism gains its momentum, it is very difficult to control despite the initial intentions of the elite. The drama of nations forced into the Soviet empire is that nationalism is not only unavoidable (due to the lack of another base for civil society) but somehow necessary as the first step in the fight for society's autonomy vis-à-vis the state.

It has to be remembered that the fight for the local language as an official one is, above all, the fight for the end of an uncontrollable and artificial state. Functions of state cannot be taken over by self-organizing society as long as the state operates with a language that is not native and imposes on society institutions (such as an educational system) that are not only instruments of control but are to some extent socially necessary. Stalin's conception of such a duality of society and state (present already at the level of culture) can be seen as a very effective instrument of control that keeps the state out of society's reach.[20]

These forces behind the revival of nationalism in Eastern Europe are not enough to explain nationalism's growing strength. Such factors as playing out frustrations inherent to the transformation itself (that cannot be channeled through the political structure) and weakening of the state and growing anarchy are also involved. These factors caused an end to the compromise with other minorities that was imposed from above and, in the past, reinforced by the totalitarian state. This is especially important in the southern republics of the former Soviet Union where national problems are nearly unsolvable due to territorial claims that cannot be met without encroaching on other groups' interests.

Demobilization of Nationalism. Unhappily, due to nationalism's multifunctionality, it is impossible to demobilize. So, was Balkanization the future of the Soviet empire? It is difficult to accept that in the Soviet context the path to progress beyond the universal totalitarian state with its nihilism is a return to national fights and intolerance, but forcible imposition of the imperial will is also unacceptable. Both create serious dilemmas for democracy in that region. It is interesting that the present wave of nationalism in the region has its own ideology, formulated in other than nationalistic terms. Paradoxically enough, this is a "Europeanism" with a peculiar vision of Eastern Europe's "return to the real track of history" and with strong Hegelian undertones. The common perception is that such a return is possible only through an imitation of both nineteenth-century capitalism and its nation-state organization, both seen as "natural moments of history."

The nineteenth century aura that is felt in Eastern Europe is also present in the two characteristic features of the new elite's mentality. First, there is a conscious feeling of participation in history combined with a belief that real socialism destroyed the possibility of change from below. Second, one can identify a strong statism in the policies of the new reform-oriented elite of Eastern Europe, also in those with a background of opposition. The devastation caused by the growing anarchization of both the economy and administrative bodies characteristic of the last stage of real socialism is the main impetus for such an attitude. Both these features of the Eastern European elites create additional dilemmas for democracy in that region.

The "soft" form of nationalism (the third of the forms mentioned) has a tendency to change with time into a harder one, as the evolution of the

Ukrainian illustrates. During preparations for 1990 local elections at the republican level, the most characteristic attitude was "autonomy for reform," not the claim for "immediate independence." A strong anti-fundamentalist orientation made possible contacts of the opposition with Communist party reformers. It also allowed for the exploitation of the façade institutions to overcome technical electoral difficulties created by the apparatus (as, for instance, the problems of registration of independent organizations, a precondition for presenting one's own candidates).[21]

The Democratic Bloc created independent organizations that helped in locating alternative candidates on lists formally prepared by façade institutions (as for instance, cultural or professional organizations that were created from above but had now changed their orientation). This tactic made it possible to win. But immediately after electoral victory a deep split occurred in the new reform-oriented center, and nationalistic slogans were reinforced. Such radicalization was also observed after the general election in Poland in 1989, though without strong nationalist rhetoric.

The Emerging State

Exclusionary Corporatism. In the new political situation a new type of state emerges in Eastern Europe. One striking feature here is that the state has to operate in a pattern of "exclusionary corporatism" to demobilize a society that had formed itself into a political entity in a fundamentalist or nationalistic way. A surge of such demobilization techniques of rule is visible—from Poland to Romania and to the former Soviet Union, though in each case the techniques are different. Other new features are already seen in new forms of dependent states following the new pattern of segmentation of the economy: the ambiguity of the presidential office; a clash between efforts to create a legal state; and a necessity to keep some extra-constitutional arrangements due to previous political agreements with Communists as well as obligations to the former Soviet Union.

Changes in political structures can be analyzed on several dimensions, including the manner of formation of the government. Looking from this angle at the Polish phenomenon of a prime minister from the previous opposition, one can say that the manner of formation of the government certainly has changed. The myth of the avant-garde that accorded the Communist party the leading role has been rejected and, if it no longer has a monopoly on power, in any case it has an exclusive right to decide who can be on the public scene, replacing this monopoly (with a certain limitation) with the principle "whoever has electoral success—is government."

Changes in the principle of forming the government did not change the language of power in a spectacular way. This is because its reformulation took place earlier, during the formation of the new center. At that time the party recognized that it was no longer able to replace or fully control social subjects and acknowledged the presence of the opposition on the public scene as legitimate. The opposition, in turn, abandoned the fundamentalist myth of moral right and the notion of freedom as its own exclusive sphere separated from the world of politics. Both sides began to use a similar language of control for the sake of the reforms.

The present stage of transformation, however, is attended by the earlier mentioned trashing of understanding when both sides appeal to the same symbols and arguments. In the public consciousness this creates an irresistible, though false, impression of continuity. Even the obvious change in the principles of forming the government escapes public attention, since often the entering government is stifled by the same persons, though this time nominated by someone else, and these new governments are still governments of a "grand coalition"—only someone else is forming them (e.g., as in Poland in 1989 when participation of the PUWP in the politically crucial ministries was allowed).

Important, though difficult to conceptualize, are changes in internal organization of the state. While institutional transformations have taken place and are still taking place in the state, there are rather slim chances of a dramatic change in state policy. Such change is made impossible by material barriers such as indebtedness, severe disequilibrium on many levels, and obligation toward the former Soviet Union, but also by the same future dilemmas and dramatic decisions concerning the manner of distributing the costs of the crisis and the reforms.

"Estates' state." Some of the changes in state organizations are obvious, such as the end of the tie of the party and the state, in the past linked by the system of nomenklatura. Today even if the same people remain in executive positions of power, "loyalty to the state and government"[22] is required of them and not loyalty to any party. Future promotions and new recruitment to the power apparatus are supposed to be based on the principle of competency, though the opposition also shows a tendency to make use of a peculiar principle of the nomenklatura that is more of a cross-mating of combatant services and loyalty than preparations to solve complicated economic and legal problems. Moreover, a clearly new element in the state system is the phenomenon of dyarchy, which is a kind of shock-absorber of the trans-

formation.[23] There are only some elements of the new situation in the domain of power, and they now deserve a more comprehensive description.

How can one describe the form of the state rising before our eyes in Eastern Europe? This is by no means a modern state of government of law (Rechsstaat) and parliamentary democracy. Neither is it a state based on corporational articulation of interests that mediate between clearly specific groups set up according to economic and occupational criteria. However, the form of domination presently being formed in Poland in certain respects is close to "consociational democracy"[24] when the elite representing well-defined segments of society (e.g., nationality or religious groups) reach a compromise and form a government on the principle of proportionality.

The formula that best fits here is the "Estates' state" (Standesstaat).[25] This is a state that appeared historically in Germany between the last phase of the feudal state of the Carolingians and absolutism. The feature of the Estates' state is a segmentation of the structures of domination, with each segment arising in a different way and having different functions. There is no universal rule that defines and is binding on all actors. These actors are collective subjects—estates—that only superficially resemble corporations.

Although, as in the corporative system, certain agreements and mediations take place between these actors, these mediations reflect the ethos of each group, "centers around which the solidarity of individuals crystallizes."[26] These groups are distinguished by different genealogies and traditions (such organizational loyalty is occurring today) and are not, like corporations, clearly defined groups with specific economic interests. Contrary to corporations (which are created from the bottom, so to say), these political estates are just now looking for their social bases, often competing with each other for the same groups and sometimes gaining the support of groups with conflicting economic interests.[27]

Thus, in Poland today, different political principles that crisscross are embodied, as in the Estates' state in various segments of the political system. A segment aspiring to become the embryo of the Rechsstaat continues in the parliament and government, limiting itself to stabilize the segment from the previous system, i.e., the PUWP. Clearly, the renamed Communist party has already ceased to be the center and source of power, just as the king in the Standesstaat changed his role in the departure from feudalism, but is beginning to function as one of the estates. The seeds of a third segment also are appearing in the form of various representations of the corporative type, e.g., some populist parties.

The emergence of segments within a political system is based on a different political rule and limits (and modifies) the actions of the others. The corporative state is no longer, like the feudal state, a collection of individuals (and vassals) and no longer serves merely to organize support for the center (king or Communist party) but is made up of collective actors. These actors represent different systems, each with its own value and ethos; though, when evaluating economic interests, differences between estates often become blurred. Thus in comparison with feudalism, or the communist party of the monocentric state, the Standesstaat assumes duality. In the latter the king/PUWP and the estates recognize each other as separate (and based on different principles) centers of power with their own spheres of domination.

Other features of the historical Standesstaat reminiscent of the type of state appearing in the first phase of the breakthrough in the system of real socialism include the roles of individual segments being established and reified through political agreements (e.g., the royal privilege for a given estate) and not through the effects of the law that is the same for all segments. Moreover, the individual segments are not organs of a modern state, since each of them appeals to a specifically different source of power.

The functions of each segment are also different, so in Poland, the "small coalition" appeals to the results of the general elections (Solidarity, Peasant party, Democratic party). The former Communist party refers to the round-table agreements and the geopolitical situation,[28] including the Ministry of Internal Affairs, while President Wojciech Jaruzelski (and his "shadow," Lech Walesa) regulate conflicts and try to affect the direction of reforms. Finally, in the Standesstaat there is no automatic regulating principle. While in Poland the former opposition formed a government after winning the elections, it did so with extra-constitutional intervention by Walesa and Jaruzelski.

The above points fully bring out the differences between the "estates"—as collective political subjects—and corporations. The political importance of corporations unmistakably comes from the power of the social groups whose economic interests they represent. In the Standesstaat the hierarchy of political estates—or the characteristic political elite—comes not only from the power of its social base but also from a certain a priori vision of the state.

This vision is guaranteeing, so to say, the political principles according to which individual segments are formed and function. In contrast to corporations, the social base of political estates as a rule is ill defined, and these estates, as ethos groups, often compete for the support of the same groups. So in contradistinction to corporations there is no exclusiveness of the represented societal section in the Standesstaat. There is less mention of representation and more about the realization (more for the society than in its name and at its request) of a particular vision of the social order.

Historical Trends. In order to understand further evolution of these structures of domination, it is useful to look at the historical development of the Standesstaat. For then and now we have to deal with characteristic transformations, including an evolution from a state of social atomization (where the masses, excluded from rule, support this or that estate, being guided either by similar material needs or emotions that spring up around symbols) toward individualization of the society. For different, though interrelated, economic interests of individuals are appearing (connected with various elements of material production), and their political and civil rights are becoming ever more clearly defined.

In the historical Standesstaat (as is happening in its modern socialist version) this evolution led to a gradual breakup of the political estates (collective political bodies operating on the base of a group ethos). Their place is being taken by corporations. At the same time this evolution will be the next stage in reducing state control of the political sphere: the first, as I wrote earlier, was the collapse of the revolutionary legitimation of power (or of traditional authority in the historical context).

This shift from the politics of ethos to the politics of economic interest will have a number of consequences, including a "deficit of legitimacy" that will be filled by greater pressure for legal legitimation. Moreover, politics will become a vocation as it became with the evolution of the historical Standesstaat. The public scene will no longer be characterized by the presence in political institutions of persons belonging to a given estate, a presence regarded as an element of their honor. Instead, it will be watching over the rules of the political game behind the scenes and putting into this game political functionaries of particular interest groups. Domination and politics no longer, as in the Standesstaat, will consist of unregulated settlement of individual cases and situations, but of a more routine and legally regulated action. Reducing state control of politics will contribute to such a separation of the social and political elite.

In the historical Standesstaat all of the aforementioned changes paved the way for the evolution to absolutism[29] and then to the modern state.

A similar evolution is in store for the version of the Standesstaat that has appeared today in the first phase of the breakthrough in the system of real socialism in Eastern Europe.

Conclusion

The key political issue faced by the new leaderships is how to demobilize forces that helped to undermine Communist rule. The important part of the democratic process in a representative system is an acceptance that some situations are insoluble and a working compromise is all that can be gained. But both fundamentalists and nationalists reject such an approach, and it is one of the main reasons that both have to be somehow demobilized.

Notes

1. See G. Poggi's analysis of German tradition of political thought, in *The Development of the Modern State*, (Stanford: Stanford University Press, 1978).

2. See G. Hegel, Philosophy of Right.

3. D. Held and J.B. Thomas in *Editors' Introduction to Social Theory of Modern Societies: Anthony Giddens and his Critics*. (Cambridge University Press, 1989), p.14.

4. See, for instance, A. Michnik's position on the need for an evolutionary strategy in *Gazeta Wyborcza*, Feb. 9, 1990.

5. The Lithuanians' decision to secede from the Soviet Union (March 1990) evoked a reaction from the Western powers similar to that of Great Britain to the XIX century crisis of Ottoman Empire.

6. J. Buchanan's remark during his lecture on "European Constitutional Opportunity," The Australian National University, Canberra, March 29, 1990.

7. F. Fukuyama, "The End of History," *National Interest*, February 1989.

8. An analysis of rituals of change in: V. Turner, *The Ritual Process* (Ithaca, N.Y., 1966.)

9. See J. Staniszkis' analysis of *October 1956 in Poland* as a ritual drama in: *Poland: Self-limiting revolution* (Princeton, N.J.: Princeton University Press, 1986).

10. See J. Staniszkis, "Form of reasoning as ideology," *Telos*, New York, 1986.

11. A peculiar twist of nationalism and religious fundamentalism is possible as well. An example: the current conflict between the Orthodox church and the Uniate church in the Ukraine. The latter was founded in 1596 as a combination of Catholicism and the Greek Orthodox religion, delegalized by Soviet authorities in 1946; Gorbachev's government rejected its relegalization. The Uniate church is treated by the emerging Ukrainian intelligentsia not only as a religion but as the symbol of Ukrainians belonging to Central Europe. Its past ability to combine elements of Western and Eastern culture is seen today as a prospect for its future role. The politicized vision of the Uniate Church is based on many historical distortions but, at the same time, is a necessary element of the emerging national identity.

12. See for instance, A. Mannanikov's electoral platform (before March 4, 1990 election) in the *Press Bulletin* of the independent Siberian Information Agency, no. 36, 1989, quoted in *Sibirskaja Gazeta*, Jan. 15, 1990. According to V. Tolz, "Informal Political groups prepare for elections in RSFSR" (in *Radio Liberty Bulletin*, Feb. 23, 1990) the Khabarovsk Popular Front asked for the proclamation of the Far Eastern Republic, demanding at the same time higher wages for specialists working in Siberia as well as "private cooperatives to build garages for private cars."

13. The reformed Communist party gained 16 percent of the votes (CDU—40 percent; SPD—around 21 percent).

14. See letters discussing access to mass media. *Tygodnik Solidarnosc*, no.12, 1990, also in the same issue, M. Zaleski's article on conflict between efforts to build a party system "from above" (out of the Solidarity Parliamentary Club) and grass-root activists.

15. An instructive example here is the supra-party bloc created in Poland from the network of so-called Citizen Committees: during preparation for the May 1990 elections to the local government position of committees (that use the Solidarity ethos as its trademark) was to reject the right of persons with any (not only communist) party affiliation to enter their electoral lists.

16. A wave of local revolutions went through Poland between January and March 1990, with the occupation of buildings owned by the late Communist party and spontaneously throwing out some managers of state enterprises that were involved in nomenklatura cooperatives.

17. One of the reasons is the end to the hard currency black market that in the past created possibilities of relatively easy take-off for those working for some time in the West.

18. Bankruptcy is linked not to efficiency but to "demand elasticity": monopoly producers of basic goods can survive without any increase of their economic efficiency.

19. Quotation from his comment during the Berlin Conference on "Progress in Freedom," in *History and Hope*, K.A. Jelenski, ed. (London: Routledge Kegan Paul, 1962), p.136.

20. An analysis of Stalin's national policy in the CPSU's Platform on Nationalities, entitled "A Strong Center and Strong Republics" (*Pravda*, Aug. 17, 1989). Also, an analysis by D. Smith "The Politics of the Russian Language" (*Radio Liberty Report on the USSR*, vol.1, no.35, Sept. 1, 1989).

21. See commentary: "Can Ruch Win the March 4 Elections in Ukraine?" K. Michalisko, *Radio Liberty Report on the USSR*, Feb. 23, 1990.

22. Expose of Prime Minister T. Mazowiecki, *Sejm*, 24 August, 1989.

23. In the first phase this was the Committee for Understanding (whose composition was described earlier in this chapter), today, in addition to this committee there is the extra-constitutional tandem of Jaruzelski and Walesa (as the "people's president"), who are capable only as a pair of playing a stabilizing role and regulating conflicts.

24. That is a pattern of democracy based on extra-constitutional agreements among elite that is renewed from time to time.

25. See Poggi, *Development of the Modern State*; also the historical writings of Otto von Gierke and Otto Hinze, *Feudalismus—Kapitalismus* (Gottingen 1970).

26. Poggi, Development of the Modern State.

27. An example is the social base of the Citizens' Parliamentary Club, which is made up of wage earners of the state sector and private farmers, groups that are clearly entering into a conflict of interests.

28. See J. Staniszkis, "The Dynamics of Breakthrough in Eastern Europe," *Soviet Studies*, Oct. 1989; also: J. Staniszkis, "Patterns of Change in Eastern Europe," *East European Politics and Society*, January 1990.

29. See North and Thomas "The Rise of the Western World" (Cambridge University Press, 1974); also: A. Giddens "Nation-State and Violence" (Cambridge Polity Press, 1985).

Epilogue: Markets and States in the Transformation of Post-Communist Europe

Kazimierz Z. Poznanski

It does not often happen that a generation witnesses the decay of a social system. The breakup of the Communist-run system taking place right now in Eastern Europe and the disintegrated Soviet Union is such a rare occurrence. This volume explores the reasons for the collapse of the system and also looks at the forces shaping the emergence of a new reality in the region. Ours is only a preliminary effort since the open breakdown of the system is a fairly recent phenomenon, and attempts to fill the gap are still in the beginning stage.

Decomposition of the System

It is difficult to predict whether this collapse will be irreversible and complete, but it is hardly conceivable that what could be called a Communist or state-socialist project will ever regain its "greatness." While many expected that the system would collapse, very few had any idea exactly how this would happen or what forces would lead to it. Scholars are compelled to explain this ongoing process of disintegration in the absence of a completely developed theory of that system.

Internal Collapse. Traditionally, social systems are seen as sets of norms and procedures designed to allow a society to meet the expectations of its members—a moral order, personal safety, and material wealth, in particular. If these needs cannot adequately be met, then the members reject the system either through gradual dismantling of it or through revolutionary means. In this case, there is an inner collapse, and society begins searching for another, more appropriate arrangement.

In another intellectual tradition, social systems are created to help one organized group—the nation-state—maximize its power relative to another one. In this conflict of interest, nation states with poorly designed systems cannot withstand competition from better ones. Inferior systems thus become a threat to the survival of a given state and ultimately such a weaker state is forced—sometimes through external intervention—to adopt the norms and procedures of its more successful rivals.

The original design of the communist system indicates that its primary purpose was to facilitate a change in the world power distribution. The state-run system of communism was expected by its founder not only to help peripheral states—such as Russia before the Bolshevik Revolution—acquire the status of frontier, capitalist states but also to provide a design on which the whole structure of the world could be patterned. (As such it fits into the category of global political movements, as defined in Janos, 1986.)

Not surprisingly, the dominant early perception of the system by its proponents was that its fate would be decided not through internal struggles but by the outcome of its competition with the capitalist alternative—the defeat of the latter. Those predicting the collapse of state socialism were anticipating not so much its internal disintegration as that an ultimate blow would be inflicted by the capitalist world (e.g., through economic blockade, military victory or "bleeding" communist countries through the arms race).

The problem with this view is that the two blocs had managed to maintain sufficient deterrent to feel secure. While tensions were not eliminated—with many regional conflicts serving as a substitute for superpower confrontation—the parties involved learned to control them through elaborate systems of security regimes. Significantly, the collapse of the system coincided with the conclusion of many first, significant agreements on weapon reduction and with de-escalating regional conflicts.

One is thus left with the competing explanation of the collapse, which focuses on endogenous forces. This is the perspective taken in this volume, even though some authors tend to put a bit more attention on external threats than do others. Thus, Bunce argues, for instance, that it was fear of adverse changes in the future configuration of power that made the former Soviet Union, with Gorbachev, instantly embark on radical reforms (very much in line with the behavior of an endangered "rational" empire, or hegemon).

While many theories have aimed at explaining the inner workings of the system, none of them seem capable of giving a complete explanation along these lines. For instance, conservative critics of state socialism have argued that the system is an aberration going against the natural desires of individuals and/or principles of economic rationality, and therefore it must collapse, as it is doing right now. At the same time they claimed that no substantive changes would take place in these societies, but they did.

The view that the system of state socialism is nonreformable and thus unable to moderate its excesses was first developed by the totalitarian school (e.g., Friedrich and Brzezinski, 1956). They portrayed the system as one in which the Communist leader could not afford changes in the basic rules without putting the whole system in immediate jeopardy. That system—and also its leadership—is acceptable—or, perhaps we should say, tolerable—to society only when totalitarian rules are intact, and when they are tampered with, the people instantly rebel. Many scholars of the totalitarian school have argued that if the system collapses, it will most likely be due to the lack of procedures for succession. When the original dictator dies, finding a substitute leader will be very difficult since potential candidates are likely to have already been eliminated. The turmoil that will follow during the formation of a new leadership has been expected by the totalitarian school to be so severe that it could bring the whole system down.

The totalitarian theorem has been challenged by the modernization school, which argues that to cope with the complex needs of their societies, the Communist leaders will replace the charismatic cast with a professional elite (see: Moore, 1966). Others have been predicting that once the original mission of the coercive system—mobilization of society for economic modernization—has been accomplished, the justification for extraordinary measures will subside (e.g., Jowitt, 1971). This view of the system as a living, dynamic one has proved to be correct. The modernization theories accounting for change did not predict the collapse of the original system but have rather stressed the inevitable emergence of its alternate version. Unable to survive in their "perverse" or "extreme" version, the communist systems were viewed as capable of continuing their existence by assuming a more normal, milder form. For this to hold, of course, people will have to eventually identify themselves with the values on which the system is based (see statement to that effect in Huntington, 1970). This part of the modernization theory has turned out to be inaccurate.

Thus, to explain the decay of the system, one has to go beyond each of these single theories or work out some modified versions of them.

Such an effort to develop a more potent framework is undertaken, I would claim, in all contributions to the volume. These are by and large preliminary efforts and it is not easy to detect some common ground in the individual approaches either to the issue of collapse or to the question of recent transition. Still, one could find an important underlying theme in most of the work combined in the book; this is the stress on the multiplicity of factors involved in the decay of the system and on the basically evolutionary nature of that collapse and its aftermath.

This particular point is well put, for instance, by Kolakowski, who stresses the casual way in which the system lost its principal attributes, leaving at the end an "empty shell" that few felt compelled either to defend or violently remove. This is echoed by some other scholars (see Jowitt, 1990) who argue that natural history, or the theory of evolution, provides the best framework for analyzing the collapse or, to use Jowitt's words, mass extinction of Communist rule—with this extinction basically seen as due to biological mechanisms of mutation rather to any physical, external threat.

It is this evolutionary nature of changes that at least in part explains why so few scholars in the field foresaw the system's collapse even when it was actually nearing its end. As in nature, evolutionary modifications are hardly noticeable even to a most devoted observer, so the outcome of that change becomes apparent only after the fact. Moreover, when change is finally realized, it tends to be seen as something sudden, as in the case of the recent reaction to the collapse of Communism. Thus, there is a marked tendency now to erroneously call the disintegration of the communist regimes in Eastern Europe revolutions (see Chirot, 1991).

While the very conclusion of the communist experiment is certainly an exciting historical event, it still has to be categorized as an evolutionary culmination rather than a revolutionary end (see Poznanski, 1991). Take Poland, where confrontation between the Communist regime and the people was more lasting and widespread than elsewhere in the region. In 1989, the regime of Jaruzelski was not particularly weak, and there were no signs of rapid demoralization of army or police. There was also no evidence of unusual lack of order, with people feeling afraid for their lives or property. Finally, some would argue, power was taken over by the opposition through negotiations or rather handed over to them by the Communist party.

Erosion of Ideology. What then was the force that destroyed the system from within? No single reason can be isolated as the cause of the inner disintegration; rather, it was the result of a number of factors. Still, certain forces have been of greater importance than others. The key point made in the volume is that most critical in the decay of state socialism has been the ideological erosion and delegitimization of the ruling regimes. The system was the product of ideology and, not surprisingly, it was the dilution of this ideology that brought it down.

The erosion of ideology was to a large extent an autonomous process and not just a response to outside developments, for instance, in the purely economic realm. To begin with, the Marxist doctrine contains numerous utopian elements (e.g., promise of a classless, stateless society) and as such could not last long. The ideological base was also damaged by the fact that so little development of the original ideas was allowed under communist rule. The early communist regimes pushed through enormous social changes, and the need for rewriting the original doctrine was particularly pressing.

Rather than rewriting the doctrine, the party had been gradually abandoning its principles. Thus, Nikita Khrushchev decided to eliminate terror by rejecting the principle of "class war," Leonid Brezhnev dropped the pretense that the party was a vanguard of the workers and began turning it into a power elite, and Mikhail Gorbachev rejected the notion that the party had an exclusive, historically sanctioned claim to power—a final surrender of ideology and the conclusion of a lengthy process. (See a very original interpretation by Jowitt, 1990.) The ideological deviations in the Soviet Union were followed by most Eastern European regimes, though not necessarily instantly, the important exceptions being East Germany, but even more Romania. (See Linden, 1986)

Most eager to pursue ideological changes were Hungary and Poland, though not for the same reason. In the case of Poland, serious regime instability—related to interparty divisions—was the factor, while in Hungary the driving force was the presence of a strong reformist wing within the party (see eloquent discussion, Comisso and Marer, 1986). Having their own dynamics, these regimes on occasion actually pursued reforms in the official ideology that anticipated (sometimes well in advance) changes in the Soviet Union. Taking Poland as an example, one finds that its political leader Wladyslaw Gomulka joined Khrushchev in dismantling the state of terror and like Brezhnev, Gomulka's successor Edward Gierek turned the party into an elite (see Poznanski, 1986). But when Wojciech Jaruzelski instituted martial law in 1981, the party lost its claim to exclusivity—the other players being the Church, the army, and "tolerated" mass opposition—the road that Gorbachev took only a few years later by formally accepting elements of political pluralism.

This brings me to another, intriguing question of what social forces—

or who—brought the communist ideology down. A frequently taken position is that the societies were the major force—with the state basically giving in under popular pressure (Bauman, 1990). However, moral rejection of the social order leads to its overthrow if people can organize themselves as a political force that thinks and acts in unity. State socialism had many built-in devices to prevent uncontrolled political mobilization, as has been suggested by totalitarian theory, so one finds it difficult, if not impossible, to explain how societies such as Poland could remove the Communist party.

The answer to this puzzling question is that the masses have not undermined the system of party monopoly on their own. Without neglecting the role of popular discontent, this volume portrays the party itself as an equal or more essential force in the collapse. This argument is most strongly presented by Bunce, who argues that it was basically the Soviet party that has been executing its own death under Gorbachev. Moreover, this self-destruction was in response not so much to the frustrated masses as to its own sense of the grim future that lay ahead of the Soviet Union if the traditional course was pursued. As Kolakowski argues, the communist system collapsed largely because the leaders stopped believing in the ideological principles, public frustration often working as a catalyst. In the early days, they studied communist doctrine and took it very seriously. But with time, succeeding generations became increasingly disinterested in the letter of the doctrine. More importantly, they grew doubtful of its practical value for the promotion of progress. As a result, the cadres lost faith in what used to be perceived as the historical mission of the apparatus.

While the totalitarian doctrine presented the communist ideology as completely alien to the respective societies, this was far from the case. There was a lot of trust in at least some of its principles among ordinary people when the system was introduced, as claimed, for instance, by Marody. This was largely due to the presence, or at least the appearance, of many universally shared values in that doctrine (e.g., communal spirit, egalitarian income distribution), but this perception has largely evaporated with time and people started viewing the ideology as a great lie (Malia, 1989).

Paradoxically, the power of the anti-party opposition has come, in part, from the communist—as formed by Stalin—system itself. By putting politics above economics, as Bunce points out, Stalinism politicized the population enormously. While the communist order was clearly succeeding in disintegrating society and changing people into party-dependents, at the same time it was also producing masses that not only shared the same views but made the party the sole entity to address grievances. This is an example of the many contradictions in the system that could not be solved in any other way but through a collapse of the system itself.

It has to be stressed, however, that the thesis on the internal nature of decay holds only for these countries as a whole. In some particular cases, such as East Germany or Czechoslovakia, the collapse of state socialism was largely brought about by the Soviet Union's refusal to provide unconditional support to atrophied leadership in the region. Jowitt (1990) makes a clear distinction between the communist regimes in the Soviet Union and in the majority of Eastern European countries. He says that evolution in the former was basically due to "biological" internal processes of mutation—while the latter were often extinguished due to "physical" threat.

Of course, the Soviet leadership could not help noticing the failures of Polish communists—lasting economic stagnation and deep distrust of the party. But this was basically taken as a warning and not much more; not, say, a threat that the example of Poland might spread to neighboring Soviet republics. Inconveniences stemming from reduced trade turnover were not of great importance for the Soviet Union either. While the Polish societal crisis damaged the image of the whole bloc, it also caused many to believe that this crisis was the price paid for "softening" communist rule.

Economic Factors. Erosion of ideology did not undermine the system on its own but in union with another force—disillusionment with economic performance. These two factors behind the collapse can be theoretically separated but not in social reality since they mutually reinforced each other throughout the whole process of gradual disintegration of the system. The ideology lost appeal because of inconsistent economic outcomes, while weakening of the ideological foundations was making the reproduction of the economy increasingly problematic.

The Communist ideology initially provided the party leaders with great confidence that the economies combining public ownership of resources and state coordination of activities guaranteed that the Soviet Union and Eastern Europe would do more than merely outperform the market countries of the capitalist world. The doctrine made the cadres believe that this economic system would take the socialist societies— mostly due to abundant technical change—out of the realm of scarcity into that of no constraints at all. They were hoping for a utopian society without an economy.

In reality, rather than introducing these societies to a world of plenty, the system designed along the ideological lines of communism kept people in the world of shortages and way behind the standards achieved by its alternative, capitalism. Most disappointing was the inability to imitate the capitalist level of consumption and not the absolute level of consumption itself, as the latter showed noticeable gains throughout the last decades of Communist rule. This "demonstration effect" should be considered the key external factor behind the collapse, though it worked mostly indirectly.

The economic failures themselves were unable to provoke a rejection of the system by these societies, but they were sufficiently painful to raise doubts about the correctness of the communist doctrine. Now, when the system is collapsing, the answer to why these economies were unable to realize their dream of plenty is still being sought. While earlier this discussion—particularly among Eastern European and Soviet scholars—was conducted with the intention to improve the working of the system, now the focus is on the question of the system's feasibility, so, in a way, the "socialist controversy" of the thirties is resurfacing today.

The liberal critics of state socialism—von Mises and Hayek (1935)—argued in the thirties that without competitive prices or market coordination, economic agents cannot make rational choices and pursue economic efficiency. They added that for competitive prices to be generated, actors have to be profit-maximizers, this in turn requiring that resources be privately owned. It followed that state socialism—with public ownership and no market—is not a viable system, except for a completely static world with no changes in tastes and techniques of production.[1]

These theoretical observations have proven to be quite accurate, for state socialism in fact showed considerable ability to provide for static efficiency—allocation of existing resources of capital and labor. Though rather crude and imperfect, the method of aggregate balances—linking inputs and outputs in particular sectors of the economy—enabled the central planners to ensure considerable coherence in the resource allocation. This ability of state socialism to ensure a strong measure of static rationality can be well illustrated with the case of trade relations involving the Soviet Union and Eastern Europe within the CMEA framework. Brada argues in this volume that regional trade institutions, while not permitting competitive prices and while relying on state monopolies, greatly opened these economies; in fact, they proved to integrate the CMEA members more than similar "custom unions" elsewhere, including the European community. Moreover, this rough regime allowed for the pattern of specialization at least in principle consistent with its factor endowments in accordance with the requirements of static rationality, (for test of consistency with Heckscher-Ohlin theorem, see Murrel, 1990a).

Early liberal critics were also correct in saying that state socialism was bound to fail in terms of dynamic efficiency—the ability to generate new needs and promote technical progress. The system left households with very limited choices and goods of inferior quality, so they missed the postwar consumer revolution. Moreover, the system caused producers not only to lag permanently behind the technical level of advanced capitalist economies—such as Western Europe—but also to be outperformed by semi-market economies of countries such as South Korea or Brazil that were way behind Eastern Europe and the Soviet Union decades ago (see Poznanski, 1987).

In fact, nowhere are the failures of these economies more apparent than in the technical realm. Also, there is probably no better test of validity of the communist doctrine than its ability to upgrade production techniques, since such ability represents the most critical source of increase in the standard of living on the longer time horizon. The crucial role of technical change was recognized by Marx (see Rosenberg, 1976), so one could argue, as Kolakowski does, that paradoxically the system, said to reflect the Marxian vision of a perfect society, has failed to meet its own fundamental criteria of economic rationality.

Interestingly, Marx argued that one of the weaknesses of market coordination was that technical choices were distorted; in particular, there was a tendency to substitute capital for labor. But state socialism, rather than solving this problem, as expected by Marx, has made technical changes even less responsive to workers by breaking the linkage between sellers and buyers. Lenin criticized capitalism in its mature form for allowing monopolies to dominate production and block technical change in order to generate rents. Without markets, however, the economies of state socialism turned almost all producers not only into monopolists but made them "lazy" ones unwilling to pursue even low risk changes.

The experience of state socialist economies also validates the hypothesis that efficient production is not only impossible without market competition but also without private property as a principle form of resource ownership and use control. By the same token, this experience unmasks the great illusion created during the "socialist controversy" by Lange (1936) that contrary to the claims of von Mises and Hayek, the state can simulate—imitate—market coordination under publicly owned resources, providing for both superior efficiency and more social justice, the latter aspect not to be discussed here. The evidence that we have in mind comes from experiments of some Eastern European countries with a modified version of the original system in which quasi-market coordination is combined with public ownership. This economic system—directly inspired by Lange—was tried in Hungary after 1968 and Poland since 1982 in expectation of raising the overall level of efficiency. These experiments—called in this volume by Kornai "re-formed socialism"—not only failed to significantly improve the low technical dynamism characteristic of the original, Stalinist model, but in fact lowered efficiency considerably in some areas (e.g., by adding inflation, reducing growth rates).

Kornai offers a theoretical framework that helps to explain this apparent paradox of pro-market reforms by Hungary and Poland. He argues that reformed socialism, similar to other forms mixing nonprivate property rights with market coordination (e.g., labor-managed model in postwar Yugoslavia) lacks consistency and thus falls into the category of "weak" systems. The only "strong" systems where logic of coordination is compatible with property forms are the capitalist economy, which combines private ownership and market allocation, and state socialism with public ownership and bureaucratic control. Shifting from a state-run socialist regime to so-called reformed socialism could not have helped much since it meant replacing a strong system with a weak one.

To fully capture the difference between the traditional and reformed version of state socialism, one has to introduce the political dimension, however. It should be recognized that the difference between Hungary and Poland in the respective period, on one side, and other state socialist countries, on the other, involved not only economic models but political structures too. Specifically, the former two countries operated much less rigid and less ideological political regimes during experimentation with "simulated markets," and this disparity also accounted for the difference in performance mentioned above.

This specific point is addressed by Poznanski, who argues that in the traditional Stalin-type model of early days, public ownership practically allowed the tyrant to arrogate to himself the right to dispense resources. Control over assets was also helped by the relative simplicity of allocative problems and willingness by the tyrant to use punitive enforcement of his rights. All this provided not only for mobilization of internal savings but also for a relatively efficient use of resources. With dispersion of power under reformed socialism, property rights became less defined and related misallocation and massive theft harder to eradicate.

The Process of Transition

Recreating Markets. With the ongoing collapse of the communist system, many obstacles to redevelopment of market institutions in Eastern Europe and the former Soviet Union have been removed. The communist system was initially intended to mitigate the imperfections of the market, but it quickly started to replace the latter. In reality, however, the market was never totally removed. Right from the start, the market—mostly in the form of illegal, or semi-legal, activities of the so-called second economy—was needed to complement the operation of the state, centralized sector.

Suffering from great economic difficulties, the countries—their leaders and people—are tempted to replace the compromised central control with a market system as fast as possible (see Murrell, 1990b). The argument is frequently forwarded that a sufficiently rapid transition is possible if only the state starts "creating" a market right away by abandoning most of the bureaucratic controls and massive divestment of public capital assets now accounting for most of the existing capital stock.

However, these societies have little savings—particularly in those economies that removed monetary overhang (like Poland in early 1990). Thus at any time they can buy only a fraction of the capital stock valued at realistic prices, so the whole process of selling assets would have to take a decade or two. The argument is made that this problem can be dealt with by making a fast transfer of public assets to the people either free of charge or at nominal prices, as widely advocated in Poland and Czechoslovakia (both of which in mid-1991 announced a massive divestment of public assets through so-called vouchers).

It should be kept in mind that if there is one important lesson from the communist experiment, it is that any social engineering on a total scale ultimately leads to disaster. Most such efforts fail right away and only a few last for a longer time, as in the case of state socialism. The Communists, of course, tried something hardly possible—perhaps totally impossible—but even realistic designs, like the idea of markets, cannot be forced upon a society without risking failure. Unfortunately, the current debate on privatization often sounds like the reverse analogue of the great socialization—issues raised after World War II and then peremptorily closed by widespread Soviet-style nationalization with known results.

The issue of privatization cannot be reduced to the purely financial aspect, i.e., making it possible for private parties to buy state assets. A key question, according to van Brabant, is what should be the motivation for privatization. If its main purpose is to improve allocative and productive efficiency, then privatization should focus on the details of how best to coordinate the service stream of existing capital assets. Moreover, it should address the question of how to ensure that assets not directly utilized by owners are not misappropriated or "stripped," and how to encourage new capital formation from gross savings with a view to obtaining maximum yield.

While distribution of shares for free, or with great discounts, solves the financial problem, it does not solve other, far more important problems. It does not help increase the number of agents available to properly allocate appropriated state capital. Without that increase, the hopes of raising efficiency through privatization may turn futile. There are already indications that aggressive acquisition of state assets by old-time managers leaves individuals that are more experienced in buying political influence than in minimizing the cost of capital (see Tardos, 1991).

Throughout the volume, the countries are seen as still being very much in what could be called a pre-market stage. They are definitely not yet fully in the category of "market societies" defined by Polanyi (1944) as those where contract, not status, is the organizing principle—a unique product of the industrial revolution. The structures that prevail in present Eastern Europe are rather markets themselves, in confined form, subjected to political structures similar to the arrangements present, as Polanyi argues, in many societies in history.

Under the existing circumstance, as Kornai and van Brabant argue, the state will have to concentrate on providing some general incentives to promote market activities and to establish an appropriate legal framework. Incentives are needed, in particular, to protect emerging private-sector agents, at least initially, against uneven rivalry from the well-established state sector. These and other incentives have to be generally—uniformly—applied to avoid the traps of reformed real socialism, i.e., overregulation. Otherwise, the private sector should be allowed to grow naturally at its own pace and to absorb state assets when ready to take on the risk.

What is implied is that the state should allow the public sector to diminish—though not necessarily completely disappear—in a spontaneous way rather than force its immediate annihilation. Instead of driving down the sale value of public assets to make them an easier target for privatization, the state should allow public enterprises to restructure themselves and reach maximum efficiency before being transferred to private hands or simply being closed down. From that perspective, the measures applied by the Polish government in 1990 namely, deep man-made recession and resignation from most forms of state assistance in order to "squeeze" the state sector, may be ill-advised, or counterproductive.

State and Market. The paradox of the transformation is that while it should reduce the role of the state in the economy, this process to succeed requires a strong state, one that is coherent, competent, and vested with substantial authority. Historical accounts such as that of Polanyi (1944) stress the critical role of states in the formation of markets during the Industrial Revolution. They were not creating markets on their own but rather responding to pressures from individual agents. Moreover, that formation was not the direct objective of states but rather a means of accomplishing other goals—the maximization of state power.

A strong state is needed to help the expansion of the private sector, since if the state is not forceful enough in pursuing its economic policies, a credibility problem will emerge, adding to the sense of uncertainty among individual agents. If the economies in those countries are going to take the form of mixed economies for an extended period of time, say, at least for twenty years (See argument by Kornai, 1990), these will be another economic rationale for a strong state—the state will have to have enough power to resist pressures from industry to gain excessive assistance (e.g., subsidies, tax rebates).

A strong state is also critical for ensuring that the political structure is stable enough to prevent destructive social conflicts related, for instance, to the fact that the transition may produce short-term costs that people will be well aware of (e.g., job losses, income reduction) while the gains that may appear in the long-run are more difficult to comprehend. Such transition is by nature divisive since it involves redistribution of both economic benefits and relative power for large segments of the society. The privatization of state assets is an obvious case in point, and the tone of the current debate on it—as in Poland where it is in the forefront of divestment—clearly speaks to that.

At the moment, Eastern Europe and most of the former Soviet Union are a case of great asymmetry—strong societies accompanied by weak states. The disintegration of Communism has meant inevitable weakening of the state, since the Communist party was also the state. It is not only that the morale of the state officials was undermined, but societal participation, so critical for the state power, was largely withdrawn as well. In the process, through self-organization and better understanding of its interests, the societies have strengthened themselves enormously (see Ekiert, 1990). This situation reverses the communist past when society was weak and the state was strong.

To change the balance in favor of the state again, there is a need, as

Staniszkis points out, to demobilize societies so that mass movements created to challenge the communist system are turned into full political participation. Here actions are driven less by moral principles than by direct interests, so societies become more diversified and thus easier for the state to manage. A weakening of many social movements has in fact been taking place recently in at least some countries, even in Poland when they were so decisive in the elimination of the Communist monopoly (of course, the most dramatic demobilization has taken place in former East Germany, forced to accept the West German political structure).

The classical view—as expressed by John Locke and Adam Smith—holds that the economic order very much determines the social one and that capitalist societies not only provide for rational allocation of resources but also create a normative order that helps markets operate. Markets are thus a powerful moralizing force that brings harmony to all—not just economic—aspects of human activity. This particular intellectual perspective on markets is called by Hirschman (1988) "doux commerce." It is also in the classical tradition to perceive normative change as coming about quickly and without cost. It is assumed that people are rational and when placed in a new institutional context, will immediately develop an appropriate set of values that involves no expense to maintain. This explains why the classical economic theory pays so little attention to the broader institutional setting in which capitalist markets operate (see Pejovich, 1990).

An interesting theoretical problem is whether markets can develop an appropriate normative order when the ethics of the pre-existing system—not just those related to economic transaction but to the totality of social interactions—are fundamentally inconsistent with those required for the working of the markets. The classical economists ignore that case. They never define the starting point because they trust that forces of rationality can always take society on the road to market order. However, scholars viewing normative order as a relatively independent reality will need to give some consideration to the question. The above question is particularly relevant in the context of contemporary Eastern Europe and the former Soviet Union, where years of communist rule left what Marody calls a "normative vacuum," or chaos. When norms are applied without a logical pattern and different meanings are attached to a single norm by various individuals, there is little guidance for functional behavior. Markets can hardly work if there is lack of trust, if people fail to meet their commitments, and if there is no sense of fairness. In that way the transition to genuine markets in Eastern Europe and the former Soviet Union is different from that experienced several decades ago in, say, Western Europe.

The contrasts between the current transition in Eastern Europe and historical patterns go much further. Thus, the lesson from nineteenth century Western Europe—including the classical pattern of political democratization in England—is that economic freedoms come first. One finds traces of the classical model only in Hungary, where the development of civil society was helped by two decades of a large second economy within which people had a chance to learn individualism—the pursuit of self-interest that is restrained, however, by a strong sense of the need to contribute to the general, collective well-being. Not surprisingly, Hungary was the first of the Eastern European countries to initiate a pluralistic political system with various parties built around articulated programs (see Szelenyi, 1989).

The rest of Eastern Europe is different since the introduction of democratic institutions is pursued there in the absence of individualism. These people have had little chance to earn their living independently in a shadow economy and instead have exhausted themselves in coping with shortages, as in Poland or the former Soviet Union, or have allowed themselves to sink into passivity, as in the case of Czechoslovakia. The opening of political space in these countries in the absence of individualism may lead to enormous instability—a governability crisis similar to that faced by the communist rulers.

The experience of England also demonstrates that in the natural process of change, civil rights come before social rights, and individual freedoms are won first and are only later followed by the limitations of individual rights for the sake of collective ends (see Marshall, 1973). In contrast, as Kolankiewicz argues in this volume, the people of Eastern Europe reasserted their social rights before acquiring civil rights. With social rights overriding civil rights, people tend thus to subordinate their own interests to those of the group or nation, and with this, differentiation of the political scene so essential for success of democratization is hampered.

Kolankiewicz argues that with the weak civil society, a re-emergence of a mono-party system and/or other elements of the traditional polity cannot be ruled out (the mid-1991 putsch in the Soviet Union alerted us to that possibility). There continues to be little participation, as illustrated in the low voter turnout in the 1990 local elections in Poland or Hungary. Symbols are still more important than substance, so political displays tend to overshadow political discourse, as, for instance, during the early 1991 presidential or late 1991 parliamentary elections in Poland. As in the past, these societies still view the state as a guarantor of social change and wait for it to solve problems.

These societies may likely have to live for the moment with a system that is neither "mass" democracy nor parliamentary, participatory democracy. As Staniszkis posits, a transitory stage between those systems may take the form of an "estate" state in which various elites will allow the formation of governments on the basis of proportional representation (regardless of the numerical results of elections if conducted and differences in political party). This is what happened with the first Polish non-communist government that emerged in 1989 from the "round table" between the Communist Party and the "acceptable" opposition, the governments formed by Walesa twice in 1991 being another case in point.

World Status. The transformation from "real socialism" will depend to a great degree on the position of Eastern European countries and the Soviet Union vis-à-vis the rest of the world. Their relative power will determine the balance of threats and opportunities from the outside world that have to be faced during the construction of a new social order in the coming years. In other words, there is an important international political economy aspect to the transition not well researched to date.

A major effort has been made in the literature on the Soviet Union and Eastern Europe in the past to determine the relative position of the communist economies in the world. Until recently this work was rather inconclusive, largely due to unevenness in the performance of these countries (e.g., relative successes of military versus civilian production) but even more because of measurement problems (i.e., distortions caused by noncovertibility of Eastern European and Soviet currencies). In addition, research has been greatly biased due to obvious ideological implications of cross-system comparisons.

The recent opening of Eastern Europe to the world economy reveals the general tendency of earlier studies to place the region way too high in the international hierarchy of power. With few exceptions (e.g., Bunce, 1985; Poznanski, 1987), these countries have been viewed as located somewhere between the "modernized" economies of the western world and the underdeveloped economies of the southern periphery. The truth is that, at least by now, Eastern Europe, but also the former Soviet Union, easily fall into the latter category. The most critical similarity is in terms of the lack of well-developed institutions to support sustainable development in an open world system.

The communist system was supposed to help the region break out of the periphery status (Skocpol, 1979) it had in pre-communist times, but in reality it didn't. It was expected to loosen up the dependence on the "modernized" core but it failed to do so, except maybe at a superficial level. In that sense, the economic strategy of the communist parties must be viewed not only as a perverse modernization (see Arendt, 1951) but also as a misguided—and thus unsuccessful—one. The nature of that process is even better captured in the phrase "junkie industrialization" coined by Michael Montias.

Now, when so many scholars are trying to define the nature of the starting point for transformation in Eastern Europe and the recently redefined Soviet Union, it seems that the appropriate description, consistent with other characterizations of the present period in the volume, is that these countries represent a periphery or semi-periphery (less, of course, in the case of Hungary and more in those of Serbia or Romania). This description appears more useful than the frequently used term "post-Communist," as the latter suggests that the remnants of the state socialist past are the key factor determining transition.

The great paradox of the anti-past, revolutionary state socialist countries is that they have never really left the past, including their peripheral status. It is thus very much that status, and not simply the logic of the communist system, that explains specific behavior of Eastern European countries and the Soviet Union during the years of Communist rule. It follows that this behavior should not differ much from that in pre-communist times and that one should be also able to trace some parallels between actions taken by communist leaders in the region and the other peripheral economies, such as those of Latin America.

In fact, there are many parallels that go back to the late twenties, when the Soviet Union adopted an autarkic growth strategy. At that time, many exporters of primary goods from Latin America were deeply hurt by depressed demand in the core and turned to the import substitution strategy of industrialization (e.g., Mexico). Similarly, both groups of countries continued this strategy well beyond the fifties though by then such strategy had long lost its economic rationale, if it had one at all, and to go further, both groups of countries are recently abandoning that strategy.

There is also a close resemblance between efforts by the communist countries after the war to change the free trade regime operated by the outside world into a more authoritarian one and the behavior of other peripheries. While this struggle by the communist party states often appeared to be driven by sheer ideological conviction, it was in fact also a self-defensive effort of vulnerable states to shift the power equation in their favor. Unable to compete with the capitalist world on its own

216 Kazimierz Z. Poznanski

terms, the Soviet Union made an effort to change it that was similar to the well-documented effort of the backward economies (termed by Krasner [1985] as "structural conflict").

If one adopts the periphery-frontier paradigm, not necessarily in its neo-Marxist form, it should not come as a surprise that Eastern Europe may be returning to, say, certain prewar political styles. References by Staniszkis to current political life drifting to pro-government blocs—and proliferation of extra-constitutional bodies—point in that direction. In this, recent developments resemble the unsuccessful interwar attempt to develop a working multi-party system, which concluded with a reversal to strong presidential rule, a single dominant bloc supporting the government, and a weak parliament.

Prewar ideological currents are reappearing as well, a thought that one finds, for instance, in Kolakowski's argument that the communist ideology was defeated, paradoxically, by the two forces it predicted to be doomed by historical forces—nationalism and fundamentalism. Staniszkis also identifies these two traditional motivations—regaining national sovereignty and religious revival—as the key ones in mobilizing Eastern European societies and the Soviet people against Party rule. These two currents continue to dominate the political scene after the communist decay.

Conclusion

The communist system has been viewed by many scholars for decades as a permanent alternative to the capitalist order or even as its ultimate replacement. Current events in Eastern Europe and the former Soviet Union—but also in still-communist China—suggest that these scholars might have been incorrect. Those who have been debating that doctrine and arguing that the communist system cannot last are correct on that account, but most often they claimed that this collapse would be due to a shock and would thus occur abruptly, which has not been the case at all.

In fact, the breakdown of the system was the product of a lengthy evolutionary change that started with de-Stalinization. This initial modification of the official Leninist ideology was followed by many others. The loss of faith in the communist promise and process—methods of accomplishing the ideal—had been the primary, though probably not the sole, reason for the eventual decay of the system and the nonrevolutionary form it has taken, at least in Eastern Europe (for an opposing view, see Chirot, 1990). Still, one cannot rule out the possibility that changes in the disintegrated Soviet Union, already very stressed, will yet result in an openly violent collapse into "states."

Now the countries that managed to dismantle the basic institutions of communism have embarked on the reconstruction of some form of market capitalism. It could be said that these societies are returning to the process of capitalist formation called by Polanyi (1944) the "great transformation." Since this process follows an unsuccessful effort to replace their semi-capitalist economies with a socialist project, the current attempt could be seen as the great transformation in reverse. While Polanyi expected socialism to emerge from capitalism to cure alienation, the sequence in Eastern Europe is proving to be just the opposite.

Since the communist decay was a slow, scarcely observable process, one might expect the formation of the alternative system to be gradual as well. This has been in fact one of the main features of the great transformation as it started in England and the Netherlands. However, one should not rule out the possibility that nonrevolutionary collapse could yet be followed by revolutionary change. Historically, in this less developed part of Europe, elites, frustrated with the lag behind their affluent western neighbors, have tended to opt for radical solutions—one of them being the communist project. Hopefully, history will not repeat itself and the region will be saved another failed modernization effort.

Notes

1. Under those conditions, the inherited price structure can be replicated indefinitely to provide adequate signals for economic agents and private property may not be needed as an incentive for proper use of resources, since some state coercion or inducements will suffice.

Bibliography

Arendt, H. 1951. *The Origins of Totalitarianism*. New York: Hacourt Brace.

Bunce, V. 1985. "The Empire Strikes Back: The Transformation of the Eastern Bloc from a Soviet Asset to a Soviet Liability." *International Organization*, vol. 39 no. 1.

Chirot, D. 1991. "What Happened in Eastern Europe in 1989?" In: D. Chirot, ed. *The End of Leninism and the Decline of the Left: The Revolutions of 1989*. Seattle: University of Washington Press.

Comisso, E. and P. Marer. 1986. "The Economics and Politics of Reform in Hungary." In: E. Comisso and L. Tyson, eds. *Power, Purpose, and Collective Choice*. Ithaca: Cornell University Press.

Ekiert, G. 1990. "Transition from State Socialism in East Central Europe." *States and Social Structures Newsletter*. Social Science Research Council, No. 12 (Winter).

Friedrich, C. and Z. Brzezinski. 1956. *Totalitarian Dictatorship and Autocracy*. New York.

Fukuyama, F. 1989. "The End of History." *National Interest* (February).

Hayek, F., ed. 1935. *Collectivist Economic Planning*. London: Routledge and Kegan Paul.

Hirschman, A. 1988. "A Rival Interpretation of Market Society." *Journal of Economic Literature*.

Hungtington, P. 1970. "Social and Institutional Dynamics of the One-Party System." In P. Hungtington and C. Moore, eds. *Authoritarian Politics in Modern Society: The Dynamics of Established One-Party Systems*. New York.

Janos, A., ed. 1976. *Authoritarian Politics in Communist Europe*. Berkeley, CA: UC-Berkeley: Institute of International Studies.

_____. 1986. *Politics and Paradigms: Changing Theories of Change in Social Science*. Stanford: University of California Press.

Jowitt, K. 1971. *Revolutionary Breakthroughs and National Development: The Case of Romania, 1945–1966*. Berkeley, CA.

_____. 1983. Soviet Neo-Traditionalism: The Political Concept of a Leninist Regime. *Soviet Studies*, no. 35 (July).

_____. 1990. *The Leninist Extinction*. In: D. Chirot.

Kornai, J. 1990. *The Road to a Free Economy*. New York: Norton Press.

Krasner, S. 1985. *Structural Conflict*. Berkeley: University of California Press.

Lange, O. 1936. "On the Economic Theory of Socialism." *Review of Economic Studies*, vol. 4, no. 1–2.

Linden, R. 1986. "Socialist Parties and the Global Economy: the Case of Romania." *International Organization*, vol. 40 (Spring).

Malia, Z. 1989. "Stalin's Mausoleum." *Daedalus* (Winter).

Marshall, T. 1973. Class, Citizenship and Social Development. Westport, Conn.

Mises, L. 1920. "Economic Calculation in the Socialist Commonwealth." In: F. Hayek. 1935.

Moore, B. 1954. Terror and Progress, USSR: Some Sources of Change and Stability in the Soviet Dictatorship. Cambridge: Cambridge University Press.

_____. 1966. The Social Origins of Dictatorship and Democracy. Boston.

Murrell, P. 1990a. The Nature of Socialist Economies: Lessons from Eastern European Foreign Trade. Princeton: Princeton University Press.

_____. 1990b. "Big Bang versus Evolution: East European Economic Reforms in the Light of Recent Economic History." *PlanEcon Report*, vol. VI, no. 26 (June 29).

Pejovich, S. 1990. "A Property Rights Analysis of Perestroika." *Communist Economies*, vol. 2, no. 2.

Polanyi, K. 1944. *The Great Transformation: The Political and Economic Origins of Our Time*. Boston: Beacon Press.

_____. 1968. *Primitive, Archaic and Modern Economics*. Garden City, NY: Anchor Books.

Poznanski, K. 1986. "Economic Adjustment and Political Process: Poland Since 1970." In: E. Comisso and L. Tyson, eds.

_____. 1987. *Technology, Competition and the Soviet Bloc in the World Market.* Berkeley: UC-Berkeley, Institute of International Studies.

Rosenberg, N. 1976. "Karl Marx on the Economic Role of Science." In: *Perspectives in Technology.* Cambridge: Cambridge University Press.

Skocpol, T. 1979. State and Social Revolutions: A Comparative Analysis of France, Russia, and China. Cambridge: Cambridge University Press.

Szelenyi, I. 1989. "Eastern Europe in an Epoch of Transition: Towards a Socialist Mixed Economy." In: V. Nee and D. Stark, eds. *Remaking the Economic Institutions of Socialism.* Stanford: Stanford University Press.

About the Contributors

Jozef C. Brada. Professor of Economics, Arizona State University. He has held visiting appointments at the Osteuropa Institut and Stanford University. He has also served as a consultant to the United Nations, the OECD, the World Bank, and the U.S. government. He currently serves as a trustee of the National Council for Soviet and East European Research, a director of the American Association for the Advancement of Slavic Studies, and the editor of the *Journal of Comparative Economics.* His research has centered on foreign trade of the socialist countries and the organization and behavior of enterprises and farms in these countries.

Among his recent books are *Economic Adjustment and Reform in Eastern Europe and the Soviet Union* (Duke University Press, 1988), *Money, Incentives and Efficiency in the Hungarian Economic Reform* (Sharpe, 1990), and *Reforming the Ruble: Monetary Aspects of Perestroika* (New York University Press, 1990). Articles include "Soviet Subsidization of Eastern Europe: The Primacy of Economics Over Politics?" *Journal of Comparative Economics,* 1988; "Economic Integration among Developed, Developing and Centrally Planned Economies: A Comparative Analysis," *Review of Economics and Statistics,* 1985.

Valerie Bunce. Professor of Political Science, Cornell University. The bulk of her work deals with the issues of the relationship between politics and economics in Soviet and Eastern European societies, and between domestic and international political economy of these countries. Books: *Do New Leaders Make a Difference: Executive Succession and Public Policy Under Capitalism and Socialism* (Princeton: Princeton University Press, 1981). Articles include "Decline of a Regional Hegemon: The Gorbachev Regime and Reform in Eastern Europe," *Eastern European Politics and Societies,* 1989; "The Polish Crisis of 1980–1981 and Theories of Revolution," in T. Boswell, ed. *Revolution and the World System,* 1989; "The Empire Strikes Back," *International Organization,* 1985.

Leszek Kolakowski. Professor of Philosophy, University of Chicago /University of Oxford. Graduated in 1953 Warsaw University. During 1950–59, professor and chairman of History of Philosophy section, Warsaw University. Since then he has taught at McGill University (visiting professor, 1968–69), University of California-Berkeley, 1969–70; Yale University, 1975; and University of Chicago, 1981–present. Received McArthur fellowship 1983, Erasmus Prize 1984, and Jefferson Award 1986. Foreign Member of American Academy of Arts & Sciences. Member of University of Chicago's Committee on Social Thought.

Published about thirty books, including *Toward a Marxist Humanism* (New York: Grove Press, 1968); *Husserl and the Search for Certitude* (New Haven: Yale University Press, 1975); *Religion If There Is No God* (New York: Oxford University Press, 1982); *Socialist Idea: A Reappraisal*, 1974; *Main Currents of Marxism* (Oxford: Clarendon Press, 3 volumes), 1978; *Bergson* (Oxford: Oxford University Press, 1985); *Marxism and Beyond*, 1968, *Conversation with the Devil*, 1972; *Modernity on Endless Trial* (University of Chicago Press, 1990); *The Presence of Myth* (Chicago: University of Chicago Press, 1989); *Metaphysical Horror*, 1989.

George Kolankiewicz. Professor of Sociology, University of Essex, England. Specializing in political life of communist societies and most recently on sociology of privatization in post-communist societies. Books include *Social Groups and Polish Society* (with D. Lane) (London, 1986). Among major articles: "Poland and the Politics of Permissible Pluralism," *Eastern European Politics and Societies*, 1988; "Bureaucratised Political Participation and its Consequences in Poland," *Politics*, 1983; "The Polish Question: Andropov's Answer," in L. Schapiro and J. Godson, eds., *Soviet Politics on Dissent and Emigration* (London, Macmillan, 1984).

Janos Kornai. Professor of Economics, Department of Economics, Harvard University. Also Professor and Chairman, Economics Department, Institute of Economics, Hungarian Academy of Sciences. Major publications include *Overcentralization of Economic Administration* (Oxford University Press, 1959); *Mathematical Planning of Structural Decisions* (North Holland: 1967), *Anti-Equilibrium* (Amsterdam, North Holland, 1971); *Rush Versus Economic Growth* (Amsterdam, North Holland, 1972); *Economics of Shortage*, (Amsterdam, North Holland, 1980); *Non-Price Control*, 1981; *Growth, Shortage and Efficiency* (1982); *Contradictions and Dilemmas* (Cambridge: the MIT Press, 1985); *Vision and Reality, Market and State* (Hempsted: Harvester Press, 1990); *The Road to a Free Economy—Shifting from a Socialist System: The Example of Hungary* (New York: Norton, 1990).

Articles include "Hard and Soft Constraint," *Acta Oeconomica*, vol. 25, 1980; "Equality as a Category of Economics," *Acta Oeconomica*, vol. 30, 1983; "Has the Hog Cycle Ceased to Exist?" *Acta Oeconomica*, vol. 20, 1981; "The Chinese Economic Reform as Seen by a Hungarian Economist" (with Z. Da'niel), *Acta Oeconomica*, vol. 30, 1986; "Individual Freedom and Reform of the Socialist Economy," *European Economic Review*, March 1988; "The Hungarian Reform Process: Visions, Hopes, and Reality," *Journal of Economic Literature* (1986); "The Soft Budget Constraint," *Kyklos* (1986).

Mira Marody. Professor of Sociology, University of Warsaw, Poland. Books: *Mental Legacy of Real Socialism: Polish Society on the Threshold of the 1990s*, London: Aneks, 1991. Articles include "Collective Sense and Social Order," in *Crisis and Transition: Polish Society of the 1980's*, London: Berg Publishers, 1987; "Antinomies of Collective Subconsciousness," *Social Research*, 1988; "Perceptions of Politics and Political Participations," *Social Research*, 1990.

Kazimierz Z. Poznanski. Professor of International Studies, H.M. Jackson School of International Studies, University of Washington, Seattle. Ph.D. in Economics. Concentration on economics of technological change, international competition, and theory of economic systems. Fellow at the Woodrow Wilson School, Princeton University. Consultant for the World Bank, the United Nations and the Joint Economic Committee of the U.S Congress. Books: *Technology, Competition and the Soviet Bloc in the World Market*, University of California-Berkeley, 1987; *From Socialist Planning to Capitalist Market: Transition Process in Poland, 1970–1991*, London: Macmillan, 1992.

Articles include "Costs of Domination, Benefits of Dependence" (with P. Marer) in J.Triska, ed., *Dominant Powers and Subordinate States*, Duke University Press, 1986; "Opportunity Costs in Soviet Trade with East Europe: Discussion of Methodology and New Evidence," *Soviet Studies*, 1988; "The CPE Aversion to Innovations: Alternative Theoretical Explanations," *Economics of Planning*, 1989; "Privatization of Polish Industry," *Soviet Studies*, 1991.

Jadwiga Staniszkis. Professor of Sociology, University of Warsaw and the Polish Academy of Science. Frequently visiting professor (1991 at the Department of History, University of California-Los Angeles). Major recent books include *Poland's Self-Limiting Revolution* (Princeton: Princeton University Press, 1984); *The Ontology of Socialism* (Oxford: Oxford University Press, 1991); *The Dynamics of Breakthrough in Eastern Europe* (Berkeley: California University Press, 1991).

Articles include "Political Articulation and Collective Property Rights," in Watson, ed., *Crisis and Transition*, 1988, London; "Dilemata der Demokratie in Osteurope," in Deppe, Dubiel, and Rodel, eds. *Demokratischer Umbruch in osteuropa*, 1991, Suhrkamp. Major recent articles: "Martial Law in Poland," *Telos*, no. 16, Winter, 1982–83; "The Dynamics of Breakthrough in Eastern Europe," *Soviet Studies*, October 1989; "Patterns of Change in Eastern Europe," *Eastern European Politics and Society*, January 1990; "History and Chance," *Deutschland Archive*, Frankfurt, 1990.

Jozef M. van Brabant. Section Chief, the United Nations, New York. Ph.D. in Economics, Yale. Major interest in the foreign trade regime and policies of the Soviet Union and East Europe. Consultant for the World Bank, the European Economic Community, the North Atlantic treaty Organization. Major Books: *Bilateralism and Structural Bilateralism in Intra-CMEA Trade*, Rotterdam: Rotterdam University Press; *East European Cooperation—the Role of Money and Finance*, New York: Praeger, 1977; *Socialist Economic Integration*, Cambridge: Cambridge University Press, 1980; *Adjustment, Structural Change and Economic Efficiency*, Cambridge: Cambridge University Press, 1987; *Centrally Planned Economies and International Economic Organizations*, Cambridge: Cambridge University Press, 1990; *Remaking Eastern Europe: On the Political Economy of Transition*, Boston: Kluwer Academic Press, 1991 (forthcoming). Articles include: "Socialist World Market Prices," *Osteurope-Wirtschaft*, 1970; "Long-term development credits and Socialist Trade," *Weltwirtschaftliches Archiv*, 1971.

About the Book and Editor

In this timely interdisciplinary volume, a renowned group of scholars provides a fresh look at transformation in Eastern Europe and the former Soviet Union. They argue that this lengthy and largely uncontrollable process will follow a different path from that blazed by Western democracies. The contributors perceive this process as a painful one, marked by trials and reversals. The most striking and current example of this uneven process considered is the attempted August coup and the subsequent fragmentation of the Soviet Union. Attributing the collapse of state socialism to ideological erosion combined with economic deterioration, the contributors contend that all major segments in these societies—including the party itself—participated in bringing the system down.

Kazimierz Z. Poznanski is professor of international studies at The Henry M. Jackson School, University of Washington.

Index